CAMBRIDGE STUDIES IN ECONOMIC HISTORY
**Published with the aid of the Ellen McArthur Fund**

GENERAL EDITOR
M. M. POSTAN
*Professor of Economic History in the University of Cambridge*

# CANTERBURY CATHEDRAL PRIORY

BELL HARRY TOWER, CANTERBURY CATHEDRAL

"Templum autem divo Thomae sacrum, tanta majestate sese erigit in coelum, ut procul etiam intuentibus religionem incutiat". (Erasmus, *Peregrinatio Religionis Ergo*.)

# CANTERBURY CATHEDRAL PRIORY

*A Study in Monastic Administration*

BY

R. A. L. SMITH

CAMBRIDGE
AT THE UNIVERSITY PRESS
1969

Published by the Syndics of the Cambridge University Press
Bentley House, 200 Euston Road, London N.W.1
American Branch: 32 East 57th Street, New York, N.Y. 10022

Standard Book Number: 521   07688   9

First published 1943
Reissued 1969

First printed in Great Britain at the University Press, Cambridge
Reprinted in Great Britain by
William Lewis (Printers) Ltd, Cardiff

# Contents

# Editorial Preface

Dr Smith's book fills a double rôle. Ecclesiastical historians will find in it a detailed discussion of the administration of a great monastic house. The students of economic history will welcome an account of the Priory's estates in Kent, and yet another addition to the collection of histories of individual monastic landlords. But in Dr Smith's version the two subjects are neither separate nor self-contained. The changes in the agrarian economy and in the administration of the estates are reflected in the financial administration of Christ Church; and the clarity with which this connexion is brought out is one of the book's most commendable features.

A link between the two topics is also provided by the chronological and personal high-lights in the history of the Cathedral Priory. Dr Smith has been able to show that the Priory fully shared in the great 'boom' of the thirteenth century. Not only were its revenues augmented, its estates enlarged, its economy diversified, but its internal administration was reformed and improved. All this was very largely the work of one man. Great men abounded in the history of monastic estates in the thirteenth century: there was Roger Ford, Michael of Amesbury, Richard of London and a host of others to redeem the fortunes of Glastonbury, Peterborough, Bury, Battle. But none of these men left so deep a mark or so lasting a memory as did Henry of Eastry. Henry's exceptional position among monastic leaders has been for a long time known to historians: an acquaintance for which the *Literae Cantuarienses* in the Rolls Series is largely responsible. More recently Dr J. F. Nichols has drawn attention to Henry of Eastry's work as an economic administrator and reformer, and Dr Nichols's verdict has now been fully endorsed by Dr Smith. Let us hope that sooner or later enough material will be found for a yet fuller study of Henry's personality and activities.

Yet, from the point of view of both its chronology and its

leadership, the most original feature of the Priory's economic history is not its high fortune in the thirteenth century, which it shared with other Houses, but a secondary boom in the early fifteenth century. In the light of the facts, so admirably brought out by Dr Smith, the turn of the fourteenth century and the beginning of the fifteenth appear in the life of the Priory as an Indian summer. The period witnessed a measure of economic recovery all over England, but the recovery was greater in Christ Church than elsewhere. Its revenues were apparently more stable than those of most other great estates, and the area under cultivation was even increased by the draining of the Appledore Marsh. No doubt some of the prosperity was due to the succession of efficient administrators, and especially to Chillenden and Woodnesburgh. But as the example of the thirteenth century shows, successful administrators did not appear by an accident. A profitable age bred profit-making men. Were then the circumstances of the fifteenth century kinder to Christ Church than they were to other Houses and to other estates? Did it benefit from proximity to London, the one great town to continue its progress throughout the fifteenth century? Or had the agriculture and the social structure of Kent been immunised by their earlier history from the economic storm of the late fourteenth century and from the depression of the fifteenth?

None of these questions can be answered from the evidence available to Dr Smith, but they are implied in his story. His work has been largely confined to the Kentish estates of the Priory, for it was not his intention either to extend it to the estates of the Priory in Essex and East Anglia (in part already covered by Dr Nichols's studies) or to the Kentish estates of other landlords. Let us hope that Dr Smith will one day be able to undertake the work. But even if it is done by others the stimulus of the present book will have instigated yet another important advance in the study of medieval economy and society.

The value of the book, however, is by no means exhausted by the indications which it provides to future historians. The interest and importance of Dr Smith's administrative themes could not escape even the inexpert eye of the editor. In the field more strictly economic Dr Smith has been able to find evidence illustrating all the major tendencies in medieval agrarian development. Most valuable of all is probably the evidence of the dissolution of the demesne in the twelfth century, but the readers will also note with gratitude the sections dealing with drainage, reclamation and the technique of agriculture.

M. POSTAN

PETERHOUSE

# Author's Preface

A large number of distinguished historians and antiquaries have investigated the monastic records of Canterbury Cathedral. During that golden age of medieval scholarship which preceded the Hanoverian Succession Henry Wharton at Lambeth and William Somner and Nicholas Battely at Canterbury did much to reveal the wealth of extant material, and in the following century and a half a small group of antiquaries made further contributions to our knowledge. The second half of the nineteenth century saw a great advance in the critical study of Christ Church records, thanks to the labours of Willis, Stubbs, and Dr J. Brigstocke Sheppard. All investigators of Christ Church history are particularly indebted to Dr Sheppard, who not only published a series of valuable texts but also issued the Reports on the Canterbury archives for the *Historical Manuscripts Commission* and compiled many calendars and indexes for the Dean and Chapter Library. Finally, in our own day several scholars, such as the Rev. C. E. Woodruff, Dr Armitage Robinson, and Dom David Knowles, have published texts and studied special aspects of Christ Church history. The *Memorials of Canterbury Cathedral*, compiled by the Rev. C. E. Woodruff in conjunction with the late Canon Danks and published in 1912, still remains the best general account of the history of the Cathedral Priory.

While, however, the politico-religious and architectural history of the Priory has now, for the most part, been treated in exhaustive detail, its administrative and economic history has been strangely neglected. This is all the more remarkable, since the records which survive for such a study at Canterbury and elsewhere are peculiarly abundant. Dr J. F. Nichols, it is true, has written an admirable thesis on the history of the Christ Church property in the Essex custody (London, Ph.D. 1930), but he largely relied on the material at Lambeth Palace and in the British Museum and of set purpose only skimmed the surface of the records at Canterbury. This work attempts to fill the gap and to give a tolerably complete account of the administrative and economic history of

Christ Church, based largely on the manuscript material in the Canterbury archives. In the chapters on estate management attention has been largely focused on the Kentish group of manors, for Dr Nichols' study of the Essex custody and the comparative unimportance of the manors in other counties made it usually superfluous for me to venture further afield.

The pleasant duty remains of acknowledging the assistance afforded to me by a number of scholars. To the late Professor Eileen Power, that most inspired of teachers and kindest of friends, I owe constant help and encouragement extending over a period of four years. Her profound interest in all problems of medieval history, and the infectious enthusiasm with which she inspired her students, need receive no emphasis from me. Mr W. P. Blore, Hon. Librarian of the Dean and Chapter Library, Canterbury, has spared no pains in granting me every facility for study and has often supplied me with long transcripts of documents in his custody. To the Dean and Chapter I owe the special privilege of being allowed to work for long hours in their library. Professor M. M. Postan has helped me greatly with criticism and advice and has also written the editorial preface. My friend Dom David Knowles, O.S.B., has read the proofs and in frequent correspondence and discussion has given most freely of his unrivalled knowledge of English monastic history. I also gratefully acknowledge the kind assistance of Professor A. Hamilton Thompson, Professor C. W. Previté-Orton, Dr H. M. Cam, Dr I. J. Churchill, Dr G. G. Coulton, Mrs Dorothy Gardiner, Miss M. A. Babington, and Mr W. G. Urry. Like so many other students, I have received innumerable courtesies from the officers of the British Museum, the Lambeth Palace Library, the Trinity College Library, the Library of Cambridge University, and the Cambridge University Press. The Fellows of Trinity College, by electing me to a research studentship in the summer of 1939 and to a Fellowship in the autumn of 1941, enabled me to complete this work in the ideal surroundings of their beautiful College.

R. A. L. S.

MAY 1942

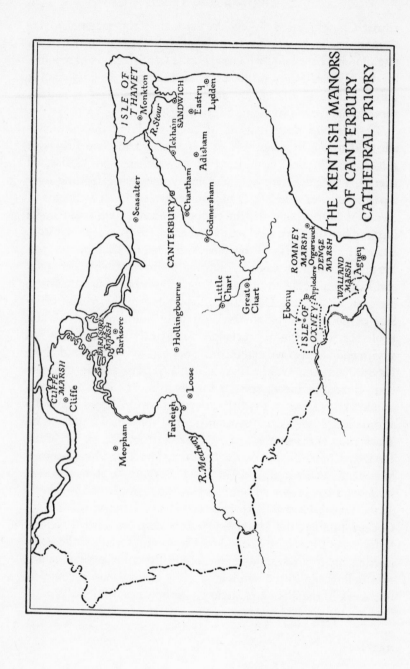

# CANTERBURY CATHEDRAL PRIORY

❖

## Chapter One

### THE MONASTIC COMMUNITY AND ITS REVENUES

The foundation of the cathedral church of Christ at Canterbury by St Augustine is a cardinal event in European history. It marked the true starting-point in the diffusion of Latin Christianity in this country. While, however, the mission of St Augustine and the work of his immediate successors in the see of Canterbury have been recounted by innumerable chroniclers from Bede onwards, the character of the early community at Christ Church has only recently been elucidated by historians.[1]

The history of the cathedral *familia* in the period of just over 450 years that stretched between its first establishment and the reorganization effected by the Norman archbishop, Lanfranc, may be read in four distinct chapters. The first phase lasted from 597, the year of the arrival of St Augustine, until c. 610. In this period of thirteen years or so the archbishop and his monks lived a quasi-regular life with the non-monastic clerks, who became part of the archbishop's entourage during the first years of his rule. The foundation of the abbey of SS. Peter and Paul (later St Augustine's) outside the walls of the city reduced the strictly monastic elements in the archiepiscopal *familia*. The second phase may be said to last from c. 610 to c. 660. Full monastic life was established by Archbishop Laurence and probably continued for some time before undergoing a gradual decline. After the accession of Theodore of Tarsus to the see in 668 the community at Christ Church consisted of clerks who led a semi-regular life with their

[1] See Dr J. Armitage Robinson, 'The Early Community at Christ Church, Canterbury' in *Journal of Theological Studies* (1926), XXVII, pp. 225–40, and Dom David Knowles, 'The Early Community at Christ Church, Canterbury', *ibid.* (1938), XXXIX, pp. 126–31.

bishop. This state of affairs lasted for well over 300 years. It was only in 997, when Archbishop Aelfric had returned from Rome with the pallium, that monks were re-introduced at Christ Church.[1] The fourth and last phase is represented by the period stretching from the year 997 to the Conquest. The monastic life was maintained at Christ Church, although discipline was much relaxed during the episcopate of Stigand (1052–70), who was a notorious pluralist and absentee. So when Lanfranc became archbishop of Canterbury in 1070, the monks who formed his cathedral chapter, though sadly diminished in numbers, could claim a continuous tradition of observance that stretched back seventy-three years. The *Statuta* assumed the knowledge and practice of the Benedictine Rule and dealt in great detail with disciplinary and liturgical questions.[2] The great Norman archbishop was able to build on a solid foundation of monastic tradition inherited from the Saxon past.

From the time of Lanfranc until the Dissolution the cathedral monastery of Christ Church was one of the most important and largest houses in the country, ranking with abbeys such as Glastonbury, St Albans, and Bury St Edmunds, and even surpassing them in its peculiarly privileged relationship to the archbishop. The political influence and scholastic achievements of the monastery do not fall within the scope of this study. It may, however, be emphasized that the part played by the monks in national politics in the twelfth and thirteenth centuries was one of no mean importance. Woolnoth was probably correct in affirming that the priorate of Henry of Eastry (1285–1331) marked 'the commencement of the decline of the political influence of the convent of Christ Church'.[3] The contribution of the monks to learning

[1] See *J.T.S.* XXVII, p. 240 and Dom T. Symons, 'The Introduction of Monks at Christ Church, Canterbury', *ibid.* (1926), XXVII, pp. 409–11.

[2] The text of the *Statuta* of Lanfranc is to be found in Migne, *P.L.* CL, pp. 443–516. The thesis of Edmund Bishop in *The Bosworth Psalter* (1908), p. 63, that the *Statuta* were intended only for the monks of Christ Church was cautiously accepted by Dr Armitage Robinson in his article on 'Lanfranc's Monastic Constitutions' in *J.T.S.* (1909), X, pp. 375–88.

[3] W. Woolnoth, *A History and Description of Canterbury Cathedral* (1816), p. 32.

forms a long and honourable chapter in the history of the priory.[1]

Lanfranc intended that there should be 150 monks at Christ Church and during his energetic rule the numbers gradually increased.[2] At his death in 1087 there were 100 monks and this number had risen c. 1125 to between 140 and 150.[3] At the end of the twelfth century, c. 1190, there were still 140 monks, but in 1207 only a little over half that number, 77, were to be found at Christ Church.[4] The sharp decline in numbers may be attributed in large part to the long and expensive struggles of the convent with Baldwin and Hubert Walter. Lanfranc's statutory number always remained impossible of achievement. In 1298 the numbers had actually sunk to below 30,[5] as a result of the monastic championship of Archbishop Winchelsey in his quarrel with the Crown and the violent action of Edward I in attempting to starve the monks into submission.[6] Less than twenty years later, in 1315, the number had increased again to 73[7] and there were 65 monks at Christ Church in 1330.[8] The monastery was exceptionally fortunate in escaping the worst ravages of the Black Death,[9] but in 1376 there were only 46 monks and Simon of Sudbury gave strict orders that the number should be increased.[10] Lists of monks compiled in the late fifteenth century show that there were 87 monks at Christ Church in 1451,[11] 91 in 1455,[12] 73 in 1465,[13] 80 in some unknown year of Sellyng's priorate (1472–94),[14] and 62 at the

[1] The volume on Canterbury College by Mr W. A. Pantin, shortly to be published by the Oxford Historical Society, should do much to reveal the scholastic activity of the Christ Church monks.
[2] A. J. Macdonald, *Lanfranc* (1926), p. 141.
[3] Dom D. Knowles, *The Monastic Order in England*, 943–1216, p. 714.
[4] *Epistolae Cantuarienses*, ed. W. Stubbs (Rolls Series, 1866), p. xxxii.
[5] *Register Winchelsey* (Canterbury and York Soc.), pp. 257–58.
[6] *H.M.C.* App. to Vth Report, p. 433.
[7] Cant. MS. M 13, xiii, mem. 9.      [8] *Ibid.* mem. 23.
[9] Only four monks died of the pestilence, *Literae Cantuarienses*, ed. J. B. Sheppard (Rolls Series, 1888), II, pp. xxii–xxiii.
[10] Wilkins, *Concilia*, III, p. 110.      [11] Cant. MS. E. VI.
[12] Cant. MS. M 13, xvii, mem. 10.
[13] *H.M.C.* App. to IXth Report, p. 105.
[14] Cant. MS. D.E. 74.

turn of the century.[1] Dr J. B. Sheppard's analysis of the records of the professions and deaths of Canterbury monks from 1214 to the Dissolution shows that 'there were usually from 70 to 80 brethren on the books at one time'.[2] The community was therefore a large one without in any way coming up to the expectations of Lanfranc or to the standard of the great Continental houses.

The priory of Christ Church was one of that group of cathedral monasteries which were almost peculiar to England in the middle ages.[3] The archbishop was both the abbot of the monks and the *persona* of the cathedral church.[4] The first archbishops of Canterbury after the Norman Conquest were abbots *de facto* as well as *de jure*, living the common life with their monks in church and cloister. This was the intention of Ethelwold and Lanfranc, the two who did most to propagate the system of cathedral monasteries in this country. In the event, however, 'the golden age of patriarchal rule in the cathedral monasteries was of short duration. At Canterbury the best was over with Anselm's death, though his successor, and perhaps Theobald a little later, were in the same tradition.'[5] Becket, we know, lived with his monks when opportunity allowed,[6] but at the end of the twelfth century the prolonged quarrels of monks and archbishops, continued at intervals in the following century, finally sundered the paternal relationship. The archbishop became the titular abbot of the monastic community, and the prior assumed for all practical purposes the functions of abbot.[7]

Long before the archbishop ceased to lead the common life with his monks a separation had been made of the lands of the two parties. The *familia* at Christ Church had a small separate

[1] Cant. MS. D.E. 25.     [2] *Lit. Cant.* II, p. xxii.

[3] See the chapter on 'The Cathedral Monasteries and the Bishops' Abbeys' in Dom Knowles' *The Monastic Order in England*, 943–1216, pp. 619–31.

[4] Lanfranc explicitly equated bishop and abbot in his *Statuta*: Migne, *P.L.* CL, pp. 482–83.

[5] Knowles, *op. cit.* p. 624.

[6] W. H. Hutton, *Thomas Becket* (1926 ed.), p. 259.

[7] This was explicitly recognized by Archbishop Pecham, who in 1282 made reference to the prior of Christ Church, 'qui in absentia nostra abbatis geris officium', *Reg. Epist. J. Peckham* (Rolls Series, 1884), II, p. 398.

endowment at least as early as 799 and Archbishop Wulfred (805–32) substantially increased their revenues.[1] It seems more than likely that the separate endowment of the community remained intact until the Conquest, although there is no evidence at hand to support this supposition.[2] The Domesday Monachorum is clear and definite in its distinction between the lands of archbishop and monks.[3] In the middle of the twelfth century the monastery fell into dire financial straits and the prior asked the archbishop, Theobald, to undertake the administration of the conventual estates.[4] The arrangement proved to be far from satisfactory and served as an evil precedent for Archbishop Baldwin, who forcibly took certain of the estates into his own hands and retained them for a considerable period. After this, the two properties remained distinct and no further disputes are recorded.

The highest privilege which the monks enjoyed was that of electing the archbishop of Canterbury, who was also their abbot.[5] In the twelfth century 'in every Canterbury election after Anselm's death a deputation from the monastic chapter either freely elected or at least went through the form of choosing the archbishop'.[6] It was the threat to their right of election which the monks read into the proposals of Baldwin, Hubert Walter, and Edmund Rich to erect colleges of secular canons that lay at the root of the long controversies at the end of the twelfth century and in 1238–40.[7] The *cause célèbre* of 1205–6 is another aspect of the same struggle for freedom of election.[8] Once the monks had vindicated their rights in conflict with the archbishop, they were exposed to a like

[1] See Dr J. Armitage Robinson in *J.T.S.* XXVII, pp. 235–38.

[2] See B. W. Kissan, 'Lanfranc's Alleged Division of Lands between Archbishop and Community' in *Eng. Hist. Rev.* (1939), LIV, pp. 285–93.

[3] *V.C.H. Kent*, III, pp. 261–64.

[4] Gervase, *Opera*, ed. W. Stubbs (Rolls Series, 1879), I, pp. 143–45.

[5] The privilege was confirmed to the monks by Pope Hadrian IV in 1158: *Papsturkunden in England*, ed. W. Holtzmann (1935), II, pp. 288–89.

[6] Dom Knowles, *op. cit.* pp. 627–68.

[7] The conflict of the monks with Baldwin and Hubert Walter is recounted at great length by Stubbs in *Epist. Cant.* pp. vii–clxxxvii. For the dispute with Edmund Rich, see Gervase, *Opera*, II, pp. 130–85.

[8] See Dom D. Knowles, 'The Canterbury Election of 1205–6' in *Eng. Hist. Rev.* (1938), LIII, pp. 211–20.

B

menace from the papacy which, by its system of provision, increasingly tended to set aside the canonical elections of the monks in favour of its own nominees.[1] By the fifteenth century freedom of election had become largely fictitious, although the outward forms were still religiously observed.[2]

After he had ceased to live with his monks, the archbishop still enjoyed certain rights in his cathedral priory, of which the most important was the right of visitation as diocesan ordinary.[3] The injunctions (*injunctiones*) which the archbishops issued subsequent to visitation covered every aspect of monastic life. The regulations of Pecham (1279–92)[4] and the elaborate series of *statuta* issued by Winchelsey in 1298[5] were particularly detailed in this respect. The archbishop also issued periodical commands to the priory on matters quite unconnected with the *comperta* of visitations. For example, Winchelsey forbade the monks to retain John of St Clare in their council in 1299,[6] and two years later he stopped the monks from going on pilgrimage.[7] The archbishop therefore retained much of the autocratic power of an abbot, while ceasing to exercise a personal rule.

In four ways other than that of visitation the monks were obliged to recognize the authority of their titular abbot. The archbishop appointed certain senior obedientiaries and servants

---

[1] Thus the papacy set aside two elections in 1229–32 (Gervase, *Opera*, II, pp. 128–29). The provision of Boniface in 1242, Kilwardby in 1270, and Pecham in 1279 followed in the next half century (*ibid.* II, pp. 198–200, 272–73, 291). Winchelsey was freely elected by the monks in 1294 (Wilkins, *Concilia*, II, pp. 188–94), but papal and royal influence was predominant in elections in the fourteenth and fifteenth centuries.

[2] See the formula used at the election of Archbishop Bourchier in *H.M.C.* App. to IXth Report, p. 103.

[3] The development of the machinery of episcopal visitation in the thirteenth century has been fully described by Mr C. R. Cheney in *Episcopal Visitation of Monasteries in the Thirteenth Century* (1931).

[4] See *Reg. Epist. J.P.* I, pp. 341–48; II, pp. 399–400 and *passim*.

[5] *Reg. Winchelsey*, pp. 813–27.

[6] *Lit. Cant.* I, pp. 27–28. The clerk in question, a canon of St Paul's, was accused by Winchelsey of pluralism and illegitimacy: *Reg. Winchelsey*, pp. 452–53.

[7] *Reg. Winchelsey*, pp. 413–14.

in the monastery, received the profession of novices, exercised a measure of seignorial jurisdiction, and claimed *exennia* from the manors of the priory at Christmas and Easter. The appointment of obedientiaries and the adjustment of the relationship between the *baronia* of the archbishop and the *libertas* of the monks by the Boniface composition in 1259 may be properly considered elsewhere.[1] The right of the archbishop to receive the profession of novices was often a subject of keen dispute. Pope Gregory IX (1227–41) granted the prior of Christ Church the privilege of receiving the profession of novices during vacancies in the archiepiscopal see,[2] and in the fourteenth century the priors attempted to vindicate this right for themselves *sede plena* as well as *sede vacante*. In spite of repeated requests addressed to the archbishop[3] they were unable to establish a right in this matter. The primate clung tenaciously to his privilege.

The history of the *exennia* has been briefly recounted by Stubbs.[4] It will suffice to say that Anselm appropriated these Easter and Christmas offerings from the manors to the cellarer's department for the use of the sick and strangers. Theobald retained the *exennia* after restoring the property which he had been asked to administer,[5] but Archbishop Richard returned them to the monks. Baldwin's appropriation of the *exennia* was one of the opening moves in the long dispute. In the issue of this struggle the *exennia* from a number of the manors remained the permanent possession of the archbishop. They were rendered to the primate from year to year and are to be found in the serjeants' accounts of the priory and in scattered notices.[6]

Quite apart from their official relationships, the archbishop and monks came into contact in a number of personal and unofficial ways. The archbishop normally kept one of the monks as a

---

[1] See Chapters Three and Six.

[2] *H.M.C.* App. to VIIIth Report, p. 318.

[3] See *Lit. Cant.* I, pp. 18, 128, 294–95, 389–90; II, pp. 131–32, 160–63, 166, 216, 244–46.

[4] In his introduction to *Epist. Cant.* p. xxx.

[5] Gervase, *Opera*, I, p. 145.

[6] See, for example, Archbishop Reynolds' receipt for the payment of the *exennia* in 1326 in *Lit. Cant.* I, p. 165.

chaplain and a liaison officer.[1] This chaplain, one may notice, played a conspicuous part at visitations by reason of his superior knowledge of the life of the convent. On one occasion at least an archbishop lived on terms of friendly intimacy with the prior of Christ Church. The correspondence of Archbishop Walter Reynolds (1313–27) and Prior Henry of Eastry (1285–1331) affords abundant proof of a close personal relationship in which the archbishop often sought advice and counsel from the prior.[2] The personal relations of Prior Eastry with Reynolds' successor, Meopham (1328–33), are interesting in that they represented the very reverse of the official connection. In the first three years of his primacy Meopham was often led 'to seek advice and to submit to snubbing from old Eastry'.[3] This personal factor of character and temperament must certainly not be ignored in an estimate of the manifold relationships of archbishop and monks.

In the twelfth and thirteenth centuries a conflict took place between the prior and chapter and the archdeacon of Canterbury over questions of jurisdiction. The archdeacon appears to have claimed a seat in chapter, for Archbishop Theobald was obliged to decree that the archdeacon should sit on the footstool of the archiepiscopal throne (*in subpedaneo sedis archiepiscopi*) and then only when the monks summoned him for special occasions.[4] Pope Alexander III exempted the clerks, servants, and churches in the demesne-lands of the monks from the jurisdiction of the archdeacon in the year 1176.[5] Stephen Langton greatly increased the powers and revenues of the archdeacon of Canterbury when he appointed his brother, Simon, to the office in 1227.[6] In 1240 Simon Langton was emboldened to challenge the right of the

---

[1] *Lit. Cant.* I, pp. 36, 334.

[2] See *Lit. Cant.* I, pp. xxviii, lxxxiv–xc and *passim* and Eastry Correspondence, Cant. MS. M 13.

[3] *Lit. Cant.* I, p. xxviii.

[4] See *Lit. Cant.* III, pp. 355–56. This arrangement was confirmed by Alexander III in 1181 and by Urban III in 1187: *Papsturkunden in England*, II, pp. 409, 446.

[5] *Papsturkunden in England*, II, p. 355.

[6] I. Churchill, *Canterbury Administration*, I, p. 44. See the life of Simon Langton by Kate Norgate in *D.N.B.* XXXII, pp. 121–22.

monks to exercise provincial and diocesan jurisdiction during the vacancy of the see of Canterbury. The controversy broke out at each new vacancy during the next fifty years and no definitive settlement of the question was ever made. After the dispute of the monks with Richard de Ferryng in the 1292–94 vacancy, however, the archdeacon appears to have abandoned his claim to exercise provincial and diocesan jurisdiction.[1]

It is proposed to conclude this introductory chapter by giving a short account of the revenues of the cathedral priory. The bulk of this revenue consisted, of course, of landed property. The evidence of the Domesday Monachorum[2] and of the lists of donations of manors[3] shows conclusively that the monks had acquired by far the greater part of their lands before the end of the twelfth century. Indeed it is quite clear that the cathedral priory was primarily indebted to Saxon kings, nobles, and thegns, for its vast endowment. The lands lay in eight counties in the south and east of England—Kent, Sussex, Surrey, Buckinghamshire, Oxfordshire, Essex, Suffolk, and Norfolk—and there were also scattered properties in London, Devonshire, Ireland, and elsewhere.

The history of the Christ Church property has been recounted in great detail by Dr J. B. Sheppard in the Reports of the *Historical Manuscripts Commission*.[4] It is only necessary here to emphasize their scattered and dispersed character and to say something of the working of the Statute of Mortmain, which was enacted in 1279 to impose a check upon the acquisition of property by religious houses. Recent research has shown that the Statute of Mortmain was regularly circumvented by the religious, who paid for royal

[1] The dispute is to be read in Gervase, *Opera*, II, pp. 180–82, 251–52, 301, and in the Black Book of the Archdeacon of Canterbury, compiled some time after 1313 under the direction of the monks and summarized by Nicholas Battely in William Somner's *Antiquities of Canterbury* (1703 ed.), pp. 140–42. See also the report on the Black Book by H. T. Riley in *H.M.C.* App. to VIth Report, pp. 498–99.

[2] *V.C.H. Kent*, III, pp. 261–64.

[3] See the analysis of these lists in E. G. Box's article on 'Donations of Manors to Christ Church, Canterbury, and Appropriation of Churches' in *Arch. Cant.* (1932), XLIV, pp. 103–19.

[4] App. to Vth Report, pp. 427–62; App. to VIIIth Report, pp. 315–55.

licences to acquire land.¹ Between the years 1279 and 1334 the monks of Christ Church acquired a number of small plots of land, which were duly registered in the *Patent Rolls*.² In the latter year they received a general licence to acquire land and rent, not held in chief, to the yearly value of £6. 13s. 4d.³ These general licences were a common expedient of the Crown and a fruitful source of revenue. The other great Benedictine community at Canterbury, St Augustine's, had paid for a similar licence in the reign of Edward II to acquire land and rent to the annual value of £60.⁴ In the later fourteenth and fifteenth centuries the monks of Christ Church received general licences of this character on several distinct occasions.⁵ The Statute of Mortmain was therefore only

---

¹ See T. A. M. Bishop, 'Monastic Demesnes and the Statute of Mortmain' in *Eng. Hist. Rev.* (1934), XLIX, pp. 303–6.

² A long list of the names of donors and places is given in *Cal. Let. Pat.* 30 Edward I, pp. 72–73. See also *ibid.* 3 Edward II, p. 208; 7 Edward II, p. 33; 10 Edward II, p. 517; 15 Edward II, p. 29; 15 Edward II, p. 275; 3 Edward III, p. 448; 5 Edward III, p. 74.

³ *Cal. Let. Pat.* 8 Edward III, p. 9. Land was acquired under the terms of this licence in 1339 and 1340, *ibid.* 13 Edward III, p. 249; 14 Edward III, p. 509.

⁴ *Cal. Let. Pat.* 10 Edward III, p. 242. The monks of Pershore Abbey were granted a general licence in 1334 to acquire land to the annual value of £10: *Cal. Let. Pat.* 8 Edward III, p. 23.

⁵ In 1353, less than twenty years after the monks had acquired their first general licence to acquire land in mortmain, they received another general licence to acquire land and rent to the value of £20 a year in order to furnish their church with an altar of Our Lady (*Cal. Let. Pat.* 27 Edward III, p. 465. For land acquired under this licence see *ibid.* 28 Edward III, pp. 44, 93, 101). This was followed five years later by another general licence for acquisitions of land not exceeding £20 a year in value on behalf of the chaplains in the almonry (*ibid.* 32 Edward III, p. 93). Once again, in 1366, a general licence to acquire land and rent to the annual value of £10 was granted to the monks at the request of their patroness, Joan, lady of Mohun (*ibid.* 39 Edward III, p. 198). In 1392 the monks paid a fine of £200 to the king in order to acquire property to the annual value of £40 (*ibid.* 15 Richard II, p. 18), and in the following year the licence secured through the good offices of the lady of Mohun was renewed (*ibid.* 16 Richard II, p. 271). In 1394 the monks were allowed to acquire lands, tenements, and rents in the city of Canterbury, held of the king in free burgage, to the yearly value of £13. 6s. 8d. (*ibid.* 17 Richard II, p. 370). In 1429 Archbishop Chichele received the permission of the Crown to assign land in mortmain to the annual value of £20

a minor impediment to religious who were desirous of acquiring landed property. The growth of a system of fines and general licences served at one and the same time to augment the revenues of the Crown and to simplify the evasion of the statute by the religious orders.

The ownership of advowsons and appropriated churches constituted another valuable source of monastic revenue. A great crop of advowsons, chiefly of London churches, lay in the hands of the monks.[1] From the rectors of the churches the monks claimed an annual pension. These grants of advowsons implied full liberty to the grantees to appropriate the rectories and in most cases were promptly followed by appropriation.[2] By the year 1400 the monks of Christ Church held no less than fourteen churches in appropriation.[3] It should, however, be emphasized that the revenue from pensions and rectorial tithes was small in extent when compared with that derived from property in land.

The history of the oblations (*oblaciones*) offered at the shrines in the cathedral has already been written.[4] The powerful intercession of St Thomas, by which a number of organic diseases were

to the monks of Christ Church who, in return for this favour, were to pray for the souls of king and archbishop (*ibid.* 8 Henry VI, p. 35). The next year another general licence to acquire lands and rents to the yearly value of £16 was granted to the monks in consideration of the extensive repairs that were then being undertaken on the fabric of their church. At the same time the monks surrendered the licence which they had gained at the request of the lady of Mohun (*ibid.* 8 Henry VI, p. 67. For land acquired under the terms of this licence, see *ibid.* 22 Henry VI, p. 219). Finally, in 1475 the monks were granted privilege of acquiring in mortmain, without an inquisition *ad quod damnum*, lands, tenements, or rents to the annual value of £20 (*ibid.* 15 Edward IV, p. 541).

[1] See the list of advowsons in W. Somner's *Antiquities of Canterbury*, App. to Supplement, p. 50. The archbishops retained the right of presenting to the churches on the estates of the convent until the latter half of the fourteenth century, when they surrendered a number of advowsons to the monks.

[2] A. Hamilton Thompson, *The Premonstratensian Abbey of Welbeck* (1938), p. 34.

[3] See the list printed in Somner's *Antiquities*, p. 41.

[4] See the Rev. C. E. Woodruff, 'The Financial Aspect of the Cult of St Thomas of Canterbury' in *Arch. Cant.* (1932), XLIV, pp. 13–32.

instantaneously cured,[1] soon drew countless pilgrims to the scene of the martyrdom. In the years before the exile the offerings averaged £426. 3s. 7d. per annum and in 1220, the year of the translation of the relics, they came to no less than £1142. 5s. 0d.[2] There was a big drop in oblations in the middle of the thirteenth century but at the beginning of the next century they once more attained the pre-exilic level. It was in the latter half of the fourteenth century, 'the era of Chaucer and the *Canterbury Tales*, that the cult of St Thomas seems to have attained to its apogee'.[3] In the years 1370–83 the offerings averaged £545. 8s. 10d. The following century saw a remarkable fall in oblations. Only £66. 15s. 0d. was received from this source in 1436, and £25. 6s. 8d. in 1444. In this period oblations rarely, if ever, reached the figure of £100. At the time of the Dissolution they averaged but £36. 2s. 7d. a year.[4]

The growth of the revenues of the priory can be traced with a considerable degree of accuracy in the accounts of the treasurers.[5] In the years before the exile the income of an average year was a little over £1406.[6] In spite of the drop in oblations in the middle of the century, there was a gradual growth in revenue during the thirteenth century. In 1292 the treasurers received a sum of £2062. 16s. 11¼d.,[7] which represents approximately the average for the period. The vigorous initiative of Prior Henry of Eastry (1285–1331) was primarily responsible for the rapid increase in revenues which took place in the early part of the fourteenth

---

[1] See Dr E. A. Abbott, *St Thomas of Canterbury. His Death and Miracles* (1898), I, pp. 223–333. The cure of a number of purely nervous disorders was also attributed to the intercession of the saint. Our chief authority for these events is Benedict, a monk of Christ Church who became prior in 1175 and abbot of Peterborough in 1177. 'Great weight', wrote Dr Abbott, 'must be attached to his accounts of the early miracles' (*ibid*. p. 224).

[2] It should, however, be noticed that no less than £1154. 16s. 5d. was spent by the cellarer this year on the entertainment of pilgrims. The increase in oblations was, therefore, more than offset by the parallel increase in expenditure.                                              [3] Woodruff, *op. cit.* p. 21.

[4] *Valor Ecclesiasticus* (Rec. Comm. 1810), I, p. 8.

[5] In the fifteenth century the prior assumed the functions of a treasurer; see last chapter.

[6] Woodruff, *op. cit.* p. 16.                        [7] Cant. MS. F ii.

century. In the last year of his priorate the net revenue of the house came to just over £2540,[1] a figure that was barely maintained for the next sixty years and certainly not increased until the last decade of the century. Then, the almost universal adoption of the leasehold system and the large investments in land, which followed upon Thomas Chillenden's accession to the priorate in 1391, brought about another large increase in revenue. In 1411, the last year of Chillenden's rule, the income soared to a peak point of £4100. 1s. 9¾d.[2] This increase was not, however, maintained throughout the fifteenth century. In 1437 receipts had dropped to £2381. 18s. 0¾d.,[3] in 1454 to £2115. 10s. 8d.,[4] and in 1456 to £2059. 19s. 3d.[5] In 1468 the revenues had fallen as low as £1828. 0s. 7d.,[6] but five years later, in 1473, a considerable recovery was made and the income amounted to £2841. 3s. 3d.[7] At the time of the Dissolution the annual income of the priory averaged £2349. 8s. 5¾d.[8] The decrease in revenue in the fifteenth century may be attributed partly to the shrinkage in rents, which was due primarily to economic causes, and partly to the drop in oblations caused by civil disorder and the decline in the popular fervour for pilgrimage.

An attempt to classify a normal year's revenue shows that about two-thirds of it consisted of rents and fee-farms from the estates of the priory. Until the fifteenth century oblations constituted about a quarter of the income. The rest consisted of tithes, pensions, and miscellaneous payments of all sorts. One point must be stressed in conclusion. In the last two centuries of the middle ages the monks tended to invest money in plate and ornament rather than in land. The inventories of ornaments and jewels acquired during the fourteenth and fifteenth centuries[9] show that the monks of Christ Church attached great importance to these valuable securities. In an age of falling land-values they proved to be a far safer investment.

[1] Cant. MS. F iii.  
[2] Cant. MS. M 13, xvii, mem. 2.  
[3] *Ibid.* mem. 7.  
[4] *Ibid.* mem. 9.  
[5] *Ibid.* mem. 10.  
[6] *Ibid.* mem. 11..  
[7] *Ibid.* mem. 12.  
[8] *Valor Ecclesiasticus*, I, p. 16.  
[9] J. Wickham Legg and W. H. St John Hope, *Inventories of Christchurch, Canterbury* (1902).

# Chapter Two

## THE CENTRAL FINANCIAL SYSTEM

The twelfth century was pre-eminently the period in which the monks of Christ Church organized and consolidated their vast possessions. Under the firm rule of the Norman archbishops and a series of enlightened priors, a central financial system grew up in the priory as a framework for all future developments in household organization. It is proposed to trace the evolution of this centralized system in some detail, in order that the elaborate domestic arrangements of the monks may be fully understood.

By the middle of the twelfth century, and probably earlier, the bulk of the revenues of the priory had been divided among three obedientiaries, the cellarer, the chamberlain, and the sacrist.[1] Certain small rents in the city of Canterbury were appropriated to the upkeep of the almonry and the guesthouse.[2] There was as yet no central office of receipt. Then at some point between the years 1163 and 1167 a *dispensator* or *thesaurarius* was appointed by the monks.[3] The function of this new obedientiary was clearly defined by Pope Alexander III, who enjoined in 1179 that all the rents of the cellarer, chamberlain, and sacrist should be received by treasurers appointed by the prior and convent. The treasurers were to undertake no commitments or expenditure without the

---

[1] This arrangement was confirmed by Archbishop Theobald (1139–61) (*H.M.C.* Appendix to VIIIth Report, p. 319) and by Pope Hadrian IV in 1158: *Papsturkunden in England*, ed. W. Holtzmann, II, p. 288.

[2] See Cant. MS. R 31 from Box D in ZA, a rental of the city compiled during the priorate of Wibert (1153–67).

[3] In his detailed confirmation of the three separate obediences and household organization of Christ Church in 1163 (*Papsturkunden in England*, II, p. 299) Pope Alexander III has no mention of a treasury. The Canterbury rental (Cant. MS. R 31), which cannot be earlier than 1163, the year in which Gervase, who is mentioned therein, became a monk (see *Camb. Antiq. Soc. Publ.* XXXIV, p. 167), and cannot be later than 1167, the year of the death of Wibert, who is referred to as a living person, enumerates small rents apportioned to a *dispensator* or *thesaurarius*. We know that the treasury was built during Wibert's priorate: Woodruff and Danks, *Memorials of Canterbury Cathedral*, pp. 50–51.

express consent of the prior and convent or the advice of the *major et sanior pars*.[1] It seems highly probable that Prior Wibert, who was a man of resource and acumen, instituted this centralized system himself as a necessary simplification in the finances and a safeguard against mismanagement in the three main departments.

In the years of hectic strife before the exile of 1207 the monks maintained their central financial system intact. It is true that Baldwin confiscated the endowment which his predecessor had bestowed upon the almonry.[2] The archbishop was nevertheless obliged to restore the possessions of the priory in 1186, the year after his accession.[3] Twelve years later the long series of extant treasurers' accounts begins.[4] They bear striking testimony to the complete integrity of that central office established under Prior Wibert. It is impossible to deny that an institution which had emerged unscathed from the protracted quarrels with Baldwin and Hubert Walter was possessed of a degree of stability uncommon for such an early date.[5]

---

[1] The pope issued three bulls on 20 February 1179, confirming the individual possessions of the three obedientiaries (*Papsturkunden in England*, II, pp. 371–78). In each case he insisted 'quod redditus ipsi ad eorum custodiam deveniant, qui per priorem et conventum fuerint thesaurarii constituti, et illi de redditibus ipsis nichil ordinent vel expendant nisi de mandato prioris et conventus aut majoris et sanioris partis'.

[2] Archbishop Richard (1174–84) endowed the almonry with the revenue of three churches and their chapels (Gervase, *Opera*, I, p. 332). Pope Alexander III confirmed this grant in 1178 (*Papsturkunden in England*, II, p. 364) and again in the following year (*ibid.* p. 370). Pope Lucius III added a further confirmation (*ibid.* p. 418) before Baldwin snatched the revenues from the monks in 1186 (Gervase, *Opera*, I, p. 332).

[3] Gervase, *Opera*, I, p. 333.

[4] In the Dean and Chapter Library, Canterbury (henceforth abbreviated for reference as Cant. MS.), MS. D IV, fos. 1–16 v. contains treasurers' accounts for the years 1198–1205. Two vellum-bound volumes, F ii and F iii, contain, with two gaps (1207–13, the period of the exile, and 1337–70, with the exception of the account for the year 1350, which is extant), a continuous series of accounts for the years 1206 to 1384. Accounts supplementary to these will be indicated in the text.

[5] For the attempts at centralizing monastic finance which took place at the end of the twelfth and beginning of the thirteenth centuries, see C. R. Cheney, 'The Papal Legate and English Monasteries in 1206' in *Eng. Hist. Rev.* XLVI, pp. 443–52.

The form of the account itself bears every sign of careful organization. The grouping of the receipts displays a regard for the distinction between revenue derived from internal and external sources and for expenditure incurred with or without tally. The contraction of loans (*de empromtis*) is, however, placed on the credit side (a practice which was to become very common in medieval accountancy) and the title and dating of the earliest accounts show considerable vagaries.[1] The main principle—central control of monastic expenditure—was effectively asserted. The treasurers allotted to the obedientiaries sums which varied annually in accordance with the needs of their respective offices. If an obedientiary incurred greater expenses than his allocation warranted, the treasurers would make good his loss at the end of the year and enter their obligation in the form of a debt at the foot of their account. Often these debts dragged over several years, and a number of partial repayments (*partes solucionum*) to obedientiaries were recorded.

If the treasury was able to survive the contest with Baldwin it was exposed to still graver danger by the complete break in the life of the monastic community of Christ Church, which began on 15 July 1207 and lasted until June 1213. How thoroughly the monastic property was sequestrated is shown by the exchequer survey of 1211.[2] It might reasonably be expected that monastic institutions would undergo a radical change when the monks resumed their life at Canterbury in 1213, after six years' exile and under changed conditions. It is therefore a matter of some surprise to find that the central financial system of the priory was quite unshaken by these events. The treasury resumed its work as if uninterrupted and financial recovery was rapid and complete.[3]

[1] See R. A. L. Smith, 'The Central Financial System of Christ Church, Canterbury, 1186–1512' in *Eng. Hist. Rev.* LV, pp. 353–69. The 1198–99 account is printed in full at the end of this article.

[2] Summarized for the Essex custody of Christ Church by J. F. Nichols in *Custodia Essexae*, pp. 166–68.

[3] As compared with the year 1206, the revenue of the treasurers dropped in 1213 from £1492. 10s. 0d. to £986. 0s. 8d. (Cant. MS. F ii, fo. 53), but in 1214 the pre-exilic level was far exceeded by a revenue of £2638. 1s. 3d. (*ibid.* fo. 54 v.).

The accounts of the three years following the return from exile (1213–15) are of extraordinary interest in showing how continuity was maintained and the *status quo* resumed. In the first place, the prior of the dependent cell of Dover, who appears to have been entrusted with the offerings made at the cathedral shrines during the exile, faithfully handed over a sum of £245. 10s. 0d. before the Michaelmas audit of 1213.[1] Restitutions of property began in the same year[2] and the treasurers began to pay off debts which they had incurred before the exile.[3] In the following year property was restored to the monks on a large scale[4] and the liquidation of debts continued. By 1215 the process of restitution had been almost completed; the subsequent accounts afford little evidence of further activity in this direction.[5]

At the same time as the financial position of the priory was re-established on a firm footing, certain very clear tendencies began to manifest themselves in the policy of the treasurers. A system of large-scale borrowing was developed to enable the treasurers to increase the competence of their office and to meet the heavy expenses connected with the translation of the relics of St Thomas in 1220[6] and the negotiations at Rome which resulted in the issue of the bull of privileges by Pope Honorius III in the same year. In the pre-exilic period the treasurers had worked largely on a credit basis. They had freely borrowed from out-siders and deliberately deferred payments to obedientiaries and serjeants of the manors. As a rule, however, the amount borrowed each year approximated closely to the sums repaid,[7] and the only

---

[1] Cant. MS. F ii, fo. 53.

[2] A sum of £2. 7s. 5½d. was received 'de Willelmo Pentecoste et de aliis hominibus de minutis restitutionibus': *ibid.* fo. 52 v.  [3] *Ibid.* fo. 54.

[4] 'De restitutione ablatorum—£1129. 17s. 0d.': *ibid.* fo. 54 v.

[5] In 1220 a sum of 10s. 6d. accrued to the treasury 'de restitutione damp-norum tempore exilii nostri' (*ibid.* fo. 64 v.) and in 1227 the paltry sum of 1s. 'de quodam destrouctione [*sic*] bosci de tempore exilis' (*ibid.* fo. 71 v.).

[6] The Rev. C. E. Woodruff has drawn attention to the staggering increase in the cellarer's expenses for this year, which more than counterbalanced the increase in revenue from oblations: *Arch. Cant.* XLIV, pp. 17–18.

[7] For example, in 1201 the monks borrowed a sum of £140. 3s. 4d. and repaid £174. 2s. 2d. to their creditors (Cant. MS. D iv, fos. 10 v., 11) and in 1203 borrowed £284. 13s. 4d. and repaid £340. 7s. 10d. (*ibid.* fos. 12 v., 13).

evidence of a substantial long-term loan comes from the year 1205 when £653. 16s. 0d. was owing 'tam Christianis quam Judeis'.[1] After 1213 loans were negotiated on a far more ambitious scale for long terms and at high rates of usury.

The Jews of Canterbury[2] and Italian merchants from Rome, Siena, Bologna, Florence, and Pistoja were the two main bodies of creditors. Thus in 1213 and 1217 small debts were repaid to Jews[3] and in 1227 the Jew Solomon was repaid a sum of £49. 6s. 8d. 'sine lucro viii annorum'.[4] Italian merchants were by far the largest creditors of the priory during the thirteenth century. As early as 1199 a sum of £244. 10s. 0d. was handed over to Lombard merchants in part repayment of a debt of £333. 7s. 6d.[5] and in 1213 Romeus, a merchant of Bologna, was extending large credits to the priory.[6] In the following year John de Sancto Angelo, a Roman merchant, supplied the monks with credit for a term of seven years[7] and Laurentius, a merchant of the same city, for a term of nine years.[8] The rate of usury *per annum* demanded by these Italian merchants varied between the figures of 15 and 20 per cent. For example, in 1221 certain merchants of Rome and Siena supplied the priory with a loan of £280 and demanded yearly interest of nearly 20 per cent.[9] In 1227 a group of Italian merchants who had proffered a loan of £1870 contented themselves with an annual *lucrum* of 15 per cent prior to the repayment of the principal obligation.[10] Throughout the thirteenth century Italian credit played a role of paramount importance in the financial history of the priory. Indeed it may be said that the monks succeeded in expanding their economy in all directions largely on the basis of Italian financial capitalism.[11]

[1] Cant. MS. D iv, fo. 16 v. It is to be noticed that the monks were then entering upon the last stage of their long conflict with two successive archbishops.

[2] See M. Adler, 'The Jews of Canterbury' in *Jewish Hist. Soc. Trans.* VII, pp. 19–59.

[3] Cant. MS. F ii, fos. 54, 60 v.   [4] *Ibid.* fo. 71 v.

[5] Cant. MS. D iv, fo. 3.   [6] Cant. MS. F ii, fo. 54.

[7] *Ibid.* fo. 55 v.   [8] *Ibid.*

[9] Cant. MS. F ii, fo. 65.   [10] *Ibid.* fo. 71.

[11] For a study of the financial history of the Christ Church household, see my next chapter. On early credit transactions in general, see M. M. Postan,

At the same time as the mechanism of credit was fully organized the monks evolved a centralized system of audit. Testimony to this development is to be found in the statement of the prior of Christ Church in 1332 to the effect that 'from old time it has always been the custom that our serjeants from all parts of England should come to Canterbury to our exchequer (*a nostre Eschekier*) there to hand in their accounts, and this in the presence of certain of our brethren'.[1] The word *scaccarium* is used in the early treasurers' accounts to denote both the audit-chamber and the audit itself,[2] which doubtless took place by means of counters on a chequered table as in the royal administration.[3] At this annual audit, which took place at Michaelmas and in the weeks following, a general account was drawn up by the senior monk-auditors and called the *Assisa Scaccarii*. A number of these accounts are extant for the thirteenth and early fourteenth century.[4] The first occurs in the year 1225. In form the *Assisa Scaccarii* was somewhat analogous to a combination of the *Status Obedientiariorum* and *Proficuum Maneriorum* of Norwich cathedral priory[5] in that it digested the accounts of all the obedientiaries and manorial officials and presented them in a summarized form for the inspection of

---

'Credit in Medieval Trade' in *Econ. Hist. Rev.* I, pp. 234–61 and the bibliographical article by the same writer on 'Medieval Capitalism', *ibid.* IV, pp. 212–27.

[1] *Lit. Cant.*, ed. J. B. Sheppard, I, pp. 481–83.

[2] Thus, in their 1204–5 account the treasurers announced in respect of a debt owing to the cellarer 'et debuimus ei ad scaccarium' (Cant. MS. D iv, fo. 15 v.), and references to 'partes solucionis debitorum facte ante scaccarium' are of common occurrence (e.g. in 1213, Cant. MS. F ii, fo. 54). The annual *Assisa Scaccarii*, drawn up at the audit (see *infra*), was headed by the single word *Scaccarium*.

[3] On the meaning and use of the word *scaccarium*, see *Dialogus de Scaccario* (1902 ed.), p. 60, and R. L. Poole, *The Exchequer in the Twelfth Century*, pp. 100–2. At the head of the 1313 *Assisa Scaccarii* account of Christ Church there is a representation of a chessboard.

[4] Individual documents of this class have survived for the years 1225, 1230, 1231, 1236, 1237, 1244, 1252, 1259, 1264, 1269, 1273, 1278, 1287, 1313, 1336 (Cant. MS. M 13, xix) and there is a continuous series for the years 1252–62 enrolled in Cant. Reg. H, fos. 172–217.

[5] H. W. Saunders, *An Introduction to the Rolls of Norwich Cathedral Priory*, pp. 11–13, 17.

the auditors. But it went further than the Norwich accounts by supplying a monetary estimate of the yearly value of agricultural produce as a basis for calculating all receipts in kind. The senior monks thus had before them a complete review of the finances of the priory which enabled them to check and control departmental expenditure. Their exercise of this limited function of auditing the accounts marks the beginning of an important administrative development in the priory household, which will be fully discussed in a later chapter.

A certain similarity in procedure will be observed between the work performed by the senior monks at the exchequer (*scaccarium*) of Christ Church in the thirteenth century and that of the *barones* at the royal exchequer in the earliest stage of its evolution. In the monastic as in the royal household the senior members, who on more than one occasion styled themselves *barones*,[1] acted as an auditing body and met at a place distinct from the treasury.[2] The *archa*, which contained the revenue, was brought from the treasury to the exchequer at the time of the audit.[3] In each of the households the distinction between an exchequer of receipt and an exchequer of audit was well defined and preserved. The use of tallies, counters, and a chessboard was common to both institutions. The position of the prior was equivalent to that of the justiciar 'who has the oversight of all that is done either in the lower or upper exchequer'.[4] At the end of the process of audit a great roll was drawn up, called in the royal household the *magnus rotulus pipae* and at Christ Church the *Assisa Scaccarii*, which gave a complete account of the finances of the household. Here the resemblance ceases. The senior monks who met at the *scaccarium*

---

[1] At the head of the 1455–56 account of Prior Thomas Goldston, who was acting as treasurer, are given the names of eight monks under the title 'Barones hoc anno' (Cant. MS. M 13, xvii, mem. 10). In 1432 a monk who received a small payment from the *firmarius* of Monkton was designated a baron (Cant. MS. serjeant's account).

[2] The treasury at Christ Church was situated between the north wall of St Andrew's Chapel and the south side-aisle wall of the Infirmary hall at a short distance from the *scaccarium* or checker building in the eastern range of the infirmary cloister.

[3] Cant. MS. D iv, *passim*.          [4] R. L. Poole, *op. cit.* p. 104.

of Christ Church never possessed judicial powers like the royal *barones scaccarii*. It should also be insisted that an analogy between the two institutions can only be maintained for a limited period, the first three-quarters of the thirteenth century. By the end of that century the *seniores ad scaccarium* of Christ Church were developing functions which had no parallel in the royal administration.

While the monks were organizing a centralized system of audit and a machinery of credit in the period following their return from exile, the relation of the treasurers to the subsidiary obedientiaries was further clarified by a number of devices which made for the more effective control of the latter by the central body. This end was effected in three principal ways. The treasurers often assigned revenues to obedientiaries with an appropriation clause stating the exact nature of the expenditure contemplated. Again, as an additional safeguard against any tendencies to autonomy in the individual departments, the tenure of one office by a single obedientiary was strictly controlled. Thirdly, the influence of powerful obedientiaries was in several cases curbed by the creation of new officials, who shared the financial responsibilities of the office.

The assignment of revenues by the treasurers for a specific purpose is exemplified by the allocation of a large sum to the sacrist in 1221 for expenditure on the *nova opera*[1] and to the precentor in 1227 'ad opus refectorii'.[2] The greatest danger to financial unity was clearly the cellarer, who was able to make such large demands for the needs of his office. A rapid series of changes took place in this department, which made it impossible for any one cellarer to wield inordinate power. Thus in 1221–22 no less than three persons occupied the office at different times in the year,[3] and there was a further change made in the year which followed.[4] Some time in 1216–17 a kitchener (*coquinarius*) was created, who deprived the cellarer of his most important function —the feeding of the monastic household.[5] In the next year, however, the cellarer resumed his old function and the kitchener disappeared.

[1] Cant. MS. F ii, fo. 65 v.     [2] *Ibid*. fo. 71.
[3] *Ibid*. fo. 66 v.     [4] *Ibid*. fo. 67 v.     [5] *Ibid*. fo. 60.

c

In the period 1225–1300, which for our purpose presents a convenient unity, the treasurers of Christ Church attained their maximum influence. Administrative centralization was the hallmark of the age and the monks of Christ Church were fortunate in being governed at the end of the century by two remarkable men with a genius for organization—John Pecham, the Franciscan archbishop (1279–92), and the great reforming prior, Henry of Eastry (1285–1331). The work of these two men stabilized the financial system of the priory for a century.

Pecham summed up the financial developments of the last hundred years by ordaining in 1282 that all the revenues of the priory, save those appropriated to the almonry, should pass through the hands of the treasurers.[1] He made no exception in favour of the prior and other obedientiaries engaged in *extrinseca negocia* but rather insisted that they should have their expenditure provided for by the treasurers before leaving the priory.[2] By his regulations on the custody of the common seal[3] and the presentation of accounts by manorial officials at the annual audit[4] Pecham did much to safeguard the integrity of the centralized financial system of the priory.

The priorate of Henry of Eastry saw a radical change in the relationship of the manorial finances to the central treasury. In the earliest accounts the treasurers received cash sums *de maneriis*, a statement that implied a transaction with the individual *servientes*, whether at Canterbury or on the manors. Only customary payments of an exceptional nature were collected by the monk-wardens in person.[5] In 1273 one stage further was reached by substituting for the general term *de maneriis* the name of each *serviens* and his particular render.[6] In 1289 financial responsibility was transferred by one stroke from the *serviens* to the monk-warden (*custos maneriorum*), who henceforth made all renders

---

[1] *Reg. Epist. J.P.* ed. C. T. Martin, I, p. 341.

[2] *Ibid.* I, pp. 341–48.          [3] *Ibid.* II, p. 403.

[4] *Ibid.* II, pp. 399–400.

[5] Thus, the entry for the year 1220–21 is typical: ‘De custodibus maneriorum de Welles ad pesepaneges et ad solidatas serviencium de bracino— £9. 3s. 10½d.’: Cant. MS. F ii, fo. 65.

[6] Cant. MS. F ii.

*de custodia sua.*[1] For the next hundred years the central financial system rested on the fruitful co-operation of the treasurers and their local representatives, the four monk-wardens of the scattered estates.[2]

Before local financial responsibility to the central office had finally passed from the *servientes* to the *custodes maneriorum* the treasury had greatly increased its competence. The case of leased property is most instructive in this context. In the first half of the thirteenth century the fee-farms (*feodifirmae*) had been in the charge of a special class of rent-collectors distinct from the treasury; they received no mention in the central accounts. But in the year 1260 the treasury assumed responsibility for all fee-farms,[3] which henceforth represented a regular item in the annual account. The enrolment of wool-sales on the treasurers' accounts for the first time in the year 1288–89[4] was a further development in the same movement for financial simplicity on centralized lines.

In order that an over-simplified and distorted picture of the centralization of Canterbury finances in the latter half of the thirteenth century may not be given, it should at once be pointed out that certain classes of revenue eluded the Christ Church treasurers even at the height of their power. In the first place, the substantial rents appropriated to the almonry never fell under the control of the treasurers. The almoners had their own *servientes*, who rendered annual accounts to their master in the almonry.[5] Again, the *camera prioris* was a separately endowed institution. A long list of 'Redditus pertinentes ad Cameram Prioris' occurs in Prior Eastry's private memorandum book (c. 1322),[6] and the

---

[1] Cant. MS. F ii. The first year of Henry of Eastry's priorate, 1285–86, saw a hesitating approach to this fundamental reform. Receipts from the individual *servientes* were given in the order of the individual *custodiae*, without any reference to the administrative grouping other than the phrase *summa de maneriis usque huc* in the case of the two Kentish *custodiae*, and *summa ab alia usque huc* for the other two units.

[2] For an account of the office of monk-warden, see Chapter Seven.

[3] Cant. MS. F ii unfoliated.          [4] *Ibid.*

[5] See the accounts of the serjeants of the lands of the almonry at Monkton and Eastry in Cant. MSS. serjeants' accounts.

[6] B.M. Cott. MS. Galba E iv, fo. 34.

day-book of Priors Oxenden and Hathbrand (1331–43) shows
the prior in receipt of an income from many different sources.
Thus in 1331, besides receiving payments in cash and jewels from
the treasurers, Prior Oxenden had considerable revenues appropriated to his *camera* by the shrine-keepers (*custodes feretrorum*)
and the serjeants of several manors. The profits of the High Court
served to swell the income of the *camera prioris*. A total revenue
of £45. 14s. 7¼d. accrued to the prior's privy purse in this particular year.[1] The prior was responsible to the treasurers for his
expenditure,[2] but his *camera* so far resembled the royal institution
in that it itinerated with him, and that payments which normally
would have been made *in thesauro* were often made *in camera* in
obedience to the prior's command.[3]

In addition to the substantial revenues appropriated to the
almonry and *camera prioris*, separate property was owned by the
sacrist in the city of Canterbury, at Street near Lympne, Geddinge
in Wootton and Bernesole in Staple,[4] and two London churches
were also appropriated to this department. The anniversarian had
his own endowment.[5] Finally, the church at Halstowe was appropriated by Hubert Walter to the office of precentor, the church
at Pagham by Simon Islip for the students at Canterbury College,
Oxford. The income from Godmersham Church was specially
allocated to the cathedral fabric fund.[6] None of these revenues
passed through the hands of the treasurers. It is therefore very
unwise to make facile generalizations about the complete financial

[1] Cant. MS. D.E. 3, fo. 1.

[2] In 1282 Pecham ordained that 'tam prior quam ceteri exeuntes expensas
recipiant de thesauro....Post redditum autem prior per capellanum suum
rationem reddere bona fide de expensis saltem summarie teneatur...': *Reg.
Epist. J.P.* I, p. 342.

[3] Evidence of these payments *in camera* is afforded by Cant. MS. D.E. 3
*passim*. On the analogous functions of the royal *camera*, see T. F. Tout,
*Chapters*, I, p. 105. There is no evidence of a wardrobe distinct from the
*camera* at Canterbury.

[4] C. E. Woodruff, 'The Sacrist's Rolls of Christ Church, Canterbury' in
*Arch. Cant.* XLVIII, p. 40.

[5] A list of 'Redditus pertinentes ad Anniversarium' has survived for
c. 1300: Cant. MS. M 13, i.

[6] J. F. Nichols, *op. cit.* p. 112.

unity of Christ Church. The unity was only approximate; it never became absolute.

The theoretical omnicompetence of the treasury is clearly expressed in the two *Assisae Scaccarii* accounts which have survived for the early fourteenth century.[1] They simply give the account of the treasurers and the value of produce in terms of money, omitting altogether the accounts of the subsidiary obedientiaries. As a general picture of the priory's financial position these later *Assisae Scaccarii* are therefore quite untrustworthy. By the middle of the fourteenth century the centralized system of audit had broken down and the documents in question were no longer compiled. Professional auditors did on the manors the work which the senior monks had previously performed at the exchequer of the priory.[2]

The centralized system of accountancy makes it easier to study the solvency or insolvency of the priory at this peak period of its economy. The long priorate of Henry of Eastry (1285–1331) and those of his two successors, Richard Oxenden (1331–38) and Robert Hathbrand (1338–70), which marked the apogee of the centralized system, were a period of remarkable financial stability. This is all the more remarkable in that unfavourable weather conditions and pestilences were constantly recurrent. Floods, drought, and plague succeeded in upsetting the balance-sheets of individual manors, but the central institution stood firm.[3] Not only were the treasurers able to curb expenditure when diminished returns from a number

---

[1] The accounts are extant for the years 1313 and 1336.

[2] Thus, for example, reference is made in 1322 to the serjeant of Chartham rendering his account on the manor 'coram auditoribus dictorum prioris et conventus, ad audiendum compotos ballivorum et servientium suorum deputatis' (*Lit. Cant.* I, p. 91). Two secular auditors were present on the Kentish manors in 1337 (*ibid.* II, p. 168). Payments to professional auditors are frequently cited in the serjeants' accounts.

[3] The serjeants' accounts for the marsh manors of Ebony, Appledore, and Orgarswick-cum-Agney in south-west Kent, and of Lyden and Monkton in east Kent, are especially noticeable for the evidence they afford of financial instability and high debts incurred in years of flood. The central accounts offer a most instructive contrast, showing that the treasurers were able to recoup themselves from other sources and so preserve the financial equilibrium.

of manors dictated such a measure; they were also able to compensate themselves to a large extent by maximizing their receipts from manors least affected by the inclemency of the weather. There was much borrowing and lending—the recognized technique of all great monastic institutions at this time—but long-term credits from foreign capitalists and Jews entirely ceased. The last of these debts to Italian merchants were paid off in the first fifteen years of Eastry's priorate.[1] Henceforth credit was supplied to the treasurers by native merchant capitalists, largely in the shape of advanced payments for goods.[2]

It may, therefore, fairly be claimed that the priory as an institution greatly benefited from having its accounts placed on a centralized basis. The sure instinct which had made Pecham demand such a reform in many of the larger monasteries of the kingdom was pre-eminently justified by the practice of Christ Church under Henry of Eastry and his immediate successors. It gave an organic simplicity to the monastic accounts, and facilitated the work of the auditors and the obedientiaries in their individual departments. It can be no coincidence that the prosperity of Christ Church and its demesne farming occurred at the time when the centralized system of accounting was most firmly established.

It would seem instructive at this point to relate the Canterbury machinery to other English Benedictine systems in the middle ages. Each monastery naturally tended to develop on individual lines and there was never any period when a uniform system obtained throughout the country. There were, however, certain methods of receipt which commended themselves to many houses, and for the later middle ages it is possible to affirm that three principal systems of receipt existed in the English monasteries. First, there were monasteries in which all the funds passed through

[1] In 1285 a sum of £1376. 6s. 4d. was owing to merchants of Florence and Pistoja (B.M. Cott. MS. Galba E iv, fo. 108 v.). These debts were wiped off in the two following years (Cant. MS. F ii). After Edward I had played havoc with the goods of the priory in 1297 Prior Eastry was obliged to secure credit in the Roman Curia (Camb. Univ. Lib. MS. Ee. v, 31, fos. 78 v., 81, 84). The money was soon repaid.

[2] In 1336, for example, Richard Spycer of Fordwich and William Pynere of Sandwich were two of the creditors of the priory: Cant. MS. M 13, xix.

a central receiving office, commonly known as a treasury or bursary, before they were distributed to the conventual officials. Secondly, there were houses in which the treasurers or bursars received only that part of the income which was not apportioned to conventual officials. Thirdly, there were houses in which there was no receiving office at all, with the result that the greater part of the revenue was received by individual officers of the monastery.

These three systems may be illustrated from the practice of English Benedictine monasteries in the late medieval centuries. The eager desire of Pecham, archbishop of Canterbury (1279–92), to simplify the system of monastic accounts was largely responsible for the erection of central receiving offices in many monasteries, of which the abbeys of Glastonbury and Reading were the most renowned. The priory of Christ Church was, as has been shown, already in enjoyment of such a central office. Subsequent episcopal policy tended to favour such institutions, whose great merit lay in the comparative simplicity presented by a general survey of the. monastic accounts.[1] It cannot, however, be too clearly stressed that the central receiving office never became a universal factor in monastic organization. Indeed, the system whereby the treasurers or bursars received only that part of the income which was not apportioned to conventual officials was actually more common in the accounts familiar to us. In effect, the treasurers were placed in charge of a central reserve fund, as, for example, at the great cathedral priory of St Swithun's, Winchester.[2] It was declared at the abbey of Evesham in 1206 that the cellarer who acted as bursar 'was to have the whole care of the abbey save the incomes assigned to the offices of the monks';[3] and at Worcester cathedral priory the cellarer also acted as bursar and receiver of all the unassigned revenues.[4] This system appears to have been in force at Durham and Mr Snape has argued convincingly for its wide prevalence.[5]

---

[1] R. H. Snape, *English Monastic Finances*, pp. 39–40.

[2] *Compotus Rolls of the Obedientiaries of St Swithun's Priory, Winchester*, ed. G. W. Kitchin (Hants. Rec. Soc. 1892), p. 32.

[3] *Chronicon Abbatiae de Evesham*, ed. W. D. Macray, p. 207.

[4] *Compotus Rolls of the Priory of Worcester in the XIVth and XVth centuries*, ed. S. G. Hamilton (Worc. Hist. Soc. 1910), pp. vi–viii, 10–23.

[5] Snape, *op. cit.* pp. 42–47.

Then, again, there were those monasteries in which no central receiving office of any kind ever seems to have been created. Norwich cathedral priory is a case in point where 'there is no intermediary between the prior and the officers'[1] and at Abingdon Abbey in the period 1322–1478 there was no central receiving office, although the treasurer received substantial pensions from nearly every obedientiary and undertook building and other expenses.[2]

In the first three-quarters of the fourteenth century the centralized financial system at Christ Church was rigidly maintained. The monastery was governed by a series of enlightened priors who forbore from tampering with the central fund.[3] An anonymous chronicler, describing the condition of the house on the death of Prior Hathbrand in 1370, explicitly states that 'all the revenues of the Church after that time, and for a long time previously, were paid into the hands of the treasurers'.[4] The enrolled accounts bear witness to the complete integrity of the treasurers in fulfilling their function, a balanced economy obtained throughout the period, and any sudden fall in oblations was met by a cutting down of food supplies. Only at the end of the century did sweeping changes inaugurate a new era in monastic finance.

---

[1] H. W. Saunders, *An Introduction to the Rolls of Norwich Cathedral Priory*, p. 71. See, however, the article by C. R. Cheney on 'Norwich Cathedral Priory in the Fourteenth Century' in *Bulletin of the John Rylands Library*, xx, No. I, January 1936, in which evidence is adduced for the existence of a common fund or *thesaurus* in the year 1347.

[2] *Accounts of the obedientiars of Abingdon Abbey*, ed. R. E. G. Kirk (Camden Soc. 1892), pp. 41–51.

[3] The archbishops were also solicitous for the integrity of the central office. In 1314, for example, Archbishop Reynolds ordained 'quod de thesaurariis sufficientibus qui officio domus deservirent concitatio fratrum consilio provideret, amotis illis qui tunc temporis illi officio possidebant': Reg. Reynolds, fo. 104 v.

[4] *Arch. Cant.* xxix, p. 59.

# Chapter Three

## HOUSEHOLD ORGANIZATION AND EXPENDITURE

The full account of the evolution of the central financial system of the priory has prepared the way for a study of its household organization. It has been shown in a previous chapter that the archbishop, although titular abbot of his cathedral priory, was but rarely present in the monastery after the first half of the twelfth century. For all practical purposes the prior stood *in loco abbatis* and exercised the functions normal to the head of a Benedictine monastery. Known in the late Saxon period as *decanus et munuc*,[1] the prior, as he came to be called shortly after the Conquest, was at first appointed by the archbishop.[2] In 1174, however, Pope Alexander III granted the monks of Christ Church the privilege of freely electing a prior *sede vacante*,[3] and this arrangement was confirmed by Urban III in 1187.[4] Both popes stipulated that the elect should be a member of the Canterbury community (*de congregatione vestra*), provided that one of their number was found to be suitable for the office. Urban III further enjoined that the prior should not be deposed, save for the gravest reasons.[5] In the early thirteenth century, as a result of their protracted tussles with archbishops and king and their espousal of the papal interest, the

---

[1] See Armitage Robinson, *loc. cit.* and the introduction of W. G. Searle to the Chronicle of John Stone in *Camb. Antiq. Soc. Publ.* (1902), XXXIV, pp. xiv–xviii for some observations on the pre-Conquest deans of Christ Church.

[2] Dom D. Knowles, *The Monastic Order in England*, 943–1216, p. 626. The monks appear to have been consulted on the suitable candidate for an appointment. Thus in 1149 Walter Parvus became prior 'ex consilio conventus et institutione Theobaldi archiepiscopi': Gervase, *Opera*, I, p. 141.

[3] *Papsturkunden in England*, ed. W. Holtzmann, II, p. 323.

[4] *Ibid.* II, p. 445.

[5] *Ibid.* This injunction was probably necessitated by the arbitrary action of Theobald in deposing Prior Jeremiah in 1143: Gervase, *Opera*, I, pp. 126–27.

monks acquired the privilege of freely electing their prior *sede plena* as well as *sede vacante*.[1] Be that as it may, the accounts that have survived of elections to the priorate in the later middle ages show that the archbishop retained a considerable measure of control.[2] Indeed it is probably true to say that his was the decisive voice by virtue of his position as scrutator at the elections.[3]

The part played by the prior of Canterbury in the high affairs of Church and State falls outside the proper scope of this study. His numerous journeyings to Parliament and Convocation, and his absorption in the secular business of the monastery and kingdom, are abundantly evidenced in surviving records.[4] Attention must here be concentrated on the position of the prior as a great baron and householder. For at least as early as 1165, and before the murder of Becket, the prior had his own household distinct from the establishment of the monks.[5] Not only did he have his own officials and servants, but also his own revenues[6] and guesthouses.[7] Indeed, from the social standpoint, his condition was

[1] Pope Gregory IX (1227–41) acknowledged that the election of the prior of Christ Church belonged to the monks alone: *H.M.C.* App. to VIIIth Report, p. 317.

[2] See 'Forma eligendi priorem Cantuar'', an early fourteenth-century formula enrolled in B.M. Cott. MS. Galba E iv, fo. 26 v., and the common mandate issued by an archbishop to his monks preparatory to the election of a prior in *Lit. Cant.* I, pp. 7–8.

[3] Thus in 1338 Archbishop John Stratford appointed the bishop of Chichester as his representative in the chapter-house at Canterbury 'ad scrutandum in hac parte vota omnium et singulorum monachorum ejusdem ecclesie...et ad nominandum, praeficiendum, et dandum monachis dictae Ecclesiae Priorem ydoneum': *Lit. Cant.* II, p. 193.

[4] See the expenditure listed under the heading 'Equitantibus pro negociis ecclesie' in Lambeth MSS. 242, 243 *passim*, for an exhaustive account of the travels of the prior on ecclesiastical and secular business in the last half of the thirteenth and the greater part of the fourteenth centuries. The *Calendars of Letters Patent* show the prior serving on numerous royal commissions.

[5] The famous Norman drawing of the conventual buildings, made after the water-system was completed c. 1165 and reproduced by Professor R. Willis in his *History of the Conventual Buildings of Christ Church*, p. 196, shows a *camera prioris vetus* at the north-east angle of the Infirmary cloisters and a *nova camera prioris* further to the east.

[6] See *supra*, pp. 23–24.

[7] Willis, *op. cit.* pp. 15, 94–99.

indistinguishable from that of the great feudal magnates who were his contemporaries.

The prior's establishment at Canterbury was, by the fourteenth century, divided into five separate administrative departments, the chamber (*camera*), the kitchen (*coquina*), the pantry and buttery (*panetria et botelaria*), the scullery (*scuttelaria*), and the stable (*mareschalcia*). It therefore resembled the household of Bishop Ralph of Shrewsbury more closely than the loosely knit entourage of Bishop Swinfield of Hereford, if two contemporary establishments of prelates may be cited in comparison.[1] All three households, as well as that of the abbot of St Augustine's, were nevertheless alike in having roughly the same number of officials.[2] At Christ Church in 1377 there were, in addition to the two chaplains of the prior who acted as accountants, 14 permanent officials, 6 assistants, and 2 boys, making a total establishment of 24 persons. Their offices fell naturally into the framework of the five administrative departments. The chamberlain (*camberlanus*) had charge of the *camera* and the kitchen lay under the control of the cook (*cocus*) and keeper of the spits (*hastelator*). The pantry and buttery were supervised by the butler (*botellarius*) and his boy, and a scullion (*scutellarius*) presided over the work of a washer-woman (*lotrix pannorum*) in the scullery. A farrier (*ferrator*), groom (*palefridarius*), and stableman (*stabularius*) looked after the prior's horses. To these must be added a porter (*ostiarius*), a carter (*carectarius*) and his mate, a keeper of the meadows (*custos pratorum*), and a fisherman (*piscator*).[3]

All these officials, known collectively as *armigeri domini prioris*, made heavy inroads on the revenue of their master. In 1287 the cost of their clothes alone came to £13. 6s. 5d.[4] and their wages

---

[1] See A. H. Thompson, 'A Household Roll of Bishop Ralph of Shrewsbury, 1337–38' in Collectanea of Somerset Record Soc. (1924), XXXIX, and the Household Roll of Bishop Swinfield of Hereford 1289–90 printed by Camden Soc. 1854–55.

[2] There were seventeen permanent officials in the households of Bishop Ralph and the abbot of St Augustine's, and Bishop Swinfield seems to have had approximately the same number.

[3] Cant. MS. M 13, v, mem. 2. The Norman drawing shows a fishpond due east of the church.  [4] Lambeth MS. 242, fo. 98.

were higher than those of the conventual servants. They received special gifts in money on the great feast-days and were liberally regaled with spices and confectionery. A series of extant day-books reveal the privy purse expenditure of the priors, which was kept quite distinct from the income expended by the chaplains on the upkeep of the household.[1] It consisted of sundry payments to messengers and brief-bearers (*brevigeruli*), 'tips' to the *alumni* of the neighbourhood, such as the sheriff of Kent, and gifts to the Friars Preachers, the poor, actors, and minstrels.[2] The prior had also to buy the material for his own clothes—an expensive item[3]—but all food, save spices and luxuries, was supplied to his household by the cellarer of the monastery.

The conventual establishment was at an early date placed in charge of a number of senior monks called obedientiaries (*obedientiarii*). The *Statuta* of Lanfranc, which were compiled especially for Christ Church, detail the functions of seven obedientiaries; the conventual prior, the circa, the cantor, the sacrist, the chamberlain, the cellarer, and the infirmarian.[4] Three of these, the cellarer, the chamberlain, and the sacrist, were entrusted with the administration of revenues at least as early as the middle of the twelfth century, and one more obedientiary, the almoner, was created and endowed with separate sources of income by Archbishop Richard (1174–84).[5] All the revenues of the three obedientiaries, but not those of the almoner, passed, as we have seen, through the hands of central receivers or treasurers, who were created in the last years of Wibert's priorate (1163–67). Throughout the thirteenth century the system of departmental administration gradually increased in complexity. A vast scheme of financial and administrative devolution for the purpose of expenditure accompanied, and complemented, the centralization of the bulk of the revenues in the hands

---

[1] Lambeth MSS. 242 and 243 contain sections which detail this privy purse expenditure, and Cant. MS. D.E. 3 is a day-book of Priors Oxenden and Hathbrand for the years 1331–43.

[2] Cant. MS. D.E. 3, *passim*.

[3] For example, in 1331 Prior Oxenden spent £3. 17s. on burnet cloth, 13s. 1d. on leather for a mantle and 8d. on the making of this garment: *ibid.* fo. 2.

[4] Migne, *P.L.* cl, pp. 443–516.          [5] See *supra*.

of the treasurers. Before this system is described in detail, however, it will be well to trace the process whereby obedientiaries were elected to their offices.

The system in vogue at Christ Church in the latter half of the twelfth century is admirably illustrated by a bull of confirmation issued to the priory in 1187 by Pope Urban III.[1] The archbishop appointed the prior, the sub-prior (or circa), the cantor, the sacrist, and the chamberlain, as well as three of the more important lay servants, but the monks were free to dispose of the rest of the offices as they thought fit.[2] It was strongly implied that the archbishop should take the advice of the monks in making his appointments.[3] In the vacancy of the see the monks were accorded the liberty of making all the necessary appointments.

In the early thirteenth century, as we have seen, the monks secured the papal recognition of their claim to elect the prior. In other respects the system of appointment remained unchanged, and the composition between Archbishop Boniface and the prior and convent in 1259 merely affirmed the existing custom.[4] The monks seem to have adopted the practice of submitting the names of three persons to the archbishop for appointment to those offices of which he enjoyed the patronage. The archbishop then appointed one of these three at his discretion.[5] The monks jealously guarded their right to appoint to the other offices.[6] On 6 August 1282,

---

[1] *Papsturkunden in England*, II, pp. 447–48.

[2] '...tamen in aliis amministrationibus tam interioribus quam exterioribus liberum fuit hactenus predecessoribus vestris et vobis, non requisito ipsius archiepiscopi consilio vel assensu, ponere et ab eis, cum exegit necessitas et utilitas, amovere...': *ibid.*

[3] '...communi consilio et assensu archiepiscopi vestri et vestro prefici debeant...': *ibid.*

[4] '...archiepiscopus et successores sui facient vel creabunt obédienciarios quos ipse et predecessores sui hactenus consueverunt facere vel creare consilio prioris et seniorum prout consuevit fieri requisicio': Trin. Coll. Camb. MS. O. 9/26, fo. 76 v.

[5] I. Churchill, *Canterbury Administration*, I, p. 122.

[6] In 'absolving' the almoner of Christ Church from his office in 1281, Pecham lamely excused himself by saying that '...credebamus, errore facti decepti, ipsius institutionem et destitutionem ad nos sine medio pertinere': *Reg. Epist. J.P.* I, p. 245.

Archbishop Pecham ordained that in future the appointment of all officials should be discussed at the exchequer (*scaccarium*) by the prior and at least six monks, before the nominations were made in chapter.[1]

The Franciscan reformer can hardly have anticipated the serious embarrassment caused to Robert Winchelsey, his immediate successor in the archiepiscopal see, by this procedure. For, once assembled at the exchequer, the senior monks stoutly resisted the claims of the archbishop on this very matter of nominating obedientiaries. It came about in this wise. When Winchelsey first visited his cathedral priory in 1295 he 'absolved' a number of obedientiaries from their offices. Certain of the *seniores ecclesiae*, meeting at the exchequer, declared that the ancient custom of their house required only one person to be nominated to the archbishop for appointment. Others said that the custom of the last thirty years was for three persons or at least two to be nominated to the archbishop, who was to be guided in his appointment by the advice of the prior. The senior monks finally decided to submit the name of only one person to the archbishop for appointment to each of the vacant offices. Winchelsey quickly denounced this stratagem as a breach of the customary procedure and so the senior monks met again at the exchequer and, after arriving at a preliminary decision in the archbishop's favour, subsequently decided to effect a compromise and to nominate only two persons for appointment to each office. The archbishop greeted this further defiance of his wishes with surprising moderation. He sharply reproved the prior and senior monks for their intransigence and asserted his prescriptive right to receive the nomination of three persons,[2] but nevertheless agreed to fill each of the vacant offices

[1] 'De officialibus vero ecclesiae volumus de cetero taliter provideri, ut videlicet prior, vocatis ad scaccarium senioribus sex predictis ad minus, tractet de personis magis idoneis, ad hujus modi officium exequendum, et illum nominet in capitulo pro hoc officio, cui majus et fidelius testimonium ac major fratrum numerus attestantur': *Reg. Epist. J.P.* II, pp. 403–4.

[2] He based his case on the 'laudabili consuetudine in eadem ecclesia hactenus observata ad officia singula quorum ad nos spectat provisio nominare tres de capitulo ad ea ydoneos debeatis, ut, uno eorum per nos postmodum approbato, idem ad officium hujusmodi assumatur': Cant. Reg. Q, fo. 26.

by appointing one of the two persons nominated to him. Controversy now raged between the archbishop and senior monks over an appointment to the office of penitentiary which Winchelsey had made on his own initiative. He finally gave way on this point also and agreed to appoint one of the three persons nominated by the senior monks.[1]

In the four years which followed this struggle the senior monks remained at peace with the archbishop and acquiesced in his wishes by nominating three persons whenever any household office in the patronage of the archbishop fell vacant.[2] But in 1299 the same trouble broke out again. The *seniores* met at the exchequer and decided once again to nominate only one monk for appointment to the vacant office of chamberlain. They also agreed to pursue this same policy in the future in regard to other offices, alleging in their defence the customary practice of Archbishops Edmund Rich and Boniface of Savoy.[3] This time Winchelsey took a stern line. He challenged the monks on their own chosen ground of historical precedent and showed how, in the time of his two immediate predecessors, Robert Kilwardby and John Pecham, it had been customary for three persons to be nominated.[4] Demanding that his right should in future be respected, he commanded the senior monks to submit the names of three persons without delay. The *seniores*, quelled by the angry reproof of the

[1] The whole struggle is recounted at great length in Cant. Reg. Q, fos. 25 v.–26 v.

[2] Thus in 1297 the archbishop made appointments to the vacant offices of sacrist and precentor. In each case three persons were nominated to him: *ibid*. fo. 28 v.

[3] '...et decreverunt seniores finaliter quod una persona tantum nominetur sibi ad illud officium et ad alia officia imposterum vacantia secundum antiquam consuetudinem tempore Bonifacii et E. Archiepiscoporum': *ibid*. fos. 28 v.–29.

[4] 'Nos et J. et R. predecessores nostri sumus et fuimus in possessione quod nominare debetis nobis ad singula officia tres personas ydoneas' (*ibid*. fo. 28 v.). In the lack of archiepiscopal and conventual registers for the period prior to the rule of Pecham it is impossible to say whether the contention of the senior monks had a factual basis. But the statement of certain of the *seniores* in 1295, quoted above, seems to show that the archbishop was right in claiming the historical precedent of the last thirty years.

archbishop, offered no further resistance and did as they were instructed.[1] Winchelsey had gained a decisive victory, but the whole story is illuminating in that it shows how a quorum of senior monks could long defy their archbishop and titular abbot on a fundamental matter of conventual procedure. The trouble arose again in the middle of the fourteenth century, but in a less acute form,[2] and the archbishop successfully maintained his traditional rights.

In classifying the Canterbury obedientiaries into four clearly distinct groups, it is convenient to follow the categories established by Dean Kitchin in his treatment of the officials of Winchester cathedral priory.[3] The first group centred in the prior, and consisted of the sub-prior, the third prior, and the fourth prior. The prior was strongly urged to spend as much time as possible in the cloister and to live with his monks in accordance with the Rule.[4] It was, however, inevitable that he should be absent from the cloister for long periods while engaged on official business, and so claustral priors (*priores claustrales*) were appointed to take his place and to exercise regular discipline. In Lanfranc's *Statuta* these claustral priors were called *circumitores*. They were instructed to make periodical inspections of the monastic offices and to report on any breach in discipline which came to their attention.[5] At Canterbury the sub-prior acted as the effective head

[1] Cant. Reg. Q, fos. 28 v.–29. In this same year, 1299, two other vacant offices, those of precentor and sub-prior, were filled (*ibid.* fo. 29). This system was maintained for the remaining years of Winchelsey's archiepiscopate (*ibid.* fos. 30–31) and proceeded smoothly under his successor, Reynolds (Lambeth: Reg. Reynolds, *passim*). In the archiepiscopate of Meopham the controversy broke out again in a mild form.

[2] For minor 'incidents' which took place over the appointment of obedientiaries in 1332, 1335, 1338, and 1360, see *Lit. Cant.* I, pp. 506–10; II, pp. 106–8, 216, 394–98. The priors attempted to influence the archbishop in his choice by pointing out (e.g. in 1344 and 1353: *ibid.* pp. 276–77, 318–19) the fittest of the three candidates for an office.

[3] *Obedientiary Rolls of St Swithun's, Winchester*, ed. G. W. Kitchin (Hants Rec. Soc. 1892), pp. 31–33.

[4] Archbishop Winchelsey enjoined in 1298 that 'prior sepius cum vacare poterit in claustro resideat et moretur et claustrales supervideat ut honeste se habeant et bene regantur...': *Reg. Winchelsey*, p. 815.

[5] Migne, *P.L.* CL, pp. 485–86.

of the community in the absence of the prior[1] and was always a person of some importance. Before the end of the fourteenth century he had the south aisle of the infirmary hall divided into rooms as his separate *camera* or lodging.[2] The third and fourth priors seem to have assisted the precentor in looking after the library.[3]

The second group of obedientiaries was attached to the church and consisted of the sacrist, the precentor, five shrine-keepers, an anniversarian, and one or more penitentiaries. The greater sacrist (*major sacrista*), as he is commonly called, was assisted by at least two sub-sacrists and had charge of the furniture and fabric of the church.[4] His accounts were always headed by payments for *sonitus et ornatus*—for bell-ringing and ornament—and his expenditure in wax often attained prodigious proportions. Thus in 1299–1300 he bought 1301 qr., 4 lb. of wax at a cost of £60. 7s. 7d.[5] The sacrist also made regular purchases of incense, oil, wick, leather, tin, glass, mats, and rushes for the floor of the church, and bars, wedges, and wire for the windows. He saw to the washing and repairing of the vestments and the work of the servants in the wax-chamber. His office (*domus sacristae*) was on the south side of the church[6] and he held a court for his tenants at the *campanile*. The heavier building expenses were usually met by public sub-

[1] Pope Urban III ordained in 1187 that '...si prioratum ejusdem ecclesie vacare contigerit vel priorem in locis remotis existere, subprior vel alius, qui ordini prefuerit, sicut antiqua et rationabilis ipsius ecclesie consuetudo requirit, de conventus consilio rebus vestris libere disponere possit' (*Papsturkunden in England*, II, pp. 447–48). Evidence is afforded of the sub-prior exercising the authority of the prior in the years 1325 and 1330 in *Lit. Cant.* I, pp. 142–43, 309, 320.

[2] Willis, *op. cit.* p. 56.

[3] In 1451 the prior disbursed a sum of 1s. 4d. 'pro iiii clavibus emptis pro libraria et deliberantur iii° et iiii° prioribus claustri': Cant. MS. E. vi, fo. 41.

[4] See the Rev. C. E. Woodruff, 'The Sacrist's Rolls of Christ .Church, Canterbury' in *Arch. Cant.* XLVIII, pp. 38–80.

[5] B.M. Add. MS. 6160, fo. 91 v.

[6] 'To facilitate the bringing in of such heavy stores as lead, stone, lime, etc., the sacrist's office was connected with the city by a little lane—described in the records as *venella quae tendet de Burgate street versus portam domus sacristae*': Woodruff, *op. cit.* p. 39.

scription, but the sacrist was always the responsible official for the day-to-day upkeep of the church.

The precentor or cantor (*praecentor, cantor*), assisted by a succentor and third cantor, 'ruled the choir' of the monks.[1] He was responsible not only for the music and choral effects but also for the supply and good repair of the service-books.[2] At Canterbury, as at many other monasteries, the precentor was the librarian of the community,[3] and he certainly shared with the novice-master some of the responsibility of instructing the novices in the cloister.[4] In short, the precentor was an official of much responsibility, and all were to obey him in choir 'without murmur and uproar'.[5]

The many shrines and altars in the cathedral church all had their appointed 'keepers' (*custodes*). The custody of the shrine of St Thomas alone offered full-time employment to two monks. There was also a keeper of the Corona (*custos Coronae Beati Martiris Thomae*), a keeper of the Martyrdom (*custos martirii* or *custos ensis*), and a keeper of the altar of Our Lady in the crypt (*custos Beatae Mariae in Criptis*).[6] Oblations were made by pilgrims at all these places, and so the constant presence of at least one monk was deemed a necessity. The rest of the altars in the cathedral were supervised by the sacrist and his lay staff.

The anniversarian (*anniversarius*), as his name implies, was in charge of the celebration of anniversaries or obit-days.[7] He had

[1] Winchelsey referred in 1298 to 'cantores et ceteri qui...chorum regunt': *Reg. Winchelsey*, p. 815.

[2] Simon of Sudbury enjoined in 1376 'quod praecentor faciat libros reparari, prout ad eum pertinet': Wilkins, *Concilia*, III, pp. 110–11.

[3] Woodruff and Danks, *Memorials of Canterbury Cathedral*, pp. 226, 382.

[4] *Ibid.* p. 226.

[5] 'In ipso quoque servicio omnes cantori obediant sine murmure et tumultu': *Reg. Winchelsey*, p. 814.

[6] See the list of shrine-keepers in *Lit. Cant.* III, p. 5 and the account (Cant. MS. M 13, ii, mem. 11) of the two keepers of the shrine of St Thomas for the year 1397.

[7] A list of anniversaries commemorated at Christ Church is printed by J. Dart in his *History and Antiquities of the Cathedral Church of Canterbury* (1726), pp. 21–26. Clearly the most important and sumptuous of these celebrations was that of Lanfranc (28 May); see *H.M.C.* App. to VIIIth Report, p. 326.

special rents appropriated to his office for this purpose and he was often the recipient of legacies.[1] He bought food and drink for the obit-days and in many ways acted as the pittancer of the convent.[2] Finally, mention must be made of the penitentiary (*penitentiarius*), who acted as confessor for the monks and assisted the prior in maintaining discipline.[3] It was only natural that the archbishop should assert his right to appoint this obedientiary.

The third and largest group of obedientiaries dealt with the domestic affairs of the priory. They were eight in number, the cellarer, garnerer, bartoner, fruiterer, refectorarian, chamberlain, infirmarian, and master of the novices. To these may be added the two or three treasurers and two chancellors, whose administrative work is considered fully elsewhere. The cellarer (*major celerarius*) occupied the key position in the household administration. From his office, that of universal provider, sprang all the minor household departments.[4] He supplied the monks with food and drink, ran a guesthouse for pilgrims,[5] and was assisted by a sub-cellarer and a large household staff. The large building to the west of the cloister, the *cellarium*, lay under his control and it was here that the large stock of provisions was stored. He commanded by far the largest revenues—usually about a quarter of the total income of the house—and was the undisputed head of all those who catered for the bodily needs of the brethren.

The fruiterer (*fruyterer*) only appears at the very close of the middle ages,[6] and the office probably reflects the increase in the consumption of fruit at this period. Previously the cellarer had

---

[1] See the list of rents belonging to the office c. 1300: Cant. MS. M 13, i, mem. 1.

[2] Thus he bought special allowances of food and drink for the monks in Lent and Advent.

[3] Woodruff and Danks, *op. cit.* p. 243.

[4] Dom Knowles, *op. cit.* p. 429.

[5] On the cellarer's lodging (*cellarium*) and the *aula hospitum*, or cellarer's hall, see Willis, *op. cit.* pp. 114–36. A whole court, with its gate, was appropriated to the use of this obedientiary.

[6] In the list of monks at the Dissolution. See W. Somner, *Antiquities of Canterbury*, ed. Battely (1703), App. to Supplement, p. 52.

supplied the fruit.[1] From an early date two obedientiaries, the garnerer and the bartoner, were appointed to receive the corn-supplies of the priory. The garnerer (*granetarius*) was in charge of the granary for wheat, which was situated on the north side of the *curia*.[2] Adjacent to this building was the bakery, where bread was baked for the monks and their servants under the supervision of the garnerer, after the flour had been ground at one or more of the many mills belonging to the priory in the country and in the city.[3]

The bartoner (*berthonarius*) was the official placed in charge of the *barton* (*bertona*), or home-farm, of the priory, which lay to the north of the city.[4] Here, besides a ploughland (*caruca*), managed by a serjeant (*serviens*), there were storehouses for barley and oats, a mill for grinding the corn, and a hall (*braseria* or *malthalla*) where malting took place. The bartoner was responsible for the safe delivery of the malt at the brewery in the *curia*.[5] So, between them, the garnerer and bartoner saw that the wheat, barley, and oats were made into bread and beer in accordance with precise instructions given by the monastic chapter.[6]

The monks normally took their meals in the refectory, which lay to the north of the great cloister and was placed under the

---

[1] There were apple orchards on some of the Kentish manors (e.g. Chartham) as early as the first half of the fourteenth century.

[2] It now forms part of the offices of the King's School. See Willis, *op. cit.* p. 150.

[3] Seven mills in the city, besides the barton mill (still called Barton Mills), belonged to the monks in the later middle ages (Somner, *op. cit.* p. 23). On baking regulations, see Appendix I.

[4] The 'villa juxta civitatem Dorobernie que vocatur Berthona ad quam pertinent quinque jugera et duo prata' was given to the monks by King Atulph in 832: Dugdale, *Monasticon* (1846 ed.), I, p. 96. Its place in the exempt jurisdiction of the monks was challenged unsuccessfully by the citizens of Canterbury in 1303: *Reg. Winchelsey*, pp. 467–68.

[5] He was strictly enjoined to see that all the corn received was duly malted and that none of it was sold (see Appendix I). He was given special permission by the archbishop in 1298 to journey to and from the barton without licence at the time of the receipt of the corn-supplies (*Reg. Winchelsey*, p. 825). His accounts (Cant. MS. M 13, vi and D.E. 6), many of which have survived, are a mine of information on the corn-supply system of the priory.

[6] See Appendix I.

charge of a refectorarian (*refectorarius*), who supplied the building with utensils, rushes, and other necessary equipment.[1] Strict rules governed the conduct of the monks and their servants in the refectory. No one was to enter the building except at meal times and then complete silence was to be observed.[2] The senior monks sat at a high table ánd one of their number read some edifying book from a pulpit built into the wall of the refectory. Two meals a day were commonly taken in the refectory, the dinner (*prandium*) at midday and the supper (*cena*) at or after five o'clock. An evening drink before going to bed, called a collation (*collatio*), was also part of the monastic routine. The times of these meals were apt to vary with the seasons.

Gerald of Wales commented on the sumptuous repasts served in the refectory of Christ Church at the end of the twelfth century. One Trinity Sunday he counted no less than sixteen courses and remarked upon the excellence of the cuisine. Delicacies were sent down by the prior from the high table to privileged individuals.[3] The records of a later date show that bread, fish, eggs, and poultry were the commodities most commonly consumed in the refectory. There was a bewildering variety of loaves. The bread at the monks' own tables was always made of wheat[4] and called *panis monachalis* or *panis conventus*. A black bread of inferior quality, called *fety*ʒ or *feytis* and made of barley, was eaten by a number of the more important servants. The lesser servants had to be content with *panis coquinae*, a coarse type of bread made of mixed corn. The monks also dined off small loaves called *smalpeys*, and another kind of bread was known as *playnpayn*.[5] Careful calculations were

[1] The accounts of the refectorarian for the years 1225 and 1231 are contained in Cant. MS. M 13, xix, mems. 1, 3.

[2] *Reg. Winchelsey*, pp. 817–18.

[3] Dom Knowles, *op. cit.* p. 463.

[4] We have it on the authority of Sir William Ashley that 'Beyond all controversy the bread at the monks' own tables was made of wheat': *The Bread of Our Forefathers*, p. 87.

[5] Thus in 1299–1300, 936 seams, 5 bushels of wheaten flour were used for making bread. 482 seams furnished *panis conventus*, 136 seams were made into *smalpeys*, 130 seams, 1 bushel into *playnpayn*; and 188½ seams were mixed with inferior corn to supply *feytis* and *panis coquinae*: B.M. Add. MS. 6160, fo. 94 v.

made of the amount of bread normally consumed in a week,[1] a month,[2] three months,[3] and a year;[4] the weight of the bread was also made the subject of strict regulation.[5] It is important to notice that in the first half of the thirteenth century much bread-corn was bought from outside, but that in the period 1250–1350, which witnessed the high-water mark of demesne farming, nearly all the corn was supplied from the conventual manors.[6]

Fish was bought and consumed by the monks in large quantities. A sober calculation c. 1300 tells us that the *ferculum* or dish of one monk ought to consist of 2 soles or 1 plaice, 4 herrings or 8 mackerel.[7] In 1299–1300 no less than £247. 18s. 5¼d. was spent on the purchase of fish.[8] Poultry and eggs were also regularly served at the refectory tables.[9] Large cheeses from the manors, many of which were made of ewes' milk, were a common item of consumption.

The eating of meat presented the monks with a thorny problem. St Benedict had expressly forbidden the practice, and it has been shown that 'complete abstinence from flesh-meat, save in the case of definite illness, was the rule throughout the monasteries of England between 960 and 1216; there is not a single piece of trustworthy evidence to show that meat was ever allowed in the common refectory during that period'.[10] Even before the Fourth Lateran Council, however, meat could be eaten outside the refec-

---

[1] Lambeth MS. 1212, fo. 364 and Cant. Reg. B, fo. 424.

[2] Cant. Reg. K, fo. 61.     [3] *Lit. Cant.* II, pp. 141–42.

[4] Cant. MS. F ii, fo. 56.v.

[5] B.M. Cott. MS. Galba E iv, fo. 28 v. and *H.M.C.* App. to VIIIth Report, p. 351.

[6] The accounts of the garnerer and the bartoner afford conclusive evidence on this point.

[7] *H.M.C.* App. to VIIIth Report, p. 325.

[8] B.M. Add. MS. 6160, fos. 92–93. Herrings seem to have been particularly in favour. In 1451 the cellarer bought 10,000 fresh herrings from one William Colman of Folkestone for the monks, and 5600 salted herrings for the servants. Not content with this large supply, he also bought 400 green-fish (probably cod) at Dover in the same year, and rounded off his purchases with a cask of salmon and a cask of sturgeon: Cant. MS. E. vi, fos. 35–36.

[9] Reference is made in the 1451 cellarer's account (*ibid.*) to a 'domus ubi ova et galline jacent juxta coquinam conventus'.

[10] Dom Knowles, *op. cit.* pp. 459–60.

tory under certain conditions.  By the end of the thirteenth century
the Canterbury monks were allowed to eat meat in no less than
five different places, in the prior's *camera*, the infirmary and the
Table Hall (*mensa magistri*) of the infirmary, the guesthouse, and
a special room called the *deportum*.[1]  So in practice, and in spite
of the Rule, the monks could indulge to the full their taste for
beef, mutton, and pork, all of which were supplied to them in
liberal quantities.[2]

The staple drink of the monks was of course beer, and many
thousand gallons were consumed in a year.  Gerald of Wales
remarked in the late twelfth century upon the many wines, both
mulled and clear, together with unfermented wine, mulberry wine
and mead, served in the refectory of Christ Church.[3]  The gift of
100 muys (*modii*) of wine which Louis VII made to the monks in
1179 did not grace the monastic table, as the wine, being of inferior
quality, was sold for cash by the agent of the convent in Paris,[4]
but the best French wine was shipped across to Sandwich for the
benefit of the monks.[5]

In the monastic year many occasions for celebration and feasting
were allowed.  On the obit-days of archbishops and priors special
pittances, in the shape of food allowances, were given to the
monks.[6]  When each monk celebrated in rotation the conventual

[1] *Reg. Winchelsey*, pp. 819–20. The *deportum* at Canterbury corresponded
to the flesh-frater (*misericordia*) of other houses. It was probably placed over
the buttery buildings, to the west of the vestibule of the refectory and near
to the conventual kitchen: Willis, *op. cit.* p. 61.

[2] The cellarer bought no meat in 1225 and 1231, but in 1299–1300 he
spent £142. 9s. 6d. (B.M. Add. MS. 6160, fos. 92–93) and in 1396–97
£234. 8s. 9½d. (Cant. MS. M 13, ix, mem. 2) on the purchase of meat of
various kinds.

[3] Dom Knowles, *op. cit.* p. 465.

[4] On the long and complicated history of the Wine of St Thomas, see
J. B. Sheppard's introduction to *Lit. Cant.* I, pp. lxxvi–lxxxiii; III, pp. xix–
xxiv, and A. L. Simon, *The History of the Wine Trade in England* (1906), I,
pp. 360–61.

[5] Thus in 1286 the monks purchased 85 casks of wine, 67 from France and
18 from Gascony: Cant. MS. F ii.

[6] These are detailed in the anniversarian's accounts: Cant. MS. M 13, i,
*passim*. See also Cant. MS. D.E. 26.

High Mass, an extra ration of food was allowed to him.[1] At the periodical blood-lettings and in the infirmary the monks had spices and confectionery of all sorts, and in the later middle ages the system of pittances became more and more elaborate. One is, therefore, left with the impression that the monks of Christ Church enjoyed a fairly high standard of living and suffered from no lack of variety in food or drink. It cannot be sufficiently emphasized that, from the social standpoint, the prior was a baron and the monks a squirearchy. Their standard of living differed in no essential respect from that of their compeers in the feudal hierarchy.

The chamberlain (*camerarius*) was the obedientiary who attended to the clothing, shoeing, bedding, washing, and shaving of the monks.[2] He was assisted by a sub-chamberlain[3] and managed a tailor's workshop (*sartrina*) in the precinct, where the cloth which had been purchased from outside was made into garments for the monks and their servants. Precise rules governed the size and embroidery of the black monastic habit,[4] and the purchase of black cloth was normally the leading item in the account of the chamberlain. In 1299–1300, for example, he purchased 250 ells at a cost of £30. 9s.[5] Only on rare occasions was a habit bought in a ready-made condition.[6] Grey cloth for the drawers (*femoralia*) of the monks and linen cloth for undershirts (*camisiae*) were constantly bought for the tailor's workshop.[7] In the period previous to the fifteenth century the monks purchased the best Flemish cloth for their garments. For example, they wrote in 1318 to their foreign agent, Raymond, demanding that he should purchase 200 Frisian cloths, each 4 ells in length and 1½ in breadth, of which 30 were

---

[1] In Canterbury Register J there is a long list headed 'De vino et speciebus dandis diversis officiariis ad magnam missam per thesaurarium': *H.M.C.* App. to VIIIth Report, p. 75.

[2] See Lanfranc's *Statuta* in Migne, *P.L.* CL, p. 490.

[3] Prior Eastry's prescription for the ideal character of a sub-chamberlain is contained in *Lit. Cant.* I, p. 309.

[4] *Reg. Winchelsey*, p. 813.          [5] B.M. Add. MS. 6160, fo. 99.

[6] Thus in 1286 a sum of £3. 7s. was paid 'pro habitu magistri J. de Chileham': Lambeth MS. 242, fo. 92.

[7] In 1315–16, for example, 114 ells of grey cloth were purchased for £6. 18s. 1d. and 370 ells of linen cloth for £7. 14s. 2d.: Cant. MS. M 13, xiii, mem. 9.

to be checkered (*chekerelli*) and the rest plain.[1] In the fifteenth century the great expansion of the native cloth industry enabled the chamberlain to make his purchases in this country.[2] The equipment of the dormitory was part of his work, and so blankets (*stragulae*) and coverlets or counterpanes (*coopertoria*) figure commonly in his accounts. Soap was not an expensive item. There were compulsory baths at Christmas, but bathing was optional for the rest of the year.[3] A special chamber called the *domus rasturae*, close to the sub-vaults of the water-tower, was set aside for the shaving of the monks.[4]

The infirmarian (*magister infirmorum*) was in charge of the whole wing of the monastic buildings to the east of the cloisters which consisted of a hall, a chapel, a dining-hall (*mensa magistri*), a kitchen, and a *necessarium*.[5] The infirmary 'was not merely used for the accommodation of the sick, but was the dwelling-place of those who were too infirm to take part in the regular routine of the cloister, known in most orders as *stagiarii* or *stationarii*...it was also generally used by the *minuti* or religious who were undergoing their periodical bleeding (*minutio*) for the sake of their health'.[6] Lanfranc drew up regulations for the infirmary in his *Statuta*[7] and Robert Winchelsey amplified these instructions in 1298,[8] but in 1376 Simon of Sudbury found that the infirmary was in a state of disrepair and without a master.[9] As a result of Sudbury's stern injunctions the senior monks met at the exchequer and drew up rules for the maintenance of sick monks in the infirmary.[10] The necessary officials and servants were appointed

[1] Camb. Univ. Lib. MS. Ee. v, 31, fos. 196 v.–197. See also *Cal. Let. Pat.* 30 Edward I, p. 40.

[2] In 1470 we find a robemaker of Salisbury supplying the monks with cloths (Cant. MS. D.E. 13) and about the same time the prior dealt with a clothmaker of Canterbury (Cant. MS. D.E. 14). In 1487 and 1494 a clothier of Cranbrook was supplying the monks with material: *Lit. Cant.* III, pp. 311–12 and Cant. MS. D.E. 15.

[3] Woodruff and Danks, *op. cit.* p. 242.          [4] *Ibid.*

[5] Willis, *op. cit.* pp. 52–59.

[6] A. Hamilton Thompson, *English Monasteries*, p. 113.

[7] Migne, *P.L.* CL, pp. 491–92.          [8] *Reg. Winchelsey*, p. 419.

[9] Wilkins, *Concilia*, III, pp. 110–11.

[10] *Lit. Cant.* III, pp. 4–6.

and the sick monks were accorded sundry indulgences in the shape of pittances.

The monks had their own resident physician (*medicus* or *physicus*) and bleeder (*minutor*),[1] but the prior received the attentions of a London 'specialist' or consultant, who often charged exorbitant fees.[2] Sometimes a surgeon (*cirurgicus*) was called in from outside for special operations,[3] and the monks relied heavily upon the services of local apothecaries and oculists.[4] Herbs, cordials of sweet sugar, lozenges, and ointment were lavished upon them in their sickness.[5] In 1326 Archbishop Reynolds presented them with the manor of Caldicote, to the east of the city, in order that they might recuperate there, and breathe fresher air, after bleeding.[6] We know that the monks were bled in batches and that their pain was softened by the fond expectation of pittances.[7]

The master of the novices (*magister noviciorum*) had the responsibility of teaching the Rule and the divine office to the novices in the cloister.[8] As he kept no accounts, his appearances in the records of Christ Church are infrequent. He seems to have acted as a subordinate of the precentor in the educational work of the priory.

The fourth and last group of obedientiaries, those who dealt with the external affairs of the priory, consisted of the four wardens of the manors (*custodes maneriorum*), who will be considered in

---

[1] See Lambeth MSS. 242 and 243, *passim*.

[2] Woodruff and Danks, *op. cit.* p. 256. See also *Lit. Cant.* I, pp. 120–21.

[3] In 1289 one Geoffrey Claudus was paid 3*s*. 'pro cirurgia fratrum' (Lambeth MS. 242, fo. 110 v.) and in 1291 3*s*. 4*d*. was paid 'pro sirurgia Hugonis de Sancta Margareta' (*ibid*. fo. 157).

[4] The apothecary (*apothecarius* or *speciarius*) was often the oculist as well. Thus in 1286 a sum of 1*s*. was paid to John, the apothecary, 'pro curacione oculorum domini J. de Samelleforde': Lambeth MS. 242, fo. 92.

[5] See the long list of medicines given in Cant. MS. D.E. 58 (c. 1513).

[6] '...ut confratres sanguine minuti et ceteris laboribus fatigati ibidem respirare possint et aerem haurire clariorem'. Cant. MS. Eastry correspondence, M· 13, i, 53.

[7] See Lanfranc's *statutum de sanguinis minutione* in Migne, *P.L.* CL, p. 494, and Dom Knowles, *op. cit.* pp. 455–56.

[8] Winchelsey enjoined in 1298 that 'monachi, suscepto habitu, statim in regulis ordinis instruantur et ad repetendum divinum servicium applicentur ad quod noviciorum magister cum continuacione qua convenit diligenter intendat': *Reg. Winchelsey*, p. 821.

a later chapter, and the almoner. The almoner (*elemosinarius*), who was endowed with separate revenues and assisted in his work by a sub-almoner,[1] governed the almonry buildings which lay immediately outside the gatehouse of the *curia*.[2] These consisted of a dining-hall, offices, a school,[3] and, after 1319, a chapel for six priests.[4] Like the infirmary and other major offices, the almonry was a self-contained department with its own household staff. A close inspection of the numerous extant almoners' accounts shows that at Canterbury, as at other monasteries,[5] very little of the revenue was expended in alms in the later middle ages. Indeed, an analysis of twenty-one surviving rolls spanning the years 1284–1373[6] reveals the somewhat astonishing fact that only 0·52 per cent of the almoner's income was given to the poor. It should be added, however, that large liveries of corn were distributed to the poor in the first half of this period,[7] as well as occasional gifts of cloth.[8] Nevertheless it is hard to avoid the impression that the almoner, unlike other obedientiaries, did not adequately fulfil his proper function—the maintenance of the poor at the gate. Most of his revenue was spent on the upkeep of his large household[9] and in

[1] On Prior Eastry's estimate of the characteristics suitable to a sub-almoner, see *Lit. Cant.* I, p. 309. The role of the sub-almoner on Maundy Thursday is detailed in *H.M.C.* App. to VIIIth Report, p. 326.

[2] Willis, *op. cit.* p. 152.

[3] A number of poor boys were given a free education in elementary subjects in the almonry school (C. E. Woodruff and H. J. Cape, *History of the King's School, Canterbury* (1908), p. 18). Certain monks acted as sponsors for these scholars; see *Lit. Cant.* III, pp. 4–5.

[4] *Cal. Let. Pat.* 19 Edward II, pp. 177–78.

[5] R. H. Snape, *op. cit.* pp. 112–17; Kitchin, *op. cit.* pp. 74–78; *Worcester Compotus Rolls of the Fourteenth and Fifteenth Centuries*, ed. S. G. Hamilton (Worc. Hist. Soc. 1910), pp. 49–50.      [6] Cant. MS. M 13, VIII.

[7] Thus in 1326–27, 151½ seams of mixed corn (*mixtura*) were distributed to the poor. This represents about the average amount for the first half of the century. In 1372–73 the dole had dropped to 63 quarters, 4 bushels.

[8] In 1291–92 and 1295–96 the almoner disposed of an unnamed quantity of *pannus pauperum*. The prior sometimes distributed small alms during his travels.

[9] This household increased in size as the middle ages advanced. A sum of £5. 17s. 9d. was spent on its upkeep in 1284–85, and £6. 17s. 10d. in 1317–18. In 1326–27 the expenses of the household, including the chaplains, came to £18. 19s. 10¾d. and in 1337–38 reached the sum of £22. 3s. 11d.

gifts (*oblaciones*) and allowances (*caritates*) to the brethren, who, as *pauperes Dei*, were able to claim alms on the specious ground of poverty.[1] A comparison of royal and monastic almsgiving in the later middle ages will almost certainly show that the royal household, in which almsgiving 'by the end of the thirteenth century was a regular part of household activity and substantial in amount',[2] was far more concerned with charity to the poor than the great and wealthy monastic corporations.

This elaborate hierarchy of obedientiaries, 25 in number (if we count 2 treasurers and 2 chancellors as normal, and omit the fruiterer on account of his late appearance), expended the revenues of the house under the watchful eye of the prior and the treasurers. The rest of the monks were known simply as cloister-monks (*claustrales*),[3] having no household duties allotted to them. The dangers inherent in this system of financial and administrative devolution, from the monastic standpoint, will be readily apparent. It placed the temptation of *proprietas* before the eyes of a large number of monks and withdrew them from the common life of the cloister for long intervals at a time. In spite of the anathemas pronounced on *proprietarii* by popes, councils, and general chapters,[4] the records of medieval monasticism are full of flagrant examples of this type of sinner.[5] At Christ Church, as early as 1215–16 we hear of a sum of £12. 2s. being found in the possession of a monk called Luke,[6] and at the end of the century and the beginning of the next, Archbishops Pecham and Winchelsey had to deal with some particularly bad examples of *proprietarii*.[7] A little later Archbishop Reynolds and Prior Henry of Eastry were sorely

---

[1] The phrase 'in caritatibus et donacionibus datis fratribus et aliis pauperibus diversis vicibus' occurs constantly in the almoners' accounts. It will be recalled that it was as *pauperes Dei* that monks petitioned to appropriate the revenues of parish churches.

[2] H. Johnstone, 'Poor-Relief in the Royal Households of Thirteenth-Century England' in *Speculum* (1929), IV, p. 163.

[3] In 1376 a list of the obedientiaries is accompanied by the statement: 'Omnes alii fratres mere claustrales per se nuncupantur': *Lit. Cant.* III, p. 5.

[4] G. G. Coulton, *Five Centuries of Religion*, III, pp. 360–62.

[5] *Ibid.* III, pp. 353–409.      [6] Cant. MS. F ii, fo. 57 v.

[7] See *Reg. Epist. J.P.* II, pp. 539–40, 545–46, 573–74, 627–28, and *H.M.C.* App. to VIIIth Report, p. 350.

embarrasssed by two notorious monks, Alexander of Sandwich
and Robert of Aledon, who squandered the possessions of the
priory and accumulated considerable private fortunes.[1] Cases of
the *vitium proprietatis* persist throughout the century.[2]

An equal danger to monastic life as conceived by St Benedict
was the tendency for obedientiaries to live in private apartments
and so to desert the common life of cloister, frater, and dorter.
The prior, the sub-prior, the sacrist, the cellarer, the infirmarian,
and the almoner all had their private households or *camerae* before
the end of the fourteenth century, and it is more than probable
that other obedientiaries set up house in the same way. Indeed
Simon of Sudbury explicitly enjoined in 1376 that all those *camerae*
which had recently been constructed should be destroyed.[3] How
far the system of private households had developed before the
year 1400 we do not precisely know, but it is clear that many
monks were leading only a quasi-regular life.

It remains for us to study the lay element in the household of
Christ Church. The large retinue of the prior has already been
described. The monks were also waited upon by numerous servants
who lived within the *curia*. This was the common practice in all
the great monasteries of the age, both in England and on the
Continent.[4] At Christ Church, Canterbury, as at Bury, Ramsey,
Glastonbury, and Evesham,[5] the number of servants far surpassed
the number of monks. Three of these, the steward of the guesthouse and two porters, were appointed by the archbishop.[6] The
cellarer controlled the largest number of servants in his capacity
of universal provider. The steward of the guesthouse was one of
the most important and catered for guests and pilgrims in the
Cellarer's Hall and the North Hall, commonly called Hog Hall,

[1] See *Lit. Cant.* I, *passim*.

[2] E.g. in 1331: *Lit. Cant.* I, pp. 365–67.

[3] 'Oneravit priorem, quod camerae novae inventae tollantur': Wilkins,
*Concilia*, III, pp. 110–11.

[4] See Dom U. Berlière, 'La Familia dans les Monastères Bénédictins
du Moyen Age' in *Mémoires de l'Académie Royale de Belgique* (1931),
XXIX.

[5] Coulton, *op. cit.* III, pp. 52–53.

[6] *Papsturkunden in England*, II, pp. 447–48.

where the poorer class of persons were probably housed.[1] Actors (*histriones*), minstrels (*menestralli*), harpers (*harpatores*), and trumpeters (*trumpatores*) were regularly hired to enliven the guests and, no doubt, to entertain the monks as well.[2] In 1322, besides the steward of the guesthouse and the two porters, the cellarer employed in his department the pantler and his boy, the keeper of the cloister-gate (*ostiarius*) and his boy, the pantler of the guesthouse, the watchman of the *curia*, the scullion and his boy, the soup-maker (*potagiarius*), the scullion of the refectory and his boy, the first and second cooks and their boys, the salter (who was also doorkeeper of the kitchen) and his boy, the kitchen stoker (*focarius*), the potter, the kitchen waiter, the drawer of wine and beer and his boy, the cellarer's esquire, his groom and his carter, two purveyors, the hunter and his boy, the porter of the guesthouse and his boy, another servant, and the gaoler.[3] It is hardly surprising that the cellarer was ordered by Archbishop Stratford in 1335 to effect a drastic reduction in staff.[4] Other household departments, such as the sacristy, the infirmary, the chamberlain's office, the bakery, and the brewery, also had their complement of servants.[5] The numbers tended to increase rather than diminish as the fourteenth century advanced, and it is probably true to say that by the year 1400 there were twice as many servants as monks at Christ Church.

Another class of lay persons who dwelt within the precinct of the monastery were the corrodians, appointed by king or prior. A corrody 'bore the implication of a grant of a definite supply of goods, chiefly in the form of provisions, from the common store of a religious house'.[6] It is to be contrasted with a pension and an

[1] Willis, *op. cit.* p. 15. In 1484–85 the cellarer bought utensils for Hog Hall (*Hoggehawe*): Cant. MS. M 13, ix, mem. 8.
[2] Thus in 1286 a sum of 7s. 6d. was paid to actors, harpers, and minstrels performing on the feast of the translation of St Thomas (7 July): Lambeth MS. 242, fo. 92 v. See also *ibid.* fos. 97 v., 100, 153, 157, 163, and *passim*.
[3] *H.M.C.* App. to IXth Report, p. 77.
[4] *Lit. Cant.* II, pp. 94–95.
[5] *H.M.C.* App. to IXth Report, p. 77.
[6] A. Hamilton Thompson, 'A Corrody from Leicester Abbey A.D. 1393–4' in *Trans. Leicester Arch. Soc.* (1925), p. 5.

annuity, both of which were normally grants in money. As early as the first half of the thirteenth century Pope Gregory IX (1227–41) is found promising that he would not in future intrude his nominees into corrodies in Christ Church,[1] but we have no first-hand evidence of these papal corrodians. At the end of the century the king began the practice of nominating his faithful discharged servants as corrodians at Christ Church.[2] It became customary for two royal nominees at a time to receive maintenance for life in the priory.[3] In 1336 Edward III, about to embark upon his schemes of conquest abroad and desirous of all possible help, was induced to declare that previous grants of corrodies conferred in Christ Church by kings of England should not be drawn into a precedent for the future.[4] Nevertheless corrodians continued to be nominated by the king at regular intervals during the next sixty years.[5] In 1395 Richard II repeated the stipulation of his predecessor that royal grants of corrodies should not be drawn into a precedent,[6] and soon after this date the practice seems to

[1] *H.M.C.* App. to VIIIth Report, p. 317.

[2] The first recorded grant is that made in 1293 to one John de Counvill, *Cal. Let. Close*, 21 Edward I, p. 323.

[3] A corrody was granted in 1299 to William de Alba Notel, the king's hunter (Camb. Univ. Lib. MS. Ee. v, 31, fo. 81 v.), in 1300 to Walter Dover (*ibid.* fo. 84), and in 1302 to Henry of Canterbury, a clerk of the Prince of Wales (*ibid.* fo. 92). The King's servant, John Drake, became a corrodian in 1305 (*ibid.* fos. 104, 111, 145 v.) and Edmund de Bawkewell, a clerk of Queen Isabella, in 1309 (*ibid.* fo. 113). In 1310 the monks refused to receive any further corrodians (*ibid.* fo. 114), but in the same year a discharged knight, Thomas de Bannebury, was nominated by the king (*Cal. Let. Close*, 3 Edward II, p. 267). Corrodians were also nominated in 1314 (*ibid.* 8 Edward II, p. 205), in 1316 (*ibid.* 9 Edward II, p. 329), in 1326 (Camb. Univ. Lib. MS. Ee. v, 31, fo. 251) and in 1329 (*Cal. Let. Close*, 3 Edward III, p. 552).

[4] *Cal. Let. Pat.* 10 Edward III, p. 253.

[5] Nicholas de Wycombe, the king's watchman, was granted a corrody in 1339 (*Cal. Let. Close*, 13 Edward III, p. 241) and John Herlyng, the king's yeoman, became a corrodian in 1354 (*ibid.* 28 Edward III, p. 72). In 1375 John Kent, the king's serjeant, received a corrody (*ibid.* 49 Edward III, p. 247) and in 1382 Lambert Fermer, a man of similar status, received a like grant (*ibid.* 6 Richard II, p. 208).

[6] *Cal. Let. Pat.* 19 Richard II, p. 612. This was confirmed by Henry IV in 1400: *ibid.* 1 Henry IV, p. 234.

have ceased.[1] It is highly probable that the prior appointed his faithful followers as corrodians, but little direct evidence of this practice occurs in the records.[2] The presence of these retired civil servants in the cloister and precinct, incongruous as it first seems, may well have served to lighten the monotony of the monastic routine. Stories of court life, of adventure, and of intrigue, would certainly come as a welcome relief.

A general review of the financial history of the priory shows that the house was constantly in debt, but rarely to the extent of more than one year's average income. The central machinery of credit has been already described, and it was shown that the monks pursued a policy of continual borrowing. No sooner had old debts been paid than new ones were contracted. In the middle of the twelfth century the priory was in debt,[3] and the long struggle with Baldwin and Hubert Walter drained the resources of the house. The financial recovery of the priory after the years of exile was rapid and remarkable, but in 1231 the prior was authorized to send letters of entreaty to his free tenants for help in the payment of his debts.[4] In this year the monks expended £465. 7s. 1d. in the payment of their debts, but still owed £953 to their creditors at the end of the financial year.[5] The position seems to have improved somewhat in the 'forties,[6] but in 1252 the monks were again heavily indebted to foreign merchants.[7] In 1265 tenants were once again appealed to for an aid to relieve the prior of his debts.[8] Pope Urban IV (1261–64) was induced to decree that the monks of Christ Church should not be bound to pay their debts unless they

---

[1] Henry Longdown, the king's serjeant, granted maintenance for life at Christ Church in 1401 (*Cal. Let. Close*, 2 Henry IV, p. 388), is the last royal corrodian of whom we have evidence.

[2] It should be noticed, however, that the pensioners of the convent often received food and drink as well as a sum in cash; see, for example, *Lit. Cant.* II, pp. 334–35.

[3] Gervase, *Opera*, I, pp. 127, 143.

[4] *Cal. Let. Pat.* 15 Henry III, p. 429.

[5] Cant. MS. M 13, xix, mem. 3.

[6] In 1244 the monks paid off £430. 17s. 7d. of their debts and ended the year still owing £302 to their creditors: *ibid*. mem. 6.

[7] They owed £2236—just over an average year's income: *ibid*. mem. 7.

[8] *Cal. Let. Pat.* 50 Henry III, pp. 496–97.

had been contracted for the common benefit.[1] The turbulent priorate of Thomas Ringmer (1274–85), with its costly and vexatious lawsuits, saw the priory heavily in debt.[2] One of the contributory causes of distress in this period was the heavy burden of papal taxation. These papal income taxes, imposed at frequent intervals in the thirteenth century, were specifically intended for crusading purposes and in practice met the pressing financial demands of both pope and king.[3] The crusading tenths of Edward I, which were imposed for periods of six years in 1274 and 1291, fell particularly severely upon the Christ Church monks and upon English monasteries in general.[4] Other papal exactions, such as the procurations of papal envoys[5] and payments made to the Curia for the confirmation of archiepiscopal elections,[6] also weighed heavily upon the priory in the thirteenth century. The archbishopric of Canterbury was in sorry financial straits at this time,[7] and Pecham went so far as to borrow large sums from the monks of his cathedral priory.[8] When Henry of Eastry acceded to the priorate in 1285 the convent was in debt to the tune of £4924. 18s. 4d.,[9] which represented more than the average income of two years. This marked the nadir of the priory finances.

In the last fifteen years of the thirteenth century Prior Henry of Eastry gradually paid off the debts which his predecessors had accumulated,[10] although he had to contract fresh short-term loans

---

[1] *H.M.C.* App. to VIIIth Report, p. 318.

[2] The enrolled treasurers' accounts (Cant. MS. F ii) bear witness to the increasing depression of the finances during Ringmer's priorate.

[3] For the whole subject of papal taxation, see the definitive works of Professor W. E. Lunt, *The Valuation of Norwich*, and *Financial Relations of the Papacy with England to 1327*. An income tax was first imposed upon the English clergy by Pope Innocent III in 1199.

[4] Lunt, *Financial Relations*, pp. 311–65. Note, however, the attempts of the Canterbury monks to avoid paying the 1274 tenth and to gain partial exemption from that of 1291: *ibid.* pp. 328, 352.

[5] *Ibid.* p. 566 and *passim*.　　　　　　　　　[6] *Ibid.* pp. 677–79.

[7] See Dorothy Sutcliffe, 'The Financial Condition of the See of Canterbury, 1279–1292' in *Speculum* (1935), X, pp. 53–68.

[8] *Ibid.* and *Reg. Epist. J.P.* I, p. 120.

[9] B.M. Cott. MS. Galba E iv, fo. 108 v.

[10] See *ibid.* fo. 109 and Cant. MS. F ii, *passim*.

in order to do so.¹ His reforming policy and programme for reducing expenditure² made of the first twenty years of the fourteenth century the zenith in the financial history of the priory. His achievement is all the more creditable in that constant demands from the Crown for loans were made and met during the same period.³ After 1320, however, the agricultural crisis and the repeated royal demands for loans, followed by the outbreak of the Hundred Years' War, tended to upset the finances of the priory. In 1376 Simon of Sudbury found that the monks were in debt to the extent of £1500, and ordered economies to meet the situation.⁴ The end of the century saw a distinct financial improvement.⁵

The centralization of the finances under the treasurers certainly acted as a check upon mismanagement, but the monks were constantly living beyond their income. Their large retinue of servants and costly purchases of food and drink involved an expenditure incommensurate with the revenues at their command. It required a man of the calibre of Henry of Eastry to set the finances of the priory on a stable footing, and even he was beaten by the agricultural crisis of the 'twenties. Altogether the priory had a chequered financial career, like most other great monasteries in this country.⁶ Too many factors, both internal and external, militated against permanent financial security.

¹ In 1286 he borrowed £20, and in 1287 £26. 13s. 4d., from Florentine merchants (Cant. MS. F ii). In 1296 he paid back a sum of £533. 3s. 4d. which he had borrowed from Florentine merchants (*H.M.C.* App. to Vth Report, p. 451) and in 1298–1300 contracted loans in the Roman Curia (Camb. Univ. Lib. MS. Ee. v, 31, fos. 78 v., 81, 84).

² The details of this programme are so interesting that I have printed it in full in Appendix II.

³ In 1312 the monks advanced £133. 3s. 4d. to the King (*Cal. Let. Pat.* 6 Edward II, p. 484) and in 1311 and 1313 supplied him with considerable quantities of food (*ibid.* 5 Edward II, p. 381 and 6 Edward II, p. 535). In 1313 a further loan of £200 was demanded (*Cal. Let. Close,* 7 Edward II, p. 67) and in the following year the king received £450 from the monks (*Cal. Let. Pat.* 8 Edward II, pp. 157–58). Additional royal exactions took place in the years 1315, 1316, 1317, and 1319 (*Cal. Let. Close,* 9 Edward II, p. 309; *ibid.* 10 Edward II, p. 433; *ibid.* 10 Edward II, p. 479; *ibid.* 13 Edward II, p. 203). ⁴ Wilkins, *Concilia,* III, pp. 110–11.

⁵ The improvement is to be associated with the reforms of Prior Thomas Chillenden. See my last chapter. ⁶ Snape, *op. cit.* pp. 119–42.

# Chapter Four

## THE CHAPTER, EXCHEQUER, AND CHANCERY

The elaborate departmental organization at Christ Church amply sufficed to meet the daily needs of the community. Most of the temporal business of the house was readily referred to the individual obedientiaries without any occasion arising for general consultation. There were, however, a number of matters which demanded the attention of the whole community, and it was for these questions of general reference that the monastic chapter acted as the representative body of the priory.

The early history of the Benedictine conventual chapter has already been written.[1] The daily meeting of the monks after prime, when a chapter of the Rule was read and breaches of regular discipline were confessed and corrected, gave the name of the chapter of faults (*capitulum culparum*) to an institution which was flourishing in England before the Norman Conquest. Lanfranc legislated for the daily chapter and enjoined that the profession of novices and the reception of persons into confraternity should only take place in chapter. In the twelfth century there emerged what has been called 'the juridical notion of the chapter'. The age was one of increasing definition in monastic administration and 'the multiplication of gifts and charters of all kinds, the organization of the feudal system, the development of national and the infiltration of canon law, the separation of establishments between abbot and monks, the emergence throughout Europe of corporate bodies, and of a spirit of controversial assertion of rights and liberties—all these various influences tended to transform the community "in chapter" into a deliberative body with certain customs and rights'.[2] The legal development was completed in the pontificate of Innocent III (1198–1216), who 'in his efforts to reinvigorate the monastic order throughout Europe did not hesi-

[1] Dom Knowles, *The Monastic Order in England*, 943–1216, pp. 411–17.
[2] *Ibid.* p. 413.

tate to sanction and impose upon various monasteries constitutions giving considerable power to the chapter in order to check the abuse of freedom on the part of abbots'.[1]

The work of the conventual chapter of Christ Church can first be studied with precision towards the end of the thirteenth century. The great series of bound registers which Prior Henry of Eastry (1285–1331) compiled[2] give us an excellent picture of the many kinds of business transacted in chapter. The work of the chapter fell into two clearly defined categories, spiritual affairs (*spiritualia*) and temporal affairs (*temporalia*). The former included not only all the business proper to a *capitulum culparum*, but also such matters as the arrangement of liturgical services, presentations to churches and ordinations of vicarages, and the confirmation of a large number of archiepiscopal acts. It should also be recalled that the prior and chapter exercised metropolitical and diocesan juris-diction in the province of Canterbury during the vacancy of the archbishopric. Several *sede vacante* registers are extant, which show the monks exercising the spiritual jurisdiction of the primate through their own official (*Officialis*), who acted in close con-junction with the chapter.

In the temporal sphere, the work of the conventual chapter embraced a wide variety of subjects. A succession of popes and Benedictine general chapters had insisted that certain questions, such as the granting of lands and pensions and the contraction of loans, should be submitted to the monastic chapter by heads of houses. Action was only to be taken after the advice of the chapter had been ascertained and its formal assent had been given.[3] The Christ Church registers are full of these *acta in capitulo*, acts formally ratified by the conventual chapter.[4] All transactions relating to the disposal of real property were registered in this manner, and the larger financial ventures of the house, of which building enterprises and the purchase of rents are two examples,

---

[1] Dom Knowles, *op. cit.* p. 416.    [2] See Bibliography.

[3] See *Chapters of English Black Monks*, ed. W. A. Pantin, I, pp. 35–36, 50, 65–66, and *passim*.

[4] The register which is now Camb. Univ. Lib. MS. Ee. v, 31 is primarily devoted to *acta in capitulo* covering the period 1285–1331.

also required the assent of the chapter. Compositions between the priory and other persons or corporations were registered in like manner. But the chapter did not only promulgate *acta*. It also from time to time issued ordinances (*ordinationes*) dealing with a great variety of subjects, both spiritual and economic. In 1304, for example, the chapter issued ordinances on the lawful measures to be observed in weighing corn and beer, on the precautions necessary for keeping malt, on the liveries to be paid to monks while absent on the manors, and on a number of other questions.[1] Again, in 1319 the chapter promulgated a detailed ordinance on the constitution of the new chapel in the almonry.[2] Thus, whereas the *acta in capitulo* embraced a limited number of subjects, the *ordinationes factae in pleno capitulo* covered every area of monastic life. By a combination of acts and ordinances the chapter displayed itself as the supreme legislative organ of the community.

It should not, however, be supposed that questions of general importance were always referred to the whole body of monks in chapter. St Benedict himself had made a clear distinction between the transaction of weighty matters and those of lesser importance in the third chapter of his Rule. 'Whenever any weighty matters have to be transacted in the monastery', writes the Saint, 'let the abbot call together all the community and himself propose the matter for discussion. After hearing the advice of the brethren let him consider it in his own mind, and then do what he shall judge most expedient.... If anything of lesser moment has to be done in the monastery let the abbot take the advice of the seniors (*seniorum tantum utatur consilio*).'[3] The growth of canon law and of a definite conception of the *mos majorum* lent further clarity to this precept of the Rule. By the twelfth century, and perhaps even earlier, the *senior et sanior pars* was a commonplace of monastic legislation and of papal bulls of confirmation and privilege.

In a large monastery like Christ Church, Canterbury, it was inevitable that a weighty burden of responsibility should fall upon

---

[1] See Appendix I. A further set of ordinances was issued in 1318; see *ibid.*

[2] B.M. Cott. MS. Galba E iv, fo. 90.

[3] *Sancti Benedicti Regula Monachorum*, ed. Dom C. Butler (Fribourg, 1912), pp. 18–19.

the senior brethren. All through the twelfth century the *seniores ecclesiae* played a prominent part in the affairs of the priory,[1] and in their protracted quarrels with Archbishops Baldwin and Hubert Walter the senior monks learned to act as a disciplined army united in a common struggle. When the thirteenth century dawned the prior and senior monks appear to have been firmly in control of the external policy of the community. In the first half of this century the senior monks became accustomed to acting as an auditing committee and thus added financial functions to their control of *extrinseca negotia*.

A decisive stage in monastic organization throughout Europe was marked by the pontificate of Gregory IX (1227–41), who devoted much of his extraordinary energy to the codification of canon law and the crystallization of custom into precedent. In 1234 his visitors drew up special statutes for the monasteries of Westminster and Bury St Edmund's, in which the rights of the *senior et sanior pars* were fully recognized. This small body of monks, chosen at the discretion of the abbot, was to deal with the audit of accounts and other *extrinseca negotia* outside the chapter, while only matters relating to 'the welfare of souls and the great advantage of the church' were to be discussed in chapter.[2] The English bishops followed the lead given by the Papacy and issued injunctions to monasteries to the same purpose,[3] and the statutes of the Benedictine general chapters stressed the necessity of giving only summary treatment to temporal matters in the conventual chapters.[4] The increasing complexity of monastic estate

---

[1] See, for example, the relations of the senior monks with archbishop Theobald: Gervase, *Opera*, I, pp. 143–44.

[2] E. Levett, *Studies in Manorial History*, p. 15. Subsequent popes tacitly assumed that financial affairs would be dealt with by the *senior et sanior pars*; see, for example, Odo Rigaldi, *Regestrum* (1852), p. 645.

[3] Levett, *op. cit.* p. 15.

[4] At Southwark in 1249 the general chapter of the Canterbury province decreed, in regard to the conventual chapter, 'de corporalibus ibidem tractetur brevius, ut profectus spiritalis effectum debitum sorciatur' (*Chapters*, I, p. 42). The decree was repeated in almost identical words by the general chapter at Evesham 1255 (*ibid.* p. 55) and in the statutes issued after the chapter held at Reading in 1277 (*ibid.* p. 75). It should be observed that the work of the general chapters themselves fell largely into the hands of a

management, caused by the rapid development in all branches of demesne farming, was another factor which made for the institution of economic committees of chapter in many large monasteries in the latter half of the thirteenth century. Broadly speaking, it may be said that the work of these select committees of chapter centred in the function of audit, but gradually tended to become much wider in its competence and finally to absorb the more difficult tasks of temporal administration. Auditing committees of senior monks were introduced by Archbishop Pecham (1279–92) into many of the larger houses of this country at the same time as he created treasurers to receive and disburse all the revenues.[1]

At Christ Church one stage further was reached in the evolution of capitular committees during the archiepiscopate of Pecham. Finding that certain of the monks of his cathedral priory were refractory and mutinous in face of the disciplinary action of the austere prior, Thomas Ringmer (1274–85), Pecham laid immense stress on the right of the *seniores* to tender advice and counsel on all questions.[2] He even went so far on 9 November 1281 as to establish a council of six senior monks to control the prior in all his actions.[3] The prior became in effect a constitutional monarch, limited and guided by that *mos majorum* of which the *seniores* were the authentic spokesmen and custodians. It was almost inevitable that the exchequer should become the meeting-place of this council

small group of *diffinitores* (*Trans. Royal Hist. Soc.* Fourth Series, X, p. 226) who drafted legislative decrees and performed other important tasks.

[1] See, for example, his injunctions for Rochester cathedral priory in 1283 (*Reg. Epist. J.P.* ed. C. T. Martin, II, pp. 622–23) and for Bardney Abbey in 1284 (*ibid.* III, pp. 824–25).

[2] Pecham wrote to Thomas Ringmer on 5 January 1281, insisting that 'in correctionibus igitur viriliter te habeas et prudenter, agens omnia de illorum consilio seniorum quos nulla macula criminis noveris infamatos': *Reg. Epist. J.P.* I, p. 160.

[3] *Reg. Epist. J.P.* I, p. 246. Pecham further defined the powers of this council of six in 1282 (*ibid.* I, pp. 341–42; II, p. 401). The monks had previously insisted that the prior should act only upon the advice of a council of twelve monks (*ibid.* I, p. 346). A good precedent for Pecham's action can be found in that of Hugues d'Anjou who c. 1200 'défendait à l'abbé de Cluny de rien faire sans un conseil composé de douze moines' (M. P. Lorain, *Histoire de l'Abbaye de Cluny* (1845), p. 148).

of monks, and it is not surprising to find Pecham ordaining on
6 August 1281 that in future the appointment of all officials should
be discussed *ad scaccarium* by the prior and at least six senior
monks before the nominations were made in chapter.[1] The centre
of gravity in temporal administration was slowly being shifted
from the *capitulum*, where the whole body of monks assembled,
to the *scaccarium*, the resort of the *senior et sanior pars*.

In the priorate of Henry of Eastry (1285–1331) the evolution
was completed. One of the first acts of the new prior was to
commission the building of a new and impressive *camera ad
scaccarium* above the old one in the eastern range of the infirmary
cloisters in close proximity to the treasury.[2] He rapidly enlarged
the powers of the senior monks who met here so that, by the end
of the thirteenth century, it is possible to say that this select committee of chapter fulfilled four distinct functions. It audited
accounts, nominated obedientiaries, decided certain questions
touching upon the daily life of the monks, and issued ordinances
on the economy of the priory. The audit of accounts and the
appointment of obedientiaries have been discussed at length elsewhere, but the other functions of the senior monks merit some
consideration here. A word first as to the personnel of the *seniores
ad scaccarium*. In 1305 this body was defined as 'the prior and all
the seniors and obedientiaries of the church'.[3] In 1323 'the prior,
the sub-prior, and the greater part of the chapter' forgathered at
the exchequer. Usually the committee was simply designated as
the *seniores et saniores fratres* meeting *ad scaccarium* to determine
some specific issue.

Important questions affecting the internal life of the priory were
regularly deliberated upon by the senior monks at the exchequer.
In the year 1300, for example, this capitular committee decided to
readmit Thomas Ringmer, an ex-prior, who had divided his time
after his resignation in 1285 between the Cistercian abbey of

[1] *Reg. Epist. J.P.* II, pp. 403–4.
[2] The 'camera ad scaccarium cum diversorio' was built between the years
1285 and 1290 (Willis, *History of the Conventual Buildings of Christ Church*,
p. 185). It was a three-storeyed building and 'plainly a continuation of the
chamber accommodation of the Norman one' (*ibid.* p. 102).
[3] B.M. Cott. MS. Galba E iv, fo. 73 v.

Beaulieu and a hermitage.[1] The intricacy of monastic procedure at Christ Church at this time is revealed by the fact that Prior Eastry, having secured this unpalatable decision from the body of *seniores*, sought the advice of certain other members of the chapter, whose reverse opinion was more acceptable to him.[2] The outcome of these divided counsels was that Thomas Ringmer was made a non-resident pensioner of the priory for the rest of his life.

In Henry of Eastry's priorate (1285–1331) the *seniores ad scaccarium* began to issue ordinances on the economic policy of the house. They covered the widest range of subjects in the greatest detail. The sequence of extant ordinances begins in 1288 with a statement of the annual food farm due to be rendered from the Kentish manors and of the deficiencies to be made good in the return of that year.[3] In 1300, 1305, and 1309 the *seniores* turned their attention to such questions as the sale of corn, the care of cattle and sheep, and the marling of land.[4] The important question as to whether the priory should invest money by the purchase of new land was decided by the *seniores ad scaccarium* in 1323.[5] Nor did they neglect problems of household expenditure. In 1322 they issued an ordinance which determined the wages of all servants within the *curia* of the priory,[6] and in 1326[7] and 1328[8] they came to decisions upon the endowment of the almonry.

[1] *Reg. Winchelsey*, p. 373. For an account of the career of Thomas Ringmer, see Woodruff and Danks, *Memorials of Canterbury Cathedral*, pp. 134–35.

[2] Winchelsey admonished Prior Eastry, declaring that 'vos postea quosdam de capitulo fecistis secrecius informari, quorum nomina bene novimus, ad contradicendum illi reconciliationi': *Reg. Winchelsey*, p. 373; cf. *ibid*. p. 378.

[3] It is entitled 'Ordinacio facta ad scaccarium in die quatuor coronatorum de blado mittendo domi anno regni Edwardi XVI'; see Appendix I.

[4] *Ibid*. They were almost certainly guided in their ordinances on agricultural practice by Walter of Henley's *Treatise on Husbandry* and an anonymous treatise on the same subject, which were enrolled in several of the conventual registers. In many details the language of the ordinances corresponds closely to that of these thirteenth-century manuals on estate management.

[5] *Lit. Cant.* I, p. 104.    [6] B.M. Cott. MS. Galba E iv, fo. 95 v.

[7] Cant. MS. M 13, viii, mem. 31.

[8] Dugdale, *Monasticon* (1817 ed.), I, p. 104.

The fortunate survival of a day-book of Priors Oxenden and Hathbrand for the years 1331–43, in which many of the intimate affairs of the monastery were recorded, has made it possible for us to gain a very clear picture of the economic aspect of the work of the senior monks at the exchequer under Prior Eastry's successors. They issued ordinances on the annual income of the penitentiary,[1] on the wages of monastic servants at Caldicote,[2] and the sum of money to be levied by a monk-warden from his group of manors.[3] They are found grappling with knotty problems connected with the purchase of land.[4] In a word, the *seniores ad scaccarium* were able, by the issue of ordinances, to exercise a decisive influence upon the life of the priory and to determine the general lines of its economy.

It must not be imagined that the influence of the chapter on temporal administration was entirely superseded by that of the senior monks who met at the exchequer. The point cannot be too strongly stressed that the latter body was in its origin, and remained throughout, a committee of chapter concerned with the temporal welfare of the priory. It will be remembered that in certain years, when time and circumstances allowed, ordinances were issued *in pleno capitulo* on economic questions similar to those which emanated from the *scaccarium*, and certain kinds of secular business were normally dealt with in full chapter. The grant of land, pensions, and corrodies always took place in the larger body, and the consent of all the monks was required for the contraction of loans. While the sale or lease of land was always a matter for the whole chapter, the purchase of new property was, as has been shown, often agreed upon by the senior monks at the exchequer. The logic of this procedure is obvious. Questions relating to the purchase of land called for a considerable technical knowledge, and it was only the senior monks, and especially the wardens of the manors, who would be competent to express any opinion.

The *seniores* appear to have been most active at Christ Church in the first third of the fourteenth century—that golden age of demesne farming. In 1359 they were still conducting their delibera-

---

[1] Cant. MS. D.E. 3, fo. 44 v.    [2] *Ibid.* fo. 46 v.
[3] *Ibid.* fo. 48.    [4] *Ibid.* fo. 44 v.

tions at the exchequer in the normal manner,[1] but in 1360 Archbishop Simon Islip attempted to bring about radical changes in
the administration of the priory. In the first place, he enjoined
that the business affairs of the house should be discussed only in
the presence of sixteen monks. The command was a fundamental
threat to the system of capitular committee meetings at the
exchequer, and the prior was not slow to emphasize in his reply
the fact that the size of the meetings had in the past depended upon
the nature of the business under discussion.[2] Secondly, the archbishop ordered the wardens of the manors to present accounts
each year at the exchequer.[3] This, again, was an innovation, and
the prior fell back upon the ancient customs of his house in resisting
the injunction. He strongly stressed his own rights as well as those
of the senior monks in his letter of reply.[4] Islip's main purpose
seems to have been to prevent the senior monks transacting business
other than that of audit at the exchequer by emphasizing the
necessity of capitular consent for all executive measures. His
policy marks the reversal of that of Pecham, whose tendency it
was to encourage the action of small groups within the framework
of the chapter.

It was not to be expected that Archbishop Islip would readily
succeed in destroying an institution which had taken such a firm
root in the life of the priory. Indeed, some sixteen years later we
find ten senior monks meeting at the exchequer and issuing important ordinances on the conduct of sick monks in the infirmary

---

[1] In this year a sum of £11 was assigned 'per consensum domini prioris
et seniorum in scaccario' for the repair of the malthouse at the barton: Cant.
MS. M 13, i.

[2] 'Item in ea parte minationum vestrarum qua cavetur, quod nullus
tractatus circa negotia Monasterii nostri habendus nisi in praesentia sexdecim
confratrum nostrorum haberetur, nobis visum est jus et parvitatem nostram
nimis per hoc fore restrictam, cum nostrae voluntatis existat, juxta naturam,
qualitatem, et exigentiam hujusmodi negotiorum et tractatuum, aliquando
plures, et aliquando numero minores seu pauciores, ad hujusmodi tractatum,
prout nobis videbitur, convocare, tam de jure quam de consuetudine Monasterii nostri supradicti': *Lit. Cant.* II, p. 397. I have been unable to consult
Islip's register on account of the war.

[3] *Ibid.* II, p. 396.

[4] *Ibid.* II, pp. 396–97.

and the annual income of the chamberlain.[1] In the critical first
two decades of the fifteenth century, when the central treasury of
the priory was breaking down,[2] the senior monks are known to
have played an active part in regulating financial affairs.[3] There
is evidence for an even later date—1461—that obedientiaries were
still nominated at the exchequer.[4] It seems probable that with the
well-nigh universal adoption of the leasehold system on the Christ
Church estates and the tendency towards separately endowed
obediences in the household, the work of the *seniores* was somewhat restricted in scope in the last century or so before the Dissolution. When the monks became *rentiers* the need for ordinances
on estate management disappeared, and centrifugal tendencies in
the household can only have led to a diminution of the power of
the *seniores*. Be that as it may, the work of the senior monks at
the exchequer of Christ Church must be accounted a decisive factor
in the administrative development of the priory household.

The secretarial department of the priory, where the decrees of
the chapter and *seniores* were recorded, the registers compiled, and
the business correspondence of the house conducted, was known
as the chancery (*cancellaria*). There were usually two chancellors
(*cancellarii*) who, like other monastic obedientiaries, devoted their
full time to the work of their department. They resembled less the
chancellors of cathedrals with secular chapters, who usually combined the offices of *theologus* and *scolasticus* with that of secretary,[5]
than the chancellor of the kingdom who, in the thirteenth and
early fourteenth centuries, was primarily a secretary and administ-
trator.[6] The international range of his correspondence and influence made it necessary for the prior to employ public notaries
or *tabelliones*.[7] Public notarial acts, drawn up in a formal fashion
by a class of professional *tabelliones*, served as an alternative to
sealing and were far more common in southern Europe than in

---

[1] *Lit. Cant.* III, pp. 4–6.          [2] See Chapter Twelve.

[3] See *Arch. Cant.* XXIX, pp. 78–81, and *Christ Church Letters*, ed. J. B.
Sheppard (Camden Soc. 1877), pp. 43–44.

[4] *Camb. Antiq. Soc. Publ.* XXXIV, p. 84.

[5] A. Hamilton Thompson, *The Cathedral Churches of England*, p. 21.

[6] T. F. Tout, *Chapters*, I, p. 16.

[7] Woodruff and Danks, *op. cit.* p. 225.

England, 'which remained emphatically a land of seals'.[1] In the thirteenth century, however, the notarial system began to appear in this country. In 1306 the Count Palatine, who as one of the electors enjoyed the imperial privilege of making notaries, authorized Prior Henry of Eastry to create three *tabelliones*.[2] The prior promptly created two, but the king, seeing a threat to his kingdom in the presence of notaries created by imperial authority, forbade all such *tabelliones* to exercise their office and refused to grant credit to their instruments.[3] In 1322 we find the prior asking the bishop of Winchester to appoint three papal notaries, so that he might accomplish with greater facility the judicial acts committed to him by the Holy See.[4] Although a number of notarial acts have survived,[5] the system of sealing was without a doubt always the chief means of authenticating documents at Christ Church.

In the manner of the royal chancery the secretariat at Christ Church was equipped with a system of letters patent and close and of conventual seals. The conventual register of the early fifteenth century, which is now Canterbury Register S., is entitled 'Registrum in cancellaria Ecclesiae Christi Cantuariensis, per Fratres Thomas Bungay et Alexandrum Lundon Cancellarios, factum ibidem anno Domini MCCCCmo undecimo. In quo continentur litterae patentes et clausae, et alia sub sigillo communi Dominorum Prioris et capituli emanancia.'[6]

An adequate description of the work of the monastic chancery would involve a full account of the business dealings of the convent. Grants of powers of attorney, formal communications with the archbishop and magnates, licences of every description, acquittances and recognizances—all emanated from the monastic

[1] Tout, *Chapters*, I, p. 123.
[2] Somner, *Antiquities of Canterbury*, Appendix, p. 59.
[3] *Ibid.* p. 60.
[4] *Lit. Cant.* I, pp. 80–81.
[5] These are to be found among the class of Canterbury MSS. called Chartae Antiquae.
[6] *H.M.C.* App. to IXth Report, p. 110. The register which is now Camb. Univ. Lib. MS. Ee. v, 31 is similarly entitled 'Registrum veterum cartarum et aliarum litterarum patentium et clausarum conventus tempore Henrici Prioris' (1285–1327).

chancery, signed with the common seal of the convent. The prior often transacted his official correspondence in chancery,[1] while his private correspondence was usually conducted *in camera*.

The Benedictine general chapters were much concerned with the proper use and custody of conventual seals. The chapter of the Canterbury province decreed in 1277 that the common seal should be kept under three or four keys, of which the abbot should possess one and the rest belong to monks appointed by the abbot with the consent of the convent. No contracts for loans were to be signed with the common seal until the abbot and convent, or at least the *major vel sanior pars*, had given their formal assent.[2] Five years later, in 1282, Archbishop Pecham enjoined the monks of Christ Church to keep their common seal under three keys. The prior was to have one and the other two were to be delivered to cloister brethren (*puri claustrales*) who held no monastic office. When the prior left the house on business he was instructed to hand over his key to a reliable person.[3] There is no direct evidence of any 'battle of the seals' at Christ Church, although the purchase of a false seal by the monks in 1220–21 has a sinister ring,[4] and we know that Prior Eastry had his own secret seal.[5] A special seal *ad causas* was used by the monks in the prosecution of their law-suits.[6] In 1376, when the central financial system of the priory

---

[1] Thus Prior Oxenden wrote to the proctor of the convent at the Roman Curia in 1333, stating 'Misimus etiam de cancellaria nostra Magistro Nicholao de Soleby quasdam litteras sigillatas, tangentes monasterium Sancti Augustini Cantuariae...': *Lit. Cant.* I, p. 528.

[2] *Chapters*, I, p. 66. See, also, the decree of the general chapter in 1343 in *ibid.* II, p. 42.

[3] *Reg. Epist. J.P.* II, p. 403. For the significance of this instrument of common control, see Dom U. Berlière, 'Le Sceau Conventuel' in *Revue Bénédictine* (1926), XXXVIII, pp. 288–309.

[4] '...et cum denariis datis pro falso sigillo, scilicet, lxx marce': Cant. MS. F ii, fo. 65 v. I can offer no explanation of this action.

[5] In a letter of Archbishop Reynolds to Prior Eastry in 1326 there occurs the phrase 'in quo quidem loco de Mortelake duo paria litterarum sub sigillo vestro secreto recepimus': Cant. MS. Eastry correspondence, M 13, i, 61.

[6] In 1240 two of the agents of the prior announced that they had sent letters sealed with the *sigillum ad causas* to the bishop of London, with whom the monks were then in conflict. See *H.M.C.* App. to VIIIth Report, p. 341.

was beginning to break down, Archbishop Simon of Sudbury had sharply to remind the monks of the proper use and custody of the common seal.[1] Soon after this date, however, the registers show that the common seal was being used with exemplary care.[2] By this time the conventual secretariat had become stereotyped in its methods and the monastic chancery underwent no further changes before the Dissolution.

[1] The archbishop enjoined 'quod sigillum commune melius custodiatur, et quod munimenta ardua, quae transeunt sub illo sigillo, registrentur': Wilkins, *Concilia*, III, p. 111.

[2] In the last century and a half before the Dissolution an annual wage of 6s. 8d. was paid to a *custos sigilli communis in cancellaria*: Cant. MS. M 13, xiv, mem. 8; xv, mem. 4.

## Chapter Five

### THE PRIOR'S COUNCIL

In the thirteenth century the central administration of Christ Church underwent a twofold development. In the first place, as we have seen, the senior monks adopted the practice of meeting as a capitular committee at the exchequer and there transacting much of the temporal business of the house. Their decisions were duly registered by a specialized secretariat in the monastic chancery. At the same time, however, as secular business was being drawn off from the chapter to the exchequer, the prior was building up an elaborate private council. The reasons for the creation of this institution are sufficiently clear. The growing complexity of secular business involved frequent recourse to expert legal aid. Few, if any, of the monks were in a position to furnish such assistance. The enactments of popes, bishops, and Benedictine general chapters that monks should occupy themselves as little as possible with *extrinseca negotia* were another factor which obviously made for the growth of private councils. All over England, in episcopal and baronial circles as well as in great monastic establishments, these private councils came into being in the thirteenth century.[1] By the end of that period they were an integral part of the administrative systems of most lay and ecclesiastical magnates.

At Christ Church, Canterbury, the prior's council can first be detected in the second quarter of the thirteenth century. The records of the Baldwin contest at the end of the previous century make it abundantly clear that no private council existed at that date. All the negotiations at Rome and at the royal court were carried on solely by monks.[2] Even after the return from exile the *pars sanior et discretior* of the monks continued to negotiate in

[1] E. Levett, *Studies in Manorial History*, pp. 21–40; N. Denholm-Young, *Seignorial Administration in England*, pp. 25–31; and F. M. Page, *The Estates of Crowland Abbey*, pp. 45–49.

[2] See the long list of monks actively engaged in the struggle compiled by Stubbs in *Epist. Cant.* pp. xxxvi–xxxvii.

person with the king,[1] and in the controversy with Boniface the monks relied largely on their own resources.[2] The event which appears to have stimulated the formation of a small standing council was the quarrel of the monks with the bishop of London and archdeacon of Canterbury over *sede vacante* jurisdiction. This controversy, which first became acute in 1240, involved highly technical problems of law and precedent,[3] and the monks were wise to choose Roger Cantelupe and Robert of Ludlow, two trained lawyers who enjoyed the royal favour, as their representatives in the struggle.[4] Both of these men were paid high fees by the priory and tirelessly upheld the claim of the prior and chapter to exercise diocesan and provincial jurisdiction during vacancies in the see, by canvassing the episcopate, influencing suitable persons, and making pointed appeals to historical precedent.[5] About the middle of the century two other lawyers, Hugh Mortimer, the official of the archbishop,[6] and Master Omer,[7] the

---

[1] *Cal. Let. Close*, 12 Henry III, p. 109.

[2] Woodruff and Danks, *Memorials of Canterbury Cathedral*, pp. 130–32.

[3] The best account of the conflict is that of Battely in Somner's *Antiquities of Canterbury* (1703 ed.), Part II, pp. 140–41.

[4] They were first employed by the priory in 1226–27, Cantelupe receiving 28 marks and Ludlow 30 marks (Cant. MS. F ii, fo. 71 v.). In 1230 Cantelupe received 40 marks and Ludlow 20 marks and this system of payment went on regularly until 1247. After this date payments were somewhat intermittent. Cantelupe received his last payment in 1259 and Ludlow in 1255. Some particulars of the career of Roger de Cantelupe are given by H. R. Luard in *D.N.B.* VIII, p. 447. The work of both men as royal agents is disclosed by many references in the *Calendars of Letters Patent and Close*.

[5] Their work is recounted at great length in Cant. MS. Chart. Antiq. M. 364, and Sede Vacante Scrap-Book, iii, 196, 199.

[6] Hugh Mortimer was official of the court of Canterbury in 1248 (*Cal. Let. Pat.* 32 Henry III, p. 12) and, though he does not appear to have held that position in 1251, was official again in the years 1255–56 (*ibid.* 39 Henry III, p. 398; 40 Henry III, p. 489) and in 1258 and 1261 (I. Churchill, *Canterbury Administration*, II, p. 237). He received a pension of 22 marks from the monks of Christ Church in 1255 (Cant. MS. F ii). In 1269 he was appointed archdeacon of Canterbury, an office which he held until his death in 1275: Gervase, *Opera*, II, pp. 249, 281.

[7] In 1249, Magister Omerus was paid a pension of £2 and for the next thirty-one years he rendered continual service to the priory, receiving an annual salary of £5 in his last years as well as a house in the precinct which

F

official of the archdeacon, were granted an annual pension by the monks in return for their expert advice. At this stage, therefore, the prior's council may be said to have consisted of a small group of trained lawyers, who received a yearly pension for their counsel and their championship of the jurisdictional claims of the priory.

A great increase in the membership and activities of the prior's council took place in the last quarter of the thirteenth century. This was a development in strict conformity with the spirit and temper of that age of administrative centralization and legal definition. It must also have been prompted in some measure by the labours of the strict and litigious prior, Thomas Ringmer (1274–85), who involved his house in many wearisome lawsuits.[1] When Henry of Eastry became prior in 1285 a large standing council was at hand to uphold his interests. Its personnel can be accurately studied in the enrolled treasurers' accounts, which record the pensions paid to counsellors year by year.

The composition of the council of the prior of Christ Church in the late thirteenth century corresponds in many respects to that of the private councils of other great baronial institutions.[2] The council normally consisted of four different elements. In the first place, there was a group of local landowners and gentry, useful for their personal influence, knowledge, and prestige. Secondly, the council contained a nucleus of permanent officials, consisting of the steward of the Liberty and other land agents of the priory. Thirdly, there was always a group of trained civil and ecclesiastical lawyers. Lastly, one or two celebrated judges, or itinerant justices, were commonly to be found on the council of the prior. The year 1291–92 may be conveniently chosen to illustrate the composition of the prior's council some few years after Henry of Eastry's accession. There were in all nineteen persons receiving

still bears his name (*H.M.C.* App. to IXth Report, p. 124). After 1250 he was official to the archdeacon (Somner, *op. cit.* Part II, p. 153). We find him journeying to London with the sacrist on behalf of the priory during the Dover dispute in 1274: Lambeth MS. 242, fo. 23.

[1] See 'Placita et contenciones mota contra Priorem et capitulum Cantuar' anno domini mcclxxxv, videlicet, die electionis Henrici Prioris' in B.M. Cott. MS. Galba E iv, fo. 108 v.

[2] See E. Levett, *Studies*, pp. 26–27. Cf. F. M. Page, *The Estates of Crowland Abbey*, pp. 45–46.

pensions as counsellors of the priory. First in importance stood the two royal justices, Ralph of Hengham[1] and Solomon of Rochester,[2] each of whom received a yearly pension of £5. Both were men of wide influence and notoriously corrupt,[3] and therefore peculiarly fitted for influencing judicial decisions in favour of the priory.[4] Adam of Lympne,[5] Peter of Peckham,[6] and Henry of Northwode,[7] three royal clerks, were associated with the two judges on the council. Their influence at court was clearly the explanation of the ample pensions which they received. The group of trained lawyers in the council was headed by Gilbert of St Liffard, formerly Official of the court of Canterbury and at this time bishop of Chichester.[8] It consisted of such men as John of Selveston,[9] and Philip Wyleweby,[10] canons of St Paul's, and Hugh

---

[1] He was granted his pension by the monks in 1283 (Camb. Univ. Lib. MS. Ee. v, fo. 31). For a concise account of his life, see J. M. Rigg's article in *D.N.B.* xxv, pp. 410–11.

[2] He received the first instalment of his pension in 1284 (Camb. Univ. Lib. MS. Ee. v, 31, fo. 19 v.). His life is recounted by A. F. Pollard in *D.N.B.* xlix, p. 73.

[3] A number of charges of maladministration and corruption were preferred against Hengham and Rochester in 1289–90. See the articles in *D.N.B.* and T. F. Tout, *History of England, 1216–1377*, pp. 172–73.

[4] Dr Coulton has shown (*Five Centuries of Religion*, ii, p. 36) that 'nearly all abbots enjoyed the usual advantages of the medieval capitalist in the law courts, where judges were habitually accessible to bribes'. See *ibid.* ii, pp. 37, 241, and iii, pp. 507–24.

[5] The monks granted him an annual pension of £2 in 1286 (Camb. Univ. Lib. MS. Ee. v, 31, fo. 19 v.). In 1291 the king appointed him custodian of the town and port of Sandwich: *Cal. Let. Pat.* 19 Edward I, p. 423.

[6] He was granted an annual pension of £5 in 1286: Camb. Univ. Lib. MS. Ee. v, 31, fo. 25.

[7] He was receiving an annual pension of £5 in 1291–92 (Cant. MS. F ii unfoliated). In 1289 he had travelled abroad in the king's service (*Cal. Let. Pat.* 18 Edward I, p. 335).

[8] His life is detailed by T. F. Tout in *D.N.B.* xxi, pp. 318–20 and by W. R. W. Stephens in *Memorials of the See of Chichester*, pp. 102–9. The monks granted him a sum of £33. 6s. 8d. in 1286: Camb. Univ. Lib. MS. Ee. v, 31, fo. 25 v.

[9] His pension, first granted in 1285, was one of £6. 13s. 4d. a year: Camb. Univ. Lib. MS. Ee. v, 31, fo. 23.

[10] In 1291–92 he was receiving a pension of £13. 6s. 8d. a year (Cant. MS. F ii). For his career as a prebendary of St Paul's, see Hennessy's *Novum Repertorium*, pp. 14, 23.

of Derby,[1] a London rector; all of whom were well suited to tender legal advice. The group of local magnates was headed by Thomas of Cobham, who came of an old and distinguished Kentish family. He was a clerk of high competence who ended his career as bishop of Worcester.[2] Roger Digges, the scion of another old Kentish family,[3] was also one of the council. The steward of the Liberty, John of Ridingate,[4] was of course a member, as were several other land agents of the priory. Many types of counsellor were therefore represented. In addition the prior had his proctors resident at Rome and paid a substantial pension to a cardinal *in curia*.[5]

The duty of the prior's counsellors was expressed in the words of their oath of allegiance—*patrocinium, consilium, et auxilium*.[6] Each counsellor had to swear that he would on no account reveal the secrets of the chapter. Accommodation within the precinct for one or more nights for a counsellor and his retinue, when

---

[1] In 1291–92 his pension came to £33. 6s. 8d. (Cant. MS. F ii), a sum which probably comprised the arrears of several years. In 1283 he was presented to the rectory of St Michael Royal by the prior and convent of Christ Church (Newcourt's *Repertorium*, p. 493), and in 1285 he was given powers of general attorney by the chapter (Camb. Univ. Lib. MS. Ee. v, 31, fo. 9). In 1291 he was rector of St Leonard's, Eastcheap (*ibid.* fo. 15 v.), and he died in 1307 (*ibid.* fo. 108 v.).

[2] See E. H. Pearce, *Thomas de Cobham* (1923) and the life by R. L. Poole in *D.N.B.* XI, pp. 157–58. He was granted an annual pension of £3. 6s. 8d. in 1283: Camb. Univ. Lib. MS. Ee. v, 31, fo. 19 v.

[3] There is a brief synopsis of the history of the Digges family, which lived at Digges Court at Barham, by Miss A. M. Clerke in *D.N.B.* XV, p. 70. His pension amounted to £2 in 1291–92: Cant. MS. F ii.

[4] He was granted an annual pension of £2 in 1285 (Camb. Univ. Lib. MS. Ee. v, 31, fo. 67 v.). In 1286 he was serving as steward of the Liberty (Lambeth MS. 242, fo. 92) and was granted powers of general attorney by the monks in 1295 (Camb. Univ. Lib. MS. Ee. v, 31, fo. 67 v.), and again in 1297, *ibid.* fo. 74.

[5] In the year in question, 1291–92, a certain Cardinal Benedict received a pension of £13. 6s. 8d.: Cant. MS. F ii.

[6] The common form of oath, stereotyped by the last quarter of the thirteenth century, demanded that a counsellor 'assistet nobis in ecclesie nostre negociis et fidele patrocinium, consilium, et auxilium prestabit, quocienscumque super hoc fuerit requisitus seu eciam quociens contigerit causam aliquam nos et ecclesiam nostram tangentem in presencia sua ventilari'.

occasion arose for a visit to Canterbury, was specifically granted
in the act of appointment. In regard to residence, the counsellors
fell into two classes; those who would normally reside at Canterbury and in its neighbourhood, and those who dwelt at a distance
from the priory. The first class was represented by the steward of
the Liberty, who had to seek licence from the prior to leave the
city of Canterbury for more than three days,[1] and those clerks of
legal training who had connections at court and formed part of
the daily entourage of the prior. This inner council of legal experts
accompanied the prior on his frequent travels and witnessed his
charters.[2] They advised him as to his conduct in parliament and
stood ready to offer counsel at all times.[3] The outer ring of counsellors, the justices, lawyers, and men of social position, were only
called to Canterbury for consultation at times of crisis.[4] Their
normal function was to safeguard the interests of the priory in the
law-courts by swaying judicial decisions.[5]

The public disgrace of Solomon of Rochester and Ralph of
Hengham in 1289–90 seems to have dissuaded Prior Eastry from
appointing secular judges to his council. The counsellors nominated between this date and the death of Prior Eastry in 1331 were,
for the most part, ecclesiastical lawyers. The prior always had one
or more canons of St Paul's on his council. Roger Cantelupe had
held a prebend in St Paul's for a period, and so had Solomon of

---

[1] Camb. Univ. Lib. MS. Ee. v, 31, fo. 20.

[2] The item *hostilagium* in the serjeants' accounts testifies to their presence
in the manors year by year. For charters witnessed by this inner group of
counsellors in 1299 and 1301, see Camb. Univ. Lib. MS. Ee. v, 31, fos. 82 v.,
87, 88.

[3] Thus in 1289–90 a sum of £5. 16s. 8d. was paid 'pro expensis domini
W. Lideberi et domini J. de Ifeld senescalli et aliorum ministrorum nostrorum
existencium apud Southwerk per xii dies pro parliamento domini regis' and
£2. 4s. to 'senescallo alia vice cum T. de Medmenham, J. Do., et aliis de
consilio nostro': Lambeth MS. 242, fo. 143 v.

[4] They were, for example, all summoned to Canterbury in the year of the
Black Death: *Lit. Cant.* II, pp. xxv, 291.

[5] For example, in 1289 we find Solomon of Rochester, who was for a long
period justice in eyre in East Anglia, acting as judge in a dispute between
Christ Church and Bury St Edmund's: Camb. Univ. Lib. MS. Ee. v, 31,
fo. 27.

Rochester, John of Selveston, and Philip Wyleweby. Ralph of Hengham was a prebendary of St Paul's from 1280 until his death in 1311. In 1306 Andrew Brugg, a canon of St Paul's, was appointed a counsellor with an annual pension of £3,[1] and Henry Iddesworth, who held three prebends in the same cathedral, joined the prior's council for the same fee c. 1328.[2] The connection of these persons with the capital and the central law-courts of Church and State placed them in a most favourable position for tendering advice to the prior.

Canon lawyers of eminence in the court of Canterbury shared with the canons of St Paul's, to whose number they often belonged, the distinction of being regularly nominated to the prior's council. We have seen how Hugh Mortimer and Gilbert of St Liffard, officials of the court of Canterbury, were appointed counsellors of the prior in the thirteenth century. In 1297 Roger of Rothwell, a former dean of Arches and at that time archdeacon of Bedford, became a counsellor,[3] and in 1303 John of Ros, who was to become Official of the court of Canterbury five years later, was granted the first instalment of a substantial pension.[4] Andrew of Brugg became auditor of causes in the court in 1308 and Henry Iddesworth was nominated Official by the prior and chapter during the vacancy of the see in 1333. The monks were therefore in a strong position to influence the decisions of the provincial court of appeal. To these ecclesiastical lawyers, who were nominated as counsellors during Henry of Eastry's priorate, must be added the

---

[1] Camb. Univ. Lib. MS. Ee. v, 31, fo. 106. In 1308 he was auditor of causes in the court of Canterbury: I. Churchill, *Canterbury Administration*, II, p. 242.

[2] See *Lit. Cant.* I, pp. 309, 339–40. Details of his ecclesiastical career are to be found in Hennessy's *Novum Repertorium*, pp. 8, 29, 33, 35, 407. In 1333 he was appointed official of the court of Canterbury: I. Churchill, *op. cit.* I, p. 438.

[3] He was granted an annual pension of £6. 13s. 4d. (Camb. Univ. Lib. MS. Ee. v, 31, fo. 73 v.). In 1279–82 he had been dean of Arches. I. Churchill, *op. cit.* I, pp. 64, 79.

[4] His pension amounted to £6. 13s. 4d. a year (Camb. Univ. Lib. MS. Ee. v, 31, fo. 94 v.). His life is briefly recounted by C. L. Kingsford in *D.N.B.* XLIX, p. 216, who was not, however, aware that Ros was appointed Official of the court of Canterbury in 1308: see I. Churchill, *op. cit.* I, p. 437.

famous scholar and chronicler, Adam Murimuth,[1] and Brice of Scharsted,[2] appointed proctors *in curia* in 1316 and 1319, and Michael of Berham[3] and Hugh of Forsham,[4] who became counsellors in 1300 and 1318 while occupying important positions in the archbishop's household.

Shortly before the death of Prior Eastry a new type of counsellor began to be appointed. The growth of secular jurisprudence and the encroachment of the royal courts on the sphere of the ecclesiastical tribunals made it imperative for the monks to have representatives in the central courts at Westminster. The king's bench, which under the first two Edwards became the great criminal court and court of common law,[5] was the first of these royal courts to receive attorneys (*attornati*) of the priory. In 1329 we have explicit mention of a representative in the king's bench,[6] and three years later the monks were paying not one, but two attorneys to maintain their interests in this court.[7] In 1336 they appointed an attorney in the court of exchequer,[8] and in the latter half of the century attorneys were appointed in the court of common

---

[1] See the life by C. L. Kingsford in *D.N.B.* xxxix, pp. 331–33. He was given an annual pension of £3: Camb. Univ. Lib. MS. Ee. v, 31, fo. 171.

[2] His annual pension was £2 (Camb. Univ. Lib. MS. Ee. v, 31, fo. 212 v.). He is found advising the prior on questions of church patronage in 1326 and 1327 (*Lit. Cant.* I, pp. 186–89, 237).

[3] His pension amounted to £3 a year (Camb. Univ. Lib. Ee. v, 31, fo. 16 v.). In 1310 he was a member of the archbishop's household and acted for a period c. 1308–10 as Winchelsey's chancellor (I. Churchill, *op. cit.* I, pp. 10, 17).

[4] His annual pension was £2 (Camb. Univ. Lib. MS. Ee. v, 31, fos. 194 v.–195). In 1301 he was dean of Shoreham, one of the archbishop's peculiars; he acted as commissary general in 1310 and during the vacancy in 1313, and conducted a visitation as commissary in 1316–17 (I. Churchill, *op. cit.* I, pp. 56–57, 118, 137; II, p. 231).

[5] See C. Petit-Dutaillis and G. Lefebvre, *Studies Supplementary to Stubbs' Constitutional History*, III, pp. 369–71.

[6] *Lit. Cant.* I, pp. 298–99.

[7] Their names were William de Waldegrave and William Letisant (Cant. MS. D.E. 3, fos. 65, 66 v.). Neither appears to have achieved public distinction.

[8] This man, John Titilmanstone, received an annual pension of £1 (Cant. MS. M 13, xix).

pleas.[1] Finally, in 1382 the monks appointed John Scarle, who later became chancellor, as their representative in the court of chancery,[2] which was gradually developing its jurisdiction in equity. Thus, instead of paying substantial pensions to one or more eminent secular judges in the hope that they would champion their rights in all civil suits, the monks now paid a comparatively small annual fee, usually £1, to lawyers practising in the central courts at Westminster. This was a less expensive arrangement and was also calculated to secure a more constant attention to the interests of the priory on the part of the persons concerned. At the same time as they appointed attorneys in the royal courts, the monks commissioned skilled lawyers (*jurisperiti*) to dwell with them at Canterbury and to be ever ready to tender advice.[3] The council thus underwent a considerable change in composition and structure in the last two-thirds of the fourteenth century, although canons of St Paul's, distinguished lawyers in the court of Canterbury, and magnates of local influence, continued to be appointed.[4] It still contained an inner nucleus, consisting of the steward of the Liberty and other land agents, but for the most part became a body of skilled and specialized lawyers, many of whom were constantly occupied in the business of the royal courts at Westminster.

The fourteenth-century letter-book of the priory, which forms

[1] Richard of Norwich, appointed in 1373, received an annual pension of £1 (Cant. MS. M 13, xv, mem. 5) and in 1382 William Pikhull was appointed for the same fee (*ibid.* mem. 2).

[2] His annual pension was £1 (Cant. MS. M 13, xv, mem. 2). See the account of his life by C. L. Kingsford in *D.N.B.* L, p. 399.

[3] Thus in 1350 Thomas Musbury, *jurisperitus*, was granted life maintenance at the priory (*H.M.C.* App. to VIIIth Report, p. 343), and in 1357 another *jurisperitus*, Thomas Mason, received a similar grant (*Lit. Cant.* II, pp. 354–55).

[4] John Lech, chancellor of the archbishop, who became a canon of St Paul's in 1351 (*Cal. Let. Pat.* 25 Edward III, p. 177), was appointed a counsellor in 1340 (*Lit. Cant.* II, pp. 220–21). Michael de Northburgh, who held many prebends in St Paul's and became bishop of London in 1354 (see life by C. L. Kingsford in *D.N.B.* XLI, pp. 187–88), became a counsellor in 1353 for an annual pension of £3 (*Lit. Cant.* II, p. 317) and John of Eccleshall, another canon of St Paul's, was appointed to the prior's council in 1358 (*ibid.* II, pp. 370–71). Officials of the court of Canterbury were also regularly pensioned (Cant. MS. F iii, *passim*).

the substance of the three volumes of *Literae Cantuarienses*, and the day-book of Priors Oxenden and Hathbrand, extant for the years 1331–43,[1] afford much evidence of the work of the prior's council in the period stretching from the year 1322 to c. 1350. More, it is true, can be learnt about the work of the inner group of counsellors than about that of the attorneys in the royal courts, but it is nevertheless possible to see the council functioning as a whole under a series of enlightened priors. Its work can be accurately defined as consultative and judicial. Legislative and administrative tasks were strictly confined to the chapter, exchequer, and chancery. There is only one recorded instance of the counsellors participating with the senior monks in the work at the exchequer. That was in 1333, when a joint assembly of the two bodies came to agreement on a question of land purchase.[2] Normally the two bodies were quite distinct and had markedly different functions.

The consultative work of the council may be considered first. The counsellors were frequently asked for their advice on matters relating to the ownership of real property. In 1323 Prior Henry of Eastry wrote to one William of Brewous as a prospective purchaser of the manor of Wykeham, declaring that 'we cannot so hastily be finally determined in so great an affair without the advice of our council (*sanz nostre conseil*)'.[3] The council appears to have advised the prior to effect the purchase, for in the same year the senior monks met at the exchequer and offered 2000 marks for the manor.[4] They were not, however, successful in securing it. In the following year the prior is found consulting his expert counsellors, stewards, and land agents, on the advantages to be gained from selling land at Horsleigh in Surrey.[5] Again, in 1330 John of Ifeld, steward of the Liberty, wrote to the prior giving his advice as to the form of conveyance of a piece of woodland purchased by the monks at Knowle, near Lyden. 'Sire,' he writes, 'as to the deed that James of Etchingham must execute to him who

---

[1] Cant. MS. D.E. 3.
[2] '...ordinatum fuit ad scaccarium de consensu fratrum nostrorum et aliorum secularium de consilio nostro...': Cant. MS. D.E. 3, fo. 44 v.
[3] *Lit. Cant.* I, pp. 104–5.
[4] *Ibid.* I, pp. 104–5.       [5] *Ibid.* I, p. 130.

is to be enfeoffed in the wood which you have agreed to purchase from him, see that there is therein a clause of warranty, and that he executes a release and quitclaim, of a date not later than two days or three after that of the deed. And, Sire, let him give you a letter declaring that he has released you for ever...from all manner of actions, quarrels, and demands, which he might have against you, on account of any manner of trespass, whatever it may be, from the beginning of the world down to the date of the making of the letter; for, Sire, as he now might not withdraw from the writ which he directs against you, and might make another for his wood, he could in the future have ground for trespass previously done. And therefore, Sire, it is expedient to be aware beforehand.'[1] Two years later the new prior, Richard Oxenden, wrote to James of Etchingham, stating that 'our council ...tells us that by the custom of Kent respecting *drovedennes* the oak timber and the firewood ought to belong to us, to cut and to carry at our pleasure; and that we have the right of entering our *drovedennes* for the purpose of drawing off the timber at the times at which we have been accustomed'.[2] In 1334 the possibility of seizing land in the fee of the priory at Cheam, which had been acquired by the bishop of Exeter without a licence in mortmain, was discussed at a general meeting of the council at Canterbury.[3] These questions of land purchase and the law of real property presented the inner group of counsellors with the greater part of their work.

The ownership of land and the law of property were subjects which could indeed be adequately discussed by a small group of civil lawyers and land agents. This was not the case with questions of tithe and church patronage, which were highly complex and could only be propounded by trained ecclesiastical lawyers. Thus in 1326, when the right of the bishop of Norwich to a pension from one of the appropriated churches of the monastery came into question, the prior of Christ Church sought the advice of the ecclesiastical lawyers on his council before communicating with his attorney in the diocese of Norwich. He then wrote to his

[1] *Lit. Cant.* I, pp. 348–51.          [2] *Ibid.* I, pp. 490–91.
[3] *Ibid.* II, pp. 74–75.

attorney thus: 'We send you the form of a letter which our council at Canterbury has settled to be sent by you to the said bishop of Norwich, provided that Master Geoffrey of Eton, and Master Adam Murimuth if he is in London, and Master Brice of Scharsted, and our other friends in London, agree to this form. And therefore show this form to our said friends and also tell them how the said bishop answered you formerly about our business of the church of Ash. And the advice of our said friends at London, and what they determine concerning the said letter, or any other form of letter whatsoever to be sent to the said bishop as security for the said pension, communicate to us at Canterbury, and we will cause it to be sealed, and will return it to you for delivery to the said bishop.'[1] Again, in 1337, when the ownership of the tithes of Westerham was disputed, we find one of the counsellors writing to the prior and telling him that 'I had a discussion with the Official of the court of Canterbury and other members of your council (*de consilio vestro*) at London about the revenues of your church of Westerham'.[2] The council appears to have advised that the bishop of Rochester be induced to sequestrate the profits of the benefice, for that is the course that the chapter subsequently recommended to two of their number who had the business in hand.[3] In 1370 a dispute arose between the monks and the king over the advowson of the church of Pagham, which had been recently appropriated to Canterbury College. The monks found themselves in a quandary, for, although they could produce papal bulls in defence of their claims, their *jurisperiti* advised them that the pope had no power to grant temporalities, especially if they belonged to the king.[4] The question, therefore, remained long in dispute.[5]

The counsellors rendered judicial service in a number of different ways. In the first place, as we have seen, they upheld the interests of the priory in the central courts of the kingdom. A letter sent

---

[1] *Lit. Cant.* I, pp. 186–89.
[2] *Lit. Cant.* II, p. 167. The church was appropriated to the priory in 1327: *ibid.* I, pp. 259–67.
[3] *Ibid.* II, pp. 168–69.
[4] *H.M.C.* App. to VIIIth Report, p. 342.    [5] *Ibid.* p. 348.

by the prior in 1329 to his counsellors in the king's bench, calling for immediate action against the debtors of the chapter, illustrates this, the most important, aspect of the judicial work of the council. 'It is expedient for your honour and our profit', writes the prior, 'that you take out writs of *fifa* from the rolls of the justices of the king's bench, for the debt which Sir Walter of Huntingfeild owes us by his recognizance made in the court of king's bench. And also a judgment writ for the debt that Sir Warreis of Valoynes owes us. And also other writs for the debts which Thomas Blak of Sandwich and many other debtors owe to us, as you well know, against whom we have taken out writs which ought to have been delivered to the sheriff at Trinitytide last past; which writs have never come into the sheriff's hands, nor into those of any of his clerks who have authority to receive and make return to such a king's writ; but lately our writ was found with its seal entire and no execution done, and of this we have great marvel. And therefore do you proceed so discreetly in these, and our other matters which we have to transact in the king's court, that our friends, and we ourselves, may be able to see and know that our attorneys are as diligent in conducting our business at the king's court as other attornies are for the business of their employers.'[1] The ability of the London attorneys of the priory to influence judicial decisions is exemplified by the long *causa Dovoriae*, which has been recounted in great detail elsewhere.[2] Time and time again, in disputes of this character, the monks appointed special attorneys and offered 'bribes' to judges in order to secure a decision in their favour.[3]

When business of especial importance was pending in the manorial courts of the priory, the prior appointed one or more of his counsellors to be present in court and to safeguard his interests. This occurred, for example, in 1335 after a writ of right had been sent to the manorial court at Merstham.[4] Again, in 1344 the prior appointed a *jurisperitus*, Thomas of Betenham, 'who is one of our council', to act as assessor to the serjeant of Merstham in holding

---

[1] *Lit. Cant.* I, pp. 298–99.
[2] C. R. Haines, *Dover Priory*, pp. 59–110. See, especially, pp. 101–3.
[3] See, for example, *Lit. Cant.* II, pp. 2–5 and *passim*.
[4] *Lit. Cant.* II, pp. 102–3.

the court as 'certain matters of high import' were about to come up for discussion.[1] No instance of the council acting as a court of appeal from the manorial courts has come to my notice, but a study of the manorial court-rolls may well afford evidence of this practice.[2]

Judicial business connected with the estates of the priory was, of course, normally transacted in the manorial courts and the High Court of the prior at Canterbury. There were, however, occasions on which the prior and his counsellors came to a decision without any reference to the hierarchy of courts. Thus in 1333 a dispute arose between the monks and the bailiff and *communitas* of the east Kent marshes over the repair of a gutter at Lyden. The prior and a number of his counsellors went to Lyden[3] and came to an immediate decision, paying £10 to the bailiff as their share in the cost of repair.[4] Two years later the steward of the Liberty and others 'de consilio nostro' took the responsibility of reducing a fine imposed by the justices in eyre upon one Roger Hadde for damaging the property of the priory in the weald.[5]

The composition of the prior's council in the fifteenth century was similar to that in the last two-thirds of the previous century. Lawyers of distinction were appointed as attorneys in all the royal courts at Westminster[6] and proctors were kept in residence at the Roman Curia.[7] In the middle of the century the monks appointed

---

[1] *Lit. Cant.* II, pp. 273–75.

[2] I have been unable to inspect these court-rolls, which have been taken from the P.R.O. to 'a safer place' for the duration of the war.

[3] '...accessimus cum consilio nostro ad mariscum de Lyden...': Cant. MS. D.E. 3, fo. 43 v.        [4] *Ibid.* fo. 43 v.

[5] The fine was reduced from £60 to £20: *ibid.* fo. 63 v.

[6] Thus in 1436–37 John Elyot represented the priory in the king's bench, Robert Shamull in the exchequer, and Richard Shipley in the court of common pleas. John May, another *attornatus*, was probably the representative of the monks in the court of chancery (Cant. MS. M 13, xvii, mem. 7). The careers of three of these men remain obscure, but Richard Shipley is known to have acted as a justice of gaol delivery at Canterbury Castle in 1437 (*Cal. Let. Pat.* 16 Henry VI, p. 145).

[7] One William Swanne was proctor *in curia* in 1436–37 (Cant. MS. M 13, xvii, mem. 7) and a certain Clement held the position in 1453–54 (*ibid.* mem. 9).

attorneys in the court of burghmote and the *curia portae monachorum*[1] in the city of Canterbury.[2] After the accession of William Sellyng to the priorate in 1472, when the relations of the monks with the city greatly improved,[3] these attorneys were found to be no longer necessary. In that same year John Fyneux, who later became chief justice of the realm, was accorded a modest pension of 13s. 4d.[4] He was one of the very last of a long line of eminent judges and lawyers to serve on the council of the prior of Christ Church.

[1] Dr J. B. Sheppard's report on the city archives (*H.M.C.* App. to IXth Report, pp. 129–77) yields no information as to the character of this court.

[2] In 1453–54 William Tame represented the monks in both courts for a fee of 16s. 8d. (Cant. MS. M 13, xvii, mem. 9) and two years later R. Carpenter acted as attorney for the same fee (*ibid.* mem. 10).

[3] See *Lit. Cant.* III, p. xi.

[4] Cant. MS. M 13, xvii, mem. 12. He was appointed steward of the Liberty of Christ Church for life in 1475 (*H.M.C.* App. to IXth Report, p. 117). See the account of his life by J. M. Rigg in *D.N.B.* xx, pp. 342–43.

## Chapter Six

### THE LIBERTY OF CHRIST CHURCH, CANTERBURY

The early history of the Liberty of Christ Church is to be read in the series of charters granted by Saxon and Norman kings and subsequently confirmed by both king and pope.[1] The most important of these early charters were unquestionably those issued by Cnut in 1020 and William I in 1071. Their effect was to free the monks, tenants, and possessions of the church of Canterbury from all secular services save those demanded by the *Trinoda Necessitas*. Henry II went one stage further by securing the complete immunity of the monks from personal and fiscal service and, in particular, the exemption of the cathedral priory and its lands from the jurisdiction of the shire and hundred courts.[2] Richard I completed the twelfth-century development of the Liberty by a grant of freedom from assarts.[3]

The medieval history proper of the Liberty may be said, however, to begin with the composition made by Archbishop Boniface and Prior Roger in 1259.[4] Formerly there had been much confusion as to the respective rights and franchises of the archbishop and the monks of his cathedral priory. The agreement of 1259 represented a definitive settlement and stood unaltered for the rest of the middle ages. It made clear and emphatic the distinction between the *Baronia*, the franchise of the archbishop, and the *Libertas*, the franchise of the monks of Christ Church,[5] and defined

---

[1] The early history of the Liberty is detailed by J. F. Nichols in *Custodia Essexae*, pp. 51–59. See also the series of early royal charters confirmed by Henry VI in 1434 in *Cal. Let. Pat.* 12 Henry VI, pp. 415–18.

[2] *Monasticon* (1817), I, p. 105.     [3] *Ibid.* pp. 105–6.

[4] Recited in *Cal. Let. Pat.* 12 Henry VI, pp. 420–24.

[5] This fundamental distinction between *baronia* and *libertas* occurs at least as early as 1237–38 (see Nichols, *op. cit.* p. 51, quoting *Trans. Essex Arch. Soc.* XIX, New Series, p. 37). It was familiar to the hundred jurors of 1275 (*Rotuli Hundredorum*, Rec. Comm. 1812, I, p. 205). It clearly arose out of

their mutual relationship. The archbishop was to defend the liberties of the prior and convent by excommunication and interdict, as if they were his own.[1]

Soon after this agreement the reports of the hundred jurors and the *Quo Warranto* pleadings give us a very clear picture of the Liberty of Christ Church in its fully developed form. They show that the prior and monks enjoyed very extensive franchises and took an active part in the administration of the kingdom. This co-operation between the Crown and the franchise-holder is the key to an understanding of the seignorial administration of the later middle ages. It should be once more stressed that 'the antithesis between baronial and royal power, between law and privilege, between a feudal and an official type of administration...are anachronistic if applied to the thirteenth century'.[2] The monks were the king's agents in performing the king's work and were liable to have their franchise withdrawn or invaded by the sheriff and his staff if they failed in their duties.[3] There is much evidence to show that they conducted the royal administration with diligence and went out of their way to seek the co-operation of the royal justices, commissioners, and agents. For example, in 1322 the prior of Christ Church wrote to Edmund de Passele, the royal

the archbishop's exclusive responsibility for knight-service from the tenants of the church of Canterbury, although the archbishop was 'from the middle of Henry III's reign exempt in practice, if not in principle, from military duties' (H. M. Chew, *Ecclesiastical Tenants-in-Chief*, Oxford, 1932, p. 61). The prior of Christ Church repeatedly urged his freedom from all military service; see, for example, *Lit. Cant.* I, pp. 182–84, 212–19.

[1] *Cal. Let. Pat.* 12 Henry VI, p. 423. In 1331 the fact was recalled that St Thomas of Canterbury and successive archbishops 'majoris excommunicationis sententia innodaverint omnes et singulos qui jura et libertates ecclesiae suae praedictae infringere, bona etiam, seu res ipsius ecclesiae, invadere, occupare, seu detinere praesumpserint quovismodo': *Lit. Cant.* I, p. 356.

[2] H. M. Cam, *The Hundred and the Hundred Rolls* (1930), p. 203. Miss Cam has fully exemplified this statement by her study of 'The King's Government, as administered by the greater Abbots of East Anglia' in *Camb. Antiq. Soc. Proc.* (1928), XXIX, pp. 25–49.

[3] Before 1275 the sheriff required a writ *ne omittas propter libertatem* in order to enter a liberty when the franchise-holder had neglected to execute the royal commands. The Statute of Westminster, passed in that year, enabled the sheriff to enter the liberty without delay, if the officials refused to act.

commissioner of sewers, urging him to come to Monkton, the manor of the monks in the Isle of Thanet, to survey the sea-walls and watercourses. The prior concluded his letter by insisting to the royal commissioner that 'without your personal presence we shall not be able to obtain reparation for the damages which we endure in these parts, in spite of law and marsh customs'.[1]

The connecting link between the franchise of Christ Church and the royal administration was the steward of the Liberty (*senescallus Libertatis*). A *dapifer* existed at Christ Church at least as early as the second half of the twelfth century.[2] It seems almost certain that this official was the steward of the Liberty, although we have no positive indications of his functions until some eighty years later. The steward of Christ Church was usually a person of some importance in the county who also commanded influence in the royal household. Prior Henry of Eastry asked the retiring steward in 1330 for his 'good counsel as to some proper person, a knight or other, who may be living in our parts, who is able, capable and willing to intervene in those of our affairs which belong to our high steward and to manage them as you have done hitherto'.[3] Five years later, when the question of appointing a steward again arose, the prior deemed it 'advisable to have some great man to maintain our right'.[4] In the last century before the Dissolution the stewards were usually men of great distinction. John Fyneux, the future chief justice, was appointed steward of the Liberty in 1475,[5] and the office was conferred upon Henry, Earl of Essex, in 1486.[6] In 1507 the choice fell upon John Roper and John Hales.[7] Several commissions issued to stewards of the

---

[1] *Lit. Cant.* I, pp. 79–81. See also *ibid.* p. 377, where evidence is afforded of the royal justices and the steward of the Liberty determining a marsh dispute c. 1331.

[2] A Canterbury rental of the late twelfth century (Cant. MS. R 31 from Box D in ZA) mentions property owned by Bartholomeus, *dapifer noster*. A bull of Alexander III in 1163 mentions the appointment of a *dapifer* by the archbishop, but this probably refers to the steward of the guest-hall who was customarily appointed by the primate (*Papsturkunden in England*, ed. W. Holtzmann, II, p. 299).

[3] *Lit. Cant.* I, p. 337.

[4] *Ibid.* II, p. 85.

[5] *H.M.C.* App. to IXth Report, p. 117.

[6] *Ibid.* p. 118.

[7] *Ibid.* p. 120.

Liberty have survived in the Canterbury registers; some are couched in general terms[1] but others particularize the functions of the steward. Among the latter class of commissions may be cited that which was issued to John of Braydeston, steward of the Liberty, in 1334. The steward was to supervise all the manors of the priory and to hold the manorial courts when it seemed expedient for him to do so. If the property on any manor had been neglected and fallen into disrepair, the steward was to have it repaired and recoup himself from the monastic treasury. Above all, he was to uphold the rights and liberties of the church of Canterbury and its officials and tenants throughout the length and breadth of the kingdom.[2] The archbishop had his own steward with similar powers for the lands of the Barony. The steward of the Liberty was normally exempt from jury-service and all secular burdens[3] and was assisted by one or more stewards of the lands (*senescallus terrarum*),[4] who in the ordinary course of events held the manorial courts when the steward of the Liberty did not deem it expedient to do so in person. A host of minor officials, such as warreners and wood-reeves,[5] were subordinate to the steward in the administration of the Liberty.

The steward was invariably a member of the prior's council,[6] and took a prominent part in the most delicate negotiations with lords of other liberties.[7] Within the Liberty itself his powers were threefold—jurisdictional, administrative, and fiscal. It is proposed to consider each of these three aspects in turn, and thus to illustrate the complex machinery whereby the monks of Christ Church carried on the king's government within the limits of their franchise.

---

[1] See, for example, the commission issued to Henry of Hayles, steward of the Liberty in 1305, in *Reg. Winchelsey* (Canterbury and York Soc.), p. 500.

[2] *Lit. Cant.* II, p. 69.          [3] *Cal. Let. Close*, 27 Henry III, p. 33.

[4] Commissions of stewards of the lands for the year 1279 are to be found in *Reg. Epist. J.P.* I, pp. 1, 3, and from the year 1298 in *Reg. Winchelsey*, p. 291.

[5] See the commissions issued to warreners and wood-reeves in 1331 and 1335, granting powers of distraint for trespass, in *Lit. Cant.* I, pp. 405–9; II, pp. 112–14.

[6] See Chapter Five.          [7] See, for example, *Lit. Cant.* II, p. 75.

From the standpoint of jurisdiction and administration the monks of Christ Church enjoyed a double liberty.. One highly privileged area, the *curia* of the priory, enjoyed an immunity from all royal control. It was explicitly enjoined in 1447 that 'no justice of the peace or other justice, sheriff, escheator, coroner, bailiff, or other minister of the king's, shall in future make any execution within the bounds of the priory'.[1] Although the special immunity of the *curia* had never been confirmed by royal charter until this late date, the privilege had long been recognized by the royal justices. A test case arose in 1304 and was carefully recorded by the monks in many of their registers as a precedent for the future.[2] One Adam, a leathermaker,[3] killed Allexius of Westwell, a carter, within the *curia* of the priory, and immediately fled into the great hall near the outer gate, locking himself in and forbidding all access. The coroners of the lasts of St Augustine's, Shepway, and Scray, duly held an inquest before the gate of Canterbury Castle. Representatives of the hundred of Westgate and the four neighbouring vills, giving evidence, declared on their oath that Adam had in fact committed the murder. The culprit was then handed over by the steward of the Liberty to be sentenced by the justices in eyre meeting within the archbishop's palace at Canterbury. At no stage of the proceedings had the liberty of the *curia* been violated by the royal officials, and a valuable precedent had been created.

It should, however, be observed that the liberty of the *curia* of Christ Church cannot be compared, either in the area or the degree of privilege, to that of the *banlieus* of Bury St Edmunds, Ramsey, and the Isle of Ely, or even the *leuga* of Battle Abbey and the twelve hides of Glastonbury.[4] In the first place, the liberty was much smaller—something less than a square mile—and only comprised the precinct of the priory. In notable contrast to Bury, where the greater part of the borough lay within the *banlieu* of

---

[1] *Cal. Charter Rolls*, 25-26 Henry VI, p. 80.

[2] I take the following summary of the case from the Christ Church register, Trin. Coll. Camb. MS. O. 9/26, fo. 120.

[3] 'Adam dictus le corur.' *Ibid.*

[4] See Mrs M. D. Lobel's study of 'The Ecclesiastical Banleuca in England' in *Oxford Essays in Medieval History presented to H. E. Salter* (Oxford, 1934), pp. 122–40.

the abbey, the city of Canterbury represented a rival liberty. And not only the city; for the archbishop's manor of Westgate, the franchise of St Augustine's, the precinct of St Gregory's priory, and the exempt jurisdiction of the castle—the abode of the sheriff and constable—were all liberties that lay in close proximity to the priory. On all sides the monks were hemmed in by exempt jurisdictional areas and were unable to expand their influence in the city beyond the limits of the *curia*.

Secondly, the monks never possessed the right of appointing their own justices to hear pleas of the Crown or even their own coroners to keep these pleas. Nor were they allowed the privilege of hearing pleas of the Crown in the presence of the justices in eyre within their own liberty and in their own court. Their position in this respect was fully defined by the composition of 1259. 'If any one of a fee or in a fee of the prior and convent be charged or appealed of the death of a man, larceny, or other misdeed, and taken, and cannot lawfully be judged in the court of the prior and convent, the bailiff of the prior and convent shall lead him as a prisoner to the next county court and deliver him there to the bailiffs of the archbishop, who shall immediately redeliver him to the bailiffs of the prior and convent, to be kept in the prior's prison, if the case be one for imprisonment, until the next coming of the justices in eyre into those parts or of some other justice appointed to deliver the archbishop's gaol. If such a case shall arise in Essex, Suffolk, Norfolk, Buckinghamshire, Oxfordshire, and Devonshire or other counties in which the archbishop has no tenants or tenements, but the prior and convent have, then the ministers of the prior and convent, having special mandate from the archbishop in that behalf, shall, unless he shall appoint somebody else, execute the office and keep the prisoner in custody until the coming of the justices in eyre, or until the archbishop or the bailiffs of the prior and convent, at the archbishop's mandate, obtain a justice to deliver the said prison: if such prisoner has to be condemned before the said justices, the bailiffs of the archbishop shall deliver him to the said bailiffs, who shall execute the judgment.'[1] There is evidence of the justices in eyre trying the tenants

[1] *Cal. Let. Pat.* 12 Henry VI, p. 422.

of the priory by ordeal in 1195,[1] and in the subsequent centuries the jurisdiction which they exercised within the Liberty is constantly recorded.[2]

It has been shown that Henry II granted to the prior and convent exemption from the courts of shire and hundred. Three hundreds were partly in the hands of the prior when the Hundred Rolls were drawn up in the early years of the reign of Edward I. The hundred of Cornilo had three lords, the prior of Christ Church, the abbot of St Augustine's and the prior of Dover; the hundred of Eastry was shared by the prior of Christ Church and the king, and half of the hundred of Newchurch belonged to the king and half to the archbishop and prior of Christ Church.[3] In the absence of accessible records it is impossible to say who held the courts or to detail the business transacted therein. The tenants of certain manors of the priory were obliged to perform suit at the hundred courts of the archbishop. The tenants of the priory at Welles, Little Chart, and Meopham owed suit and the duty of making presentments and judgments at the archbishop's hundred courts of Colehill (*Kolehelle*) and Toltentrough (*Toltyntre*),[4] a duty which probably dated back to a time before the division of possessions between archbishop and prior had been finally accomplished. The prior and convent appointed attorneys in the archbishop's hundred courts of Colehill and St Martin's[5] and in the hundred court of Felborough[6] to safeguard their interests and to maintain the rights of their church.

The jurisdictional privileges of the priory were not of a very exceptional character. In common with a vast number of other

---

[1] Gervase, *Opera*, I, pp. 530–31.

[2] See, for example, the royal commission to the justices itinerant in the county of Kent in 1232 in *Cal. Let. Close*, 16 Henry III, p. 24. Lists of amercements imposed by them are recorded in the account-rolls of the steward of the Liberty; see *infra*.

[3] H. M. Cam, *The Hundred and the Hundred Rolls* (1930), pp. 270–72.

[4] *Cal. Let. Pat.* 12 Henry VI, p. 422.        [5] *Ibid.*

[6] *Lit. Cant.* I, p. 403. The prior and convent of Christ Church claimed in 1275 that two-thirds of the hundred of Felborough (of which the rightful lords were Isabel and Alexander of Balliol and the king) belonged to their manors of Chartham and Godmersham (*Rot. Hundredorum*, Rec. Comm. 1812, I, p. 210).

franchise-holders, the monks held the view of frankpledge in all their manors[1] and exercised the leet jurisdiction that went with this right. They also held the assize of bread and ale,[2] a liberty normally enjoyed by lords who had view of frankpledge.[3] The jurisdictional rights enjoyed by the prior of Christ Church and described in the words *sake* and *soke*, *toll* and *theam*, *infangenethef* and *utfangenethef*, meant very little in the thirteenth century.[4] The highest regalian right enjoyed by the monks was that of holding pleas of *vee de naam* (*vetitum namium*), that is, of conducting actions of replevin. They possessed this right in certain of their manors[5] and, in particular, could hold such pleas with or without writ in the central court of the prior at Canterbury.[6] It is now possible to consider in detail the courts in which these jurisdictional powers were exercised.

There were at Canterbury in the later middle ages three central courts for the tenants of the priory; the court of the prior, the court of the sacrist, and the court of the bartoner. The prior's court, which was often called the High Court (*Alta Curia*) and was held within the North Hall at three-weekly intervals,[7] was far the most important of these central tribunals. It was here that the steward of the Liberty heard and determined pleas of *vee de naam*, debt, trespass, detinue, and other personal actions arising within the lands of the monks in the county of Kent, at the suit of any wishing to complain in the court.[8] Other business was also done

[1] *Placita de Quo Warranto* (Rec. Comm. 1818), p. 325.

[2] *Ibid.*

[3] Pollock and Maitland, *History of English Law*, I, p. 569.

[4] *Ibid.* p. 567.

[5] *P.Q.W.* p. 325. Maitland tells us (*op. cit.* I, p. 574) that 'few lords claim to entertain' actions of replevin.

[6] *P.Q.W.* p. 348. Archbishop Boniface granted to the monks of Christ Church in 1259 the right of holding pleas of *vee de naam* in the prior's court at Canterbury (Trin. Coll. Camb. MS. O. 9/26, fo. 77).

[7] See *Cal. Charter Rolls*, 25–26 Henry VI, p. 78 and R. Willis, *The History of the Conventual Buildings of Christ Church, Canterbury* (1869), p. 148.

[8] *Cal. Charter Rolls*, 25–26 Henry VI, pp. 78–79. In 1447 the powers of the court were extended by allowing actions of debt, hitherto confined to amounts under 40 shillings, to be tried without any limit of the amount (*ibid.*).

here, as the extant court-rolls[1] plainly show. The free tenants of
the priory performed their acts of fealty and paid relief in this
court or were distrained for failure to do so.[2] Boys who had
reached the age of fifteen testified to the fact in the court of the
prior with the aid of witnesses, in accordance with the custom of
gavelkind.[3] The procedure of inquest was frequently employed
by the court. Thus in 1393 eighteen honest men of the view of
Eastry were asked to enquire and give evidence in a plea touching
the allegedly unjust detention of goods, and in the same year
eighteen honest men of the view of Appledore gave evidence after
enquiring into a similar case.[4] In 1394 twelve persons were appointed in court to make enquiry as to the rent owing to the
treasurers at Staple.[5]

In many respects the court of the prior at Canterbury appears
to have resembled that *curia sub fraxino* at St Albans which has
been the subject of a recent study.[6] Except in the case of pleas of
*vee de naam*, which could not be heard in many of the manorial
courts, suit to the prior's court at Canterbury seems to have been
largely dictated by convenience and the urgency of the business
in hand. The High Court of the neighbouring abbey of St Augustine's was a tribunal with very similar powers.[7] The relation
between the court of the prior at Canterbury and the court held
in the archbishop's palace was ill-defined in the early middle ages,

[1] These rolls cover the period 1295–1394, with long gaps, and plea-rolls
and lists of estreats are extant for the fifteenth century: Cant. MS. M 13, xi.
[2] Thus in 1303 a court-roll was entitled *Curia de Canon'*. It is recorded
that 'Willelmus de Wiltune fecit fidelitatem pro una domo in vico Judeorum'.
A slip of parchment, attached to this entry, has written on it the words
'De quadam domo in vico Judeorum que est de feodo canonicorum' (Cant.
MS. M 13, xi, mem. 1). For evidence of tenants of the priory journeying to
Canterbury to do fealty, see *Lit. Cant.* I, pp. 499–501; II, pp. 52–53.
[3] For example, a court-roll of the year 1393 contains the following entry:
'Ad hanc curiam venit Johannes filius Johannis Jordan de Wythstaple et
secundum consuetudinem de Gavylkenda probat etatem suam quindecim
annorum et amplius' by the testimony of three persons: Cant. MS. M 13,
xi, mem. 5.
[4] *Ibid.* mem. 5.          [5] *Ibid.* mem. 3.
[6] E. Levett, *Studies in Manorial History* (Oxford, 1938), pp. 134–47.
[7] *Cal. Charter Rolls*, 24 Henry VI, pp. 58–59.

and disputes arose.[1] The composition of 1259 clarified the situation by its stipulation that, in matters of contention between the two parties, appeal should be allowed from the prior's court to the court of the archbishop's palace.[2] It was, of course, also possible for suitors at the prior's court in the early middle ages to claim the benefits of the royal assize system in proprietary disputes, and we accordingly find one Alice being granted the Grand Assize in 1199 and the privilege of having her case transferred from Canterbury to Westminster.[3] The prior's court further resembled the *curia sub fraxino* at St Albans in that it exercised no jurisdiction in error over the manorial courts. Appeals were made to the prior in person and not to his central court.[4]

The sacrist, who held his court at the *campanile* on the south side of the cathedral[5] in the presence of the steward of the Liberty, exercised a jurisdiction which was partly franchisal and partly domanial.[6] He owned property in the boroughs of Street near Lympne, Geddinge in Wootton, and Bernesole in Staple,[7] and it was for the tenants of these possessions that the court was held.[8] Many of the tenants paid essoins, finding attendance at court a burden, and in the fifteenth century at least the business of the

---

[1] An instance of such a dispute in the year 1200 is contained in *Curia Regis Rolls*, I, p. 238.

[2] *Cal. Let. Pat.* 12 Henry VI, p. 422. The two principal courts of the archbishop's barony were those held at the palace in Canterbury and at the manor of South Malling in Sussex: *Cal. Let. Pat.* 26 Henry VI, p. 171.

[3] *Curia Regis Rolls*, I, p. 83.

[4] See 'An Early Fourteenth Century Petition from the Tenants of Bocking to their Manorial Lord' in *Econ. Hist. Rev.* (1930), II, pp. 300–7, and Dr J. F. Nichols' account of an appeal from a tenant of the manor of Milton Hall in Essex to the prior in 1247–48 in *Custodia Essexae*, p. 83.

[5] For the site of the *campanile* see Willis, *op. cit.* p. 153.

[6] I here follow the classification of seignorial jurisdiction made by Professor G. B. Adams in his article on 'Private Jurisdiction in England' in *The American Historical Review* (1918), XXIII, pp. 596–602, and adopted by Professor W. O. Ault in his study of *Private Jurisdiction in England* (1923), pp. 1–8.

[7] C. E. Woodruff, 'The Sacrist's Rolls of Christ Church, Canterbury' in *Arch. Cant.* XLVIII, p. 40.

[8] Court-rolls are extant for the fifteenth century; Cant. MS. M 13, xi, mem. 21 and Cant. MS. ii in ZA.

court was trivial in amount and sessions were held at infrequent intervals. Freeholders performed fealty and paid relief in the court and a common fine of sixpence was imposed upon the tenants. Once a year the sacrist held a view of frankpledge and this was often the only occasion on which the court was held during the year. The procedure of inquest was adopted at the view.[1] The assize of ale was commonly held at the view and tenants were amerced sixpence for being 'common brewers'. These small amercements partook of the nature of fines, paid yearly as a matter of course for the privilege of evading the assize. The sacrist's court also dealt with such common civil offences as the failure to repair waterways. Borsholders or tithing-men were elected in court. All the suitors nominated two persons and the sacrist appointed one of these to the office.[2] The profits of the court never appear to have been very considerable. After the steward's fee was paid they seldom amounted to twenty shillings.[3]

The third of the central courts of the priory was that of the bartoner. In the fifteenth and early sixteenth centuries—the only period for which evidence is available[4]—it was held at the door of the brewery (*ostium bracini*)[5] in the presence of the steward of the Liberty. The business of the court consisted solely of the payment of relief and the performance of fealty by tenants, or their distraint for failure to accomplish these acts. The bartoner seems to have exercised no manorial jurisdiction over his small number of tenants other than that of compelling attendance at his court. No criminal or civil offences are recorded in the court-rolls, which are exclusively concerned with default of suit and the failure

[1] In 1442, for example, it was decided by inquest that one Peter Conys had assaulted Richard Code in the cathedral church and should therefore be distrained for a fine of eight shillings or 10 pounds of wax *ad usum domini libertatis*: Cant. MS. M 13, xi, mem. 21.

[2] Thus in 1443 the tenants of the court nominated Thomas Salter and William Weykham for the office of Borsholder in the borough of Gedding. The sacrist appointed the former: Cant. MS. M 13, xi, mem. 21.

[3] Woodruff, *loc. cit.* p. 40.

[4] Court-rolls of the bartoner covering the years 1434–1522 are now Cant. MS. R.E. 100.

[5] On the brewery (now part of the King's School) see Willis, *op. cit.* pp. 150–51.

of tenants to fulfil the obligations of fealty and relief. In the sixteenth century, and probably earlier, the court became simply a tribunal where the tenants paid their rents. It ceased to be called a court or to exercise any judicial functions.[1] When this change occurred the steward of the Liberty ceased to be present at the door of the brewery. The attendance of the steward at the High Court and the courts of the sacrist and bartoner needs to be emphasized. It shows conclusively that the jurisdiction of the priory was centralized in his person and that a literal interpretation was given to his duty of general supervision.

The steward of the Liberty also maintained a close control of the manorial courts with the help of specially appointed deputies, the *senescalli terrarum*.[2] He is to be found attending the courts in person when important cases arose which called for his presence.[3] Dr Nichols has described for us the business transacted in the manorial courts in the Essex custody,[4] but it has been impossible to consult the court-rolls extant for the Kentish and Surrey custodies.[5] In Essex leet jurisdiction, of which 'the very heart and centre...was the right to hold the view of frankpledge',[6] was exercised once a year in the Christ Church courts. Persons were regularly fined for violation of the assize of bread and ale. Besides the exercise of this common form of franchisal jurisdiction, the manorial courts dealt with the usual civil offences, of which debt and trespass were the most frequent. The details of judicial

[1] In 1455 reliefs were still being paid at the court and distraints made. In 1499 the court was simply a rent-receiving institution.

[2] The appointment of these deputy-stewards to hold courts and exercise functions of general supervision is to be found in *Lit. Cant.* II, pp. 296–97, 348–49, for the years 1349 and 1356.

[3] Thus in 1311 the serjeant of Bocking recorded the expenditure incurred by the attendance of the steward of the Essex custody 'et vicecomitis Essexie, clericorum quorum et ballivi libertatum die S. Mathie ad letam apud Bockyng pro inquisitione generali de malefactoribus patrie facienda qui non potuerunt refutari': Cant. MS. serjeant's account.

[4] Nichols, *op. cit.* pp. 78–107.

[5] They have been deposited by the Ecclesiastical Commissioners at the P.R.O. and are now evacuated.

[6] F. J. C. Hearnshaw, *Leet Jurisdiction in England* (Southampton, 1908), p. 17.

procedure do not properly fall within the scope of this study. It should, however, be observed that ordeal-pits existed on many of the manors and that the method of proof by ordeal was freely practised until the decree of the Lateran Council in 1215, forbidding the clergy to take part in the ceremony, caused the procedure to die out quickly in this country.[1] At Canterbury in 1195 the criminous tenants of both the archbishop and prior underwent the ordeal by water in the archbishop's ditch at Westgate in the presence of the itinerant justices.[2]

In turning from the jurisdictional aspect of the Liberty to the administrative, the important privilege of returning the king's writs (*returnus brevium*) must first be noticed. There is no mention of this franchise in the royal charters of the twelfth century, but in 1244 the king instructed the sheriff of Kent to allow return of writs to the new Archbishop Boniface 'tam de feodis prioris Sancte Trinitatis quam de feodis suis propriis', and it was stated that Archbishop Edmund Rich (1234-40) had enjoyed the same liberty.[3] The composition of 1259 clearly defined the procedure to be followed in the future. It was agreed that 'the prior and convent shall have, by the hands of the archbishop or his steward for the time being, the return of all writs and precepts of the King and of summonses of the exchequer touching their fees or tenements, and the men, things and possessions in their fees in all counties of England: such writ after delivery to the sheriff, and being returned by him to the bailiffs of the archbishop, shall immediately be by them in like manner returned to the bailiffs of the prior and convent for execution, and, if the writ ought to return before the King, his barons of the exchequer, his justices in eyre or those appointed for the keeping of the Jews or other royal justices, the bailiffs of the prior and convent, immediately after office done and executed in this matter, shall deliver the return with their execution thereof to the bailiffs of the archbishop, and

---

[1] See Cant. MS. Sede Vacante Scrap-book, iii, 12, 13, 14.

[2] Gervase, *Opera*, I, pp. 530-31.

[3] *Cal. Let. Close*, 28 Henry III, pp. 267-68. In 1279 the monks claimed to enjoy the right 'sine carta et per antiquam consuetudinem': Trin. Coll. Camb. MS. O. 9/26, fo. 88.

they in their degree shall return the writ in its due course. But if any such writ of the King come which can be brought into and determined (*deduci et terminari*) in a county court or the archbishop's court, the writ after delivery by the sheriff to the archbishop's bailiffs, and by them to the bailiffs of the prior and convent, shall be dealt with and determined by the prior and convent.'[1] Return of writs was 'a highly valued right'.[2] The sheriff and his staff were excluded from the Liberty and it fell upon the steward of the Liberty to execute the king's writ by attaching, distraining, empanelling inquests, and in other ways fulfilling the royal commands. The franchise thus involved both high privileges and onerous responsibilities, and it is a tribute to the Christ Church administration that we do not hear of this liberty being abused or of the sheriff being ordered to execute writs which had been neglected by the steward.

Another administrative liberty enjoyed by the prior and convent was that of having their own gaols, pillories, tumbrils, and gallows, the latter a logical consequence of the early grants of *infangenethef* and *utfangenethef*. We are told that, in the time of Archbishop Hubert (1193–1205), there were so many prisoners in the gaol of the prior near the gate of the *curia* that some had to be accommodated in the stone chamber next to the granary (*camera lapidea ante granarium*).[3] Nothing more is heard of this temporary prison but there is much evidence to show that the gaol near the great gate was in constant use. In the early thirteenth century manorial mills and court-houses were used as gaols,[4] but at a later date all malefactors seem to have been sent to the gaol within the monastic *curia*. A royal charter of 1447 explicitly stated that 'any traitor, felon, trespasser, or evil doer, who may be arrested, attached or taken by the bailiffs of the prior and convent within the manors or fees of the prior and convent within the county of Kent' should be imprisoned in the gaol of the *curia* until it was delivered by the

[1] *Cal. Let. Pat.* 12 Henry VI, pp. 420–21.
[2] Pollock and Maitland, *op. cit.* I, p. 583.
[3] Cant. MS. Sede Vacante Scrap-book, iii, 12, 13, 14.
[4] Prisoners were confined in the mills at Hollingbourne, Great Chart, and Risborough and in the court-houses of Godmersham and West Welles; see *ibid.*

royal justices.[1] The gaoler and the porter of the great gate were obliged to swear that they would allow no prisoner to leave the *curia* without the special permission of the steward of the Liberty or his deputy.[2] Complementary to the central gaol were the gallows, pillory, and tumbril, on each of the manors.[3] The monks lacked none of the machinery for executing justice within their Liberty.

It is probable that the prior and convent valued their fiscal privileges even higher than those which were strictly judicial and administrative. The financial profits of the Liberty formed no inconsiderable item in the annual revenue of the priory. In 1314, for example, the treasurers acknowledged the receipt of £60. 12s. 4d. *de Libertate*.[4] The most important of this class of privileges was the right of the monks to claim the amercements imposed upon their own tenants and the chattels of felons and fugitives. It was stated in 1294 that the monks had enjoyed these amercements and chattels from time immemorial,[5] and the composition of 1259 explicitly recognizes their rights in this matter.[6] Each year the steward of the Liberty drew up a special account detailing the amercements imposed upon the tenants of the priory in the royal courts and at the views of frankpledge held by other lords.[7] Thus in 1429–30 a sum of £1. 8s. 7d. was received by the monks from the amercement of their tenants in the views of the king, archbishop, and other lords, and £16. 17s. 8d. from amercements imposed 'tam coram justiciariis de banco quam coram baronibus de scaccario domini regis ac justiciariis ad pacem in comitatu Kancie quam in comitatu...Surre'.[8] The monetary value of the chattels of condemned felons and fugitives was recorded by franchise-holders upon estreat-rolls which were shown

---

[1] *Cal. Charter Rolls*, 25–26 Henry VI, p. 80.
[2] B.M. Cott. MS. Galba E iv, fo. 74 v.
[3] Nichols, *op. cit.* p. 78. See also *P.Q.W.* p. 325.
[4] Cant. MS. F iii.
[5] *Cal. Charter Rolls*, 22 Edward I, p. 435.
[6] *Cal. Let. Pat.* 12 Henry VI, p. 421.
[7] These accounts are to be found in Cant. MS. M 13, xi, mems. 12–18 and Cant. MS. ZA, 21.
[8] Cant. MS. ZA, 21.

to the royal justices when they held their assize. If the liberty was allowed, the lord retained the chattels. So it came about that, when Justice Henry of Staunton held his eyre of Kent in 1313–14, he and his fellow justices were confronted by a long list of the chattels of felons and fugitives which had accrued to the priory since the last eyre. Their pecuniary value amounted to no less than £117. 3s. 9¼d.[1] The monks jealously guarded this valuable privilege and their records reveal many instances of the prior ordering the seizure of chattels.[2] Coroners were present at the seizure to see that the rights of the Crown were in no way violated.[3]

Other fiscal liberties enjoyed by the monks of Christ Church included the right to waifs and strays, treasure trove, and wreck of sea.[4] These were fairly common and not very important franchises and need not detain us here. Marriages and wardships fall into the same category.[5] The commercial monopoly of markets and fairs was of far greater importance. The monks were allowed markets and fairs in a number of their manors in the thirteenth century,[6] and in the two following centuries their commercial

[1] Cant. MS., in a wooden box in XYZ, headed 'Catalla dampnatorum et fugitivorum totius prioratus de itinere H de Stantune in comitatu Kancie'. The previous eyre appears to have been that of 1293, mentioned in Gervase, Opera, II, p. 301. Cf. the assessment of the value of seized chattels made by the abbot of Peterborough in 1285 in Chronicon Petroburgense, ed. T. Stapleton (Camden Soc. 1849), pp. 119–24. The reforming abbot of St Albans, Richard of Wallingford (1326–35), ordered the steward of the Liberty c. 1300 to draw up an annual account which should include the chattels of felons: Gesta Abbatum, ed. H. T. Riley, 1867, II, p. 206.

[2] See, for example, Lit. Cant. II, pp. 68, 242–45.

[3] The serjeant of Monkton recorded in 1300–1 the expenses 'R. senescalli et coronatoris pro inquisitione facta de catallis Ade de Geyningdone': Cant. MS. serjeant's account.

[4] The right of wreck, allowed by the justices who undertook the Quo Warranto proceedings (P.Q.W. p. 325), was asserted by the monks at least as early as 1217–18 (see Cant. MS. F ii, fo. 62: 'De hominibus nostris de Sesautre pro forisfacto de wrecco—xxxvi sol'). The right was more than once challenged in the history of the priory; see Cal. Let. Pat. 7 Edward I, p. 344 and Lit. Cant. I, pp. 411–12.

[5] Both rights were challenged as being contrary to the custom of gavelkind (Trin. Coll. Camb. MS. O. 9/26, fo. 88 and Rot. Hundredorum, I, pp. 201, 204), but the monks continued to claim the liberties in question (e.g. in 1331; Lit. Cant. I, p. 375). [6] P.Q.W. p. 325.

monopoly was greatly increased by royal grants.[1] A handsome revenue accrued from this franchise, although no individual markets and fairs on the Christ Church manors were of outstanding importance. The right of free warren, repeatedly challenged and repeatedly confirmed by the king,[2] belonged to the monks in all their demesne-lands. Finally, the prior and convent enjoyed a comprehensive exemption from the payment of all tolls, the *murdrum* fine, and other dues.[3] These negative grants had also their positive aspect—the right to exact toll from persons not enjoying a similar immunity.

A general review of the administration of the Liberty of Christ Church leaves the strong impression that the monks carried on the king's government with skill and efficiency. Conflicts were bound to arise with both the royal officials[4] and the lords of rival liberties,[5] but on the whole the monks managed their vast and unwieldy franchise with considerable success. As trustees of the Crown, their success may be largely explained by their close imitation of the methods of the royal administration.

[1] See Chapter Nine.

[2] The grant of free warren was first made to the prior and convent by Henry II (*Cal. Let. Pat.* 12 Henry VI, pp. 418–19), and then in great detail by Henry III in 1264 (*ibid.* 48 Henry III, p. 383). The royal justices denied the right to the prior in certain of his manors in 1279 (Trin. Coll. Camb: MS. O. 9/26, fo. 88 v.), but Edward I confirmed the grant of his predecessors in 1294 (*Cal. Let. Pat.* 22 Edward I, p. 62). Further royal confirmations occurred in the years 1316, 1364, and 1447 (*Cal. Charter Rolls*, 10 Edward II, p. 314; *ibid.* 38 Edward III, pp. 187–88; *ibid.* 25–26 Henry VI, p. 79).

[3] *P.Q.W.* p. 325. See also *Reg. Winchelsey* (Canterbury and York Soc.), pp. 150–52, 794, and *Lit. Cant.* II, pp. 358–59, 364–67.

[4] See *Lit. Cant.* I, pp. 280–81 and *ibid.* II, pp. 194–97, 206–7.

[5] The monks of Christ Church came more than once into conflict with the great Suffolk liberty of the monks of Bury St Edmunds. Details of the conflict are given in *Lit. Cant.* I, p. 278, and *Cal. Let. Pat.* 10 Henry IV, pp. 33–34. Nor were the relations of the monks with the Constable of Dover Castle always cordial; see *Lit. Cant.* I, pp. 362–63.

# Chapter Seven

## THE MANORIAL ADMINISTRATION

Two clearly defined characteristics differentiated the monastic and episcopal estates of medieval England from the lay fiefs. First, the greater compactness and, secondly, the possibility of a continuity of administration in the former 'makes it impossible to compare them with the more loosely knit and often transient administrative systems of the comital or baronial estates'.[1] The estates of Christ Church cannot be described as compact—the manors lay scattered in eight counties—but continuity of administration there certainly was, at least from the end of the twelfth century. A consideration of this administrative system may serve as a prelude to a detailed account of the agricultural operations on the estates.

At an early date the estates of Christ Church were separated into four administrative divisions called wardenships or custodies (*custodiae*). The east Kent custody comprised the group of manors near the coast, on the Isle of Thanet, and in the neighbourhood of Canterbury, while the custody of the weald and marshes included 'all the manors in the west of the county. The estates in Surrey, Oxford, and Buckinghamshire, formed a third custody, and those in Essex, Suffolk, and Norfolk, constituted a fourth. The property in London, and the outlying estates in Devonshire, Ireland, and elsewhere, did not fall within this system of custodies. They were administered separately by resident proctors, bailiffs, and rent-collectors.[2]

Each of the four custodies was placed in the charge of a warden, commonly called *custos maneriorum*, and sometimes *gardianus* or

---

[1] N. Denholm-Young, *Seignorial Administration in England* (1937), p. 1.
[2] On the work of the agents of the priory in London, see *Lit. Cant.* I, pp. 400–1, 484–85; II, pp. 300–1. William de Tracy, penitent after the murder of Becket, gave land at Doccombe in Devonshire to the monks (*H.M.C.* App. to VIIIth Report, p. 324). Its administration is detailed in *Lit. Cant.* I, pp. 211–12, 400, 519; II, p. 303. A full account of the Irish property is given by Dr J. B. Sheppard in his introduction to *Lit. Cant.* III, pp. xl–xlix.

*supervisor maneriorum*. The first reference to these wardens, who are nowhere hinted at in Lanfranc's *Statuta*, occurs, curiously enough, in Gervase's *Imaginatio quasi contra monachos*. The writer recalls how Baldwin expelled both the wardens (*custodes*) and the serjeants (*servientes*) when he confiscated the manors of the priory in 1186.[1] The text does not show whether the wardens were monks or laymen, but we do know that the practice of entrusting groups of manors to monks was widespread in this country in the twelfth century.[2] The first *Assisa Scaccarii* account of 1225 mentions the four wardens and shows that they were certainly monks at this period.[3] Monks continued to occupy the office, save for one brief interlude, for the rest of the middle ages.

At first, the work of the monk-wardens was largely supervisory and administrative. They exercised a general oversight of the manors and left the detailed direction of agrarian policy to the serjeants and reeves. Only when occasion demanded did they intervene to issue some specific instruction on agricultural technique or the management and repair of property. This occurred, for example, in 1225 when the warden of the east Kent custody ordered the expenditure of a sum of £22. 9s. 8d. on the improvement (*melioracio*) of the manors.[4] The control of the wardens over the manorial finances was, at the beginning, very slight. The treasurers' accounts show that they merely collected the income assigned for the payment of certain servants within the *curia* of the priory.[5] The greater part of the liveries from the manors were

---

[1] 'Servientes nostri fugati sunt, custodes exclusi, ita ut nec panniculos suos eis liceret absportare': Gervase, *Opera*, I, p. 35.

[2] Dom Knowles, *The Monastic Order in England*, 943–1216, pp. 437–38.

[3] Their names were Roger de Wrinedale, Thomas de Sancto Wallerico (Valerico), Richard de Berkesore, and William de Lega. They are all included in Cawston's list of monks: *Camb. Antiq. Soc. Publ.* (1902), XXXIV, pp. 172–73.

[4] He gave the instruction 'per consilium prioris et fratrum': Cant. MS. M 13, xix, mem. 1.

[5] In 1220 the treasurers received a sum of £1. 12s. 'de custodibus maneriorum de pesepaneges' (Cant. MS. F ii, fo. 63 v.), and in the next year £9. 3s. 10½d. 'de custodibus maneriorum et de Welles ad pesepaneges et ad solidatas serviencium de bracino' (*ibid.* fo. 65). The last entry continues with slight variations for a number of years.

taken by the serjeants and reeves in person to the treasury at Canterbury, and thus eluded the hands of the wardens.

Later in the thirteenth century a number of the wardens and other brethren appear to have been in the habit of dwelling on the estates and acting as manorial bailiffs,[1] for the austere prior, Thomas Ringmer (1274–85), forbade the practice and recalled them sharply to their duty as monks.[2] The prior was warmly supported by the Franciscan archbishop, John Pecham, who declared in 1280 that monks who dwelt outside a monastery were veritable demons, 'for a monk without a monastery is as a fish without water'. All manorial bailiffs, the archbishop commanded, should henceforth be laymen.[3] Pecham repeated the injunction in 1281, but this time he sanctioned the appointment of two responsible monks to perambulate the manors and to make all necessary corrections.[4] Later in the same year he restored the traditional system of four monk-wardens.[5] The sorry condition of the finances of the priory at this period probably induced him to modify his previous injunction. The year 1289 marked a decisive turning-point in the history of the monk-wardens. It was then, as we know, that Prior Henry of Eastry greatly enhanced their powers by

[1] Pecham informed a cardinal *in curia* in 1283 that some monks 'lasciviis et vanitatibus saeculi insistentes potius quam monasticae honestati, maneria ecclesiae et possessiones in suis manibus tenuerunt, exeuntes et discurrentes per patriam, religionis vinculo penitus dissoluto': *Reg. Epist. J.P.* II, p. 545.

[2] '...primus instituit ut maneria ecclesiae a monachorum manibus et per fideles ballivos communitati devotos custodiantur...': *ibid.* II, p. 546.

[3] *Ibid.* I, pp. 89–90.

[4] *Ibid.* I, pp. 342–43.

[5] The injunction, which was issued on 6 August 1282, gives an accurate description of the work of the monk-wardens at this juncture. 'Provideatur insuper per priorem et capituli seniores, quod duo fratres honesti et providi, quando dicetur eis per priorem de seniorum consilio, visitent pariter maneria prioratus que sunt in Kancia et duo alii maneria extra Kanciam, qui statum maneriorum ac ballivorum et praepositorum diligentiam seu negligentiam explorent sollicite, et priori et conventui referant quod invenerint in praemissis. Ita tamen quod isti supervisores nullam recipiant pecuniam in maneriis, sed praepositi eis sumptus necessarios subministrent, et expensas necessarias, si quas facturi sunt, usque ad proximum manerium juxta distantiam itineris faciendi; et de sumptibus et expensis faciant tallias monachis supradictis': *ibid.* II, pp. 400–1.

entrusting them with the render of the annual liveries (*liberationes*) from the manors.[1] Henceforth the *custos maneriorum*, and not the individual *servientes*, was held responsible for the financial returns of a *custodia*. He it was who now summed up these returns in an annual account, after consultation with the senior monks at the exchequer as to the proper livery to be drawn from each manor.

At the end of the century, in 1298, Archbishop Winchelsey issued detailed instructions for the behaviour of monk-wardens. Each warden was to be accompanied on his travels by a clerk (*clericus*) versed in manorial business and the procedure of the courts. His retinue had to be severely simple, and a following of servants was only to be allowed in special cases. The archbishop enacted that the wardens should spend the greater part of the year in attendance at the Divine Office. Immediately after the manorial officials had drawn up their accounts the wardens were to collect the liveries and pay them into the treasury before the feast of All Saints (1 November). For the rest of the year they were to dine in the refectory and live the common life with the monks. The wardens were forbidden to take any action without the previous consent of the prior, and a stern warning against wasting the goods of the house and running into debts was addressed to them and all other monks entrusted with the administration of property.[2]

A variety of sources make it possible for us to draw a detailed picture of the work of the monk-wardens in the late thirteenth and fourteenth centuries—the period when they commanded the greatest influence. The monks appointed to the office were nearly always senior and experienced men. Two examples will suffice. Geoffrey of Chilham was warden of the Surrey custody for a number of years at the end of the thirteenth century.[3] He had for long been a professed monk[4] and was entrusted with tasks of high responsibility. In 1290, for example, he was sent as the representative of the priory to the bishop of Rochester,[5] and in the same year

---

[1] See Chapter Two.                    [2] *Reg. Winchelsey*, p. 824.

[3] His name occurs in the Meopham serjeants' accounts of 1286–87 and 1291–92, and he is probably to be identified with the 'Dom. G.' in the 1300–1 account of the same manor.

[4] *Camb. Antiq. Soc. Publ.* XXXIV, p. 176.

[5] Camb. Univ. Lib. MS. Ee. v, 31, fo. 31 v.

the prior accredited him to the bishop of Bath and Wells 'pro arduis ecclesie nostre negociis vobis exponendis'.[1] He fulfilled other missions of like importance while holding the wardenship of the manors.[2] Another monk-warden of eminence was John of Gore, who was successively sub-almoner and treasurer prior to his appointment as warden of the manors of the weald and marshes c. 1315.[3] He compiled the greater part of Register J, a storehouse of information on the rural economy of the priory,[4] and represented the prior and convent in many important business transactions. If all monk-wardens were not of the same calibre as John of Gore, most of them had at least had some previous experience in household administration and estate management.[5]

Twice a year, at Easter and at Michaelmas, the monk-warden made a 'progress' (*progressus*) of all the manors in his custody.[6] He was accompanied by a clerk and one or more grooms, who looked after his horses,[7] and he was usually armed with a bow and arrows.[8] An undated letter from a monk-warden of the wealden custody to Prior Eastry (1285–1331) gives a vivid account of the 'progress' at Michaelmas. 'Next Sunday', he writes, 'I will be at

[1] Camb. Univ. Lib. MS. Ee. v, 31, fo. 32.

[2] See *ibid*. fos. 34 v., 67 v., 69, 70 v., 78, 82, 83 v., 86.

[3] He was treasurer in 1311–12 (Cant. MS. F iii), and in 1315–16 he is found in the manor of Appledore as *custos* of the weald (Appledore serjeant's account). He died in 1326 (*Camb. Antiq. Soc. Publ.* XXXIV, p. 178).

[4] The register is entitled 'Registrum Johannis de Gore de consuetudinibus ecclesie Christi Cantuar' tam infra curiam quam in civitate ac eciam in Maneriis ejusdem cum quibusdam aliis contentis': *H.M.C.* App. to IXth Report, p. 75.

[5] Prior Eastry's conception of a good *custos maneriorum* was a man 'qui sit prudens et providus, non prodigus nec bonorum communium dissipator, quodque de republica sit magis sollicitus quam de commodo suo privato': *Lit. Cant.* I, p. 309.

[6] The implication of Winchelsey's injunction in 1298 that the warden should only be absent from the monastery in the period between Michaelmas and the feast of All Saints was ignored in practice.

[7] Thus at Merstham, in 1288–89, 7 quarters were expended 'in pane servientis et messoris et i carpentarii per vices et garcionum domini custodis et aliorum supervenientium a festo Sancti Michaelis usque Gulam Augusti': serjeant's account.

[8] In 1495 the warden spent 8*d*. 'pro reparatione sagittarum' and 2*d*. 'pro cordulis emptis pro arcubus': Cant. MS. account-roll in Drawer 32.

your manor of Agney, and on the following Monday in the same part of the county. On Tuesday I hope to be at your manor of Farleigh or Great Chart, directing my steps towards Meopham, as I hear that the affairs of the almonry do not prosper there. I audited the account at Eastry on the vigil of the feast of St Michael, and I became a debtor (to the accountant) for a sum of £6. And, by the faith and obedience that I owe to you, I declare that Meopham and Freningham are not between them worth more than £4. 11s. 11¾d. as, by the grace of God, you will see for yourself.'[1] Several pocket note-books of travelling monk-wardens are extant, and show the expenditure incurred on these 'progresses'.[2] The chief item was always food and drink for the warden and his company, and the feeding and shoeing of the horses are constantly recorded. On each of the manors the serjeants afforded hospitality to the wardens and recorded the cost in their annual account.[3] The wardens were in the habit of paying for the maintenance of lights in the churches which they passed in their journey, and on occasion they gave away small sums in alms to the poor. They hired barbers and washerwomen, and 'tipped' the servants who ministered to their wants. Payments were regularly made for river transport, as also for parchment, fuel, and other necessary commodities. Their itineraries varied in detail from year to year, but they always made a practice of paying at least two visits a year to each manor in their custody. During the absence of the wardens from the priory monks were deputed to take their place in choir and received a small pittance in return for this service.[4]

Apart from their work of general oversight and supervision, the functions of the monk-wardens may be accurately described

---

[1] Cant. MS. Eastry correspondence, M 13, III, 29. The reference to the valuation of Meopham and Freningham is, of course, given in terms of the livery to be exacted. See the itinerary of the warden of the Essex custody given by J. F. Nichols, *Custodia Essexae*, pp. 139–40.

[2] These are all of fifteenth-century date and will be described in detail in my last chapter.

[3] It occurs under the heading *hostilagium*. The serjeants were enjoined to provide the warden with 'all things necessary for his consumption' during his period of residence on the manors: *Lit. Cant.* II, p. 73.

[4] Thus in 1447 a sum of 6s. 8d. was paid 'fratri custodienti servicium gardiani': Cant. MS. R.E. 40.

as financial and administrative. We have seen how Prior Henry of Eastry made them responsible for the render of the liveries from the manors in the year 1289. From this date until the Dissolution they exercised an undisputed authority over the manorial finances, subject only to the decrees of the senior monks at the exchequer. The notes which Prior Oxenden made in his day-book in 1333 reveal the nature of this authority. 'I must remember', writes the prior, 'that the reeve of Meopham told us that he will raise £16 from our manor of Meopham at the feast of the Purification in obedience to the command of the warden (*juxta ordinacionem custodis*).' Also that 'the reeve of Newington will raise £10 at the feast of the Purification by the order of the warden'.[1] The livery (*liberatio*) to be drawn from the manors was determined each year by the monk-wardens in consultation with other senior monks at the exchequer. Thus in 1333, the year which we have just considered, the senior monks ordered one of the wardens, Richard of Ickham, to raise 100 marks more than the sum which they had originally agreed upon, in order that they might repay the money loaned to them by one Jacob Frysel at the time of the election of Simon Meopham.[2] Besides receiving the liveries from manors held in demesne, the monk-wardens were also empowered to collect all fee-farms and leasehold rents. The terms of the 1322 lease of the land and stock of the manor of West Mersey in Essex to John le Doo, the steward of the Essex custody, may serve as an illustration. The lease was for a term of twelve years and an annual rent of £8 was paid to the *custos*, who received a sum of 6s. 8d. a year for supervising the stock of the manor. The cost of any new buildings which the warden might order was to be deducted from the rent of the manor.[3]

The monk-wardens not only accounted for the liveries of the demesne manors and the rents of the estates let out on fee-farm or lease, but also paid special sums into the privy purse of the prior, provided for extraordinary manorial expenditure, assisted the bailiffs and serjeants in enforcing the payment of rents, and acted as financial advisers to the prior and chapter. In the year 1331=32 the

[1] Cant. MS. D.E. 3, fo. 47.     [2] *Ibid.* fo. 48.
[3] *Lit. Cant.* I, pp. 81=84.

prior received the greater part of his private income, £22. 10s. 7d., from the treasurers, but he also took £12 from the warden of the Essex custody and £7 from the warden of the East Kent custody.[1] This practice of appropriating a small part of the livery before it reached the treasurers was commonly adopted by the priors in the last three-quarters of the fourteenth century and continued until the Dissolution. It might well have proved a serious abuse, but was never pursued on a scale large enough to introduce confusion into the finances. The cost of special agricultural operations, such as marling, was always borne by the wardens. An ordinance to this effect was passed by the senior monks at the exchequer in 1309,[2] and the accounts of the serjeants show that the decree was translated into practice. The assistance which the wardens afforded to the manorial staff in enforcing the payment of rents and services is well illustrated by the long dispute of the monks with their tenants at Monks Risborough in Buckinghamshire. The warden of the custody constantly intervened with instructions and detailed advice for the harassed stewards and bailiffs.[3] The position of the monk-wardens as financial advisers to the prior and chapter is revealed by their constant presence at the meetings of the senior monks at the exchequer. They, above all other brethren, were best equipped for giving advice on difficult problems of estate management.

There is much evidence of the diverse administrative work of the monk-wardens. A custody was far more than a convenient financial unit. It was the administrative area on which the whole manorial economy was based. Calculations as to the render of the food-farm, the number of acres sown with corn, and the number of cows and sheep agisted, were all made in terms of the four custodies.[4] The compilation of special registers for monk-wardens is another indication of the administrative importance of the custody. It cannot, however, be too often emphasized that the wardens were strictly dependent on the central administration in all their actions. They were liable to instant dismissal by the senior

---

[1] Cant. MS. D.E. 3, fo. 65.  [2] See Appendix I.
[3] See *Lit. Cant.* I, pp. 491–95; II, *passim*.
[4] See Appendix I and B.M. Cott. MS. Galba E iv, fo. 177.

monks who appointed them, and their power was severely circum-scribed by the obligation of referring to the prior for his assent to all executive measures of importance. Thus, in the case of new buildings, the warden was not allowed to begin a work which cost more than £2 on any of the manors of his custody without the previous consent of the prior.[1]

The warden acted as the agent and expert adviser of the prior in buying and leasing land. In 1336, for example, Prior Oxenden made a note in his day-book that there were '2½ acres of land at Mersham lying in our field called Burgatefeld, which Geoffrey Mot our serjeant bought for our use at the command of William of Coventry, who was then warden'.[2] Three years earlier he observed that the warden of the Surrey custody had 'let out at lease 53 acres at Walworth to several of our tenants there for £8. 7s. 6d.'[3] We know that the sale of the corn-crop was controlled by the warden of the custody of the weald and marshes,[4] and it was probably regulated in like manner by the other three wardens. The de-forestation of land and the sale of wood were also dictated by the wardens. In 1332 '26 great ashes were cut down in our wood at Welles called Brechebroke by the order of the warden, brother Thomas de Bourne, and were sold for 5 marks'. At Great Chart, in the same year, trees were cut down and sold for £25 'at the command of brother Thomas de Bourne, warden of the same place', and at Loose and East Farleigh for £3 and £6 'by the order of the same brother'.[5]

On his Easter 'progress' the warden supervised the 'culling' of stock on the manors,[6] a task which must have occupied a con-siderable amount of his time. He was sometimes called upon to testify to the quality of the crops. In 1326, a year of agricultural crisis, 40 acres sown with barley at Godmersham showed a yield of only 47 seams. The serjeant of the manor observed that there was 'non plus hoc anno quia nimis debile per testimonium cus-

---

[1] See Appendix I.
[2] Cant. MS. D.E. 3, fo. 40.
[3] *Ibid.* fo. 47.
[4] See Appendix I.
[5] Cant. MS. D.E. 3, fo. 40 v. The wardens also supervised gifts of timber; see *Lit. Cant.* I, p. 368; II, p. 55; III, p. 298.
[6] See Appendix I.

todis'.[1] In this same year of acute crisis, when many cattle and sheep died of the pestilence, the wardens were authorized to take special measures for the re-stocking of the manors. They were to order large sales of wood and to assign certain revenues for the purchase of stock.[2]

Quite apart from the control which they exercised over the disposal of land, corn, and wood, the wardens sometimes acted as the personal representatives of the prior. The serjeants' accounts often record gifts made by the order of the warden to the great men of the kingdom. In 1319–20 the serjeant of the manor of Eastry had the misfortune to impound animals belonging to the constable of Dover Castle.[3] In order to mollify the constable, who was also Lord Warden of the Cinque Ports,[4] the serjeant was ordered by the prior and warden of the custody to send gifts of corn to the constable for the next four or five years.[5] More than once the wardens ordered gifts of corn to be made to the bailiffs of the king.[6] Sometimes they acted as liaison officers between the prior and distinguished persons. In 1362, for example, the Earl of Arundel sought leave of the prior to work the iron ore at Merstham in Surrey. The prior was unable to see the earl in person but wrote to him, saying: 'Most dear Lord, be pleased to understand that we are now and always shall be ready to perform your will in all that ever we can, and therefore we have commissioned our warden to go to you, to carry out your wishes.'[7]

The wardens of the Christ Church estates have certain affinities with the high officials of some other houses. The proctor-general who supervised the estates of the abbey of Bec in this country had somewhat similar financial and administrative functions and went

[1] Godmersham, serjeant's account, 1325–26.

[2] See Appendix I.

[3] Eastry, serjeant's account, 1319–20.

[4] K. M. E. Murray, *The Constitutional History of the Cinque Ports* (1935), p. 77.

[5] Eastry, serjeant's accounts, 1320–24.

[6] Thus at Merstham, in 1288–89, 4 bushels of wheat were sent to William de Wyngeham, the king's bailiff, and at Walworth, in 1319–20, 4 bushels were also given to a royal bailiff. Both gifts were made 'per preceptum domini custodis'.

[7] *Lit. Cant.* II, pp. 420–21.

on an annual 'progress'. More closely akin to the monk-warden, perhaps, is the *senescallus forinsecus* of Ely cathedral priory, a monk who itinerated the manors and collected the annual liveries for the treasurers.[1] He also exercised administrative functions comparable to those of the Canterbury monk-warden. It must, however, be stressed that on most monastic estates in this country in the later middle ages the manors were placed in the charge of lay stewards. The exceptionally scattered character of the Christ Church and Ely manors, and the long distance of the Bec group from the mother house, doubtless accounted for the institution of monk-wardens or proctors-general. Far more than lay stewards, monk-wardens could be relied upon to exercise a strict control of the manorial administration in the interests of their own religious corporation.

In each of the Christ Church custodies the monk-warden was assisted by a lay steward (*senescallus terrarum*) who, as we have seen on a previous page,[2] held the manorial courts in the absence of the steward of the Liberty. It was natural that men of some experience and ability should be selected for this office, such as John le Doo, who compiled c. 1305-10 the magnificent series of extents for those manors in the Essex custody of which he was steward.[3] They were constantly occupied with such legal aspects of estate management as the holding of inquests and other judicial business.[4] On many occasions they acted as deputies for the monk-wardens. To take only one instance, in 1325 the steward of the manors in the custody of Surrey, Buckinghamshire, and Oxford, was instructed to supervise four manors and to sell corn, buy stock,

---

[1] *Ely Chapter Ordinances and Visitation Records,* 1241-1515, ed. Seiriol J. A. Evans (Camden Miscellany, XVII, 1940), p. 24.

[2] *Supra,* p. 86.

[3] These are to be found in B.M. Harl. MS. 1006.

[4] Thus in 1300-1 the steward of the East Kent custody and the coroner conducted an enquiry at Monkton as to the ownership of the goods of one Adam de Geyningdone (Monkton serjeant's account). In 1322-23 the steward of the same custody was at Lyden 'pro negociis marisci de Lyden' (Lyden, serjeant's account). See the commissions of enquiry addressed to stewards in *Lit. Cant.* I, pp. 86-87; II, p. 35. For the general commission of the steward of the East Kent custody in 1331, see *ibid.* I, pp. 371-72.

and repair buildings at the order of the prior, as the monk-warden was busily engaged on other manors. He was, however, to take the advice of the warden before doing any of these things.[1] Like the warden, the steward was entertained on the manors at the expense of the serjeants, when he arrived to hold the courts or to conduct enquiries. He often appears to have been present at the same time as the warden, with whom he was expected to work in the closest conjunction.

The lay officials who were placed by the monk-wardens[2] in charge of the individual manors were usually called serjeants (*servientes*), and sometimes bailiffs (*ballivi*) or reeves (*prepositi*). The common formula for the appointment of a serjeant intimated that he should 'cause the land to be ploughed, sown, and reaped, manured and cultivated, and all the waggons and plough cattle, together with the sheep, lambs, hogs, and all other kind of stock there to be managed and tended, as shall seem best to him for our profit, rendering thereof such an account as it behoves bailiffs to render, and receiving, for him and his man, what other bailiffs, holding the same office in times past, have received'.[3] The serjeants, who were assisted in directing the agricultural operations on the manors by beadles (*bedelli*), belonged to that prosperous peasant class which came into its own in the fifteenth century. They often held office for long periods at a time[4] and were only removed for reasons of misconduct, ineptitude, or old age. The subordinate relation of the serjeant to the monk-warden was clearly expressed in the oath which he took on his entry into office. 'I, R. of Deopham of the parish of Pecham,' runs this oath, 'on such and such a day and year of the reign of Edward, received from Dom. J.

---

[1] '...et quod praemissa omnia exequamini, per vos et alios ydoneos quos ad hoc duxeritis deputare, communicato consilio praedicti custodis nostri cum praesens fuerit in maneriis nostris praedictis': *Lit. Cant.* I, pp. 146–47.

[2] In 1360 the prior of Christ Church referred in a letter to the archbishop to 'ballivi et prepositi sub ipsis custodibus, et per ipsos deputati': *Lit. Cant.* II, p. 396.

[3] *Lit. Cant.* II, pp. 307–9.

[4] See the chronological lists of serjeants (incorrectly styled 'beadles') printed in *Bulletin of the Institute of Historical Research* (1931), VIII, pp. 140–50.

de North the charge (*custodia*) of such and such a manor with all its appurtenances, to administer truly and faithfully and to answer to the same for all kinds of stock found on the same manor, and to render a faithful account to the same for all the rents, proceeds, and profits arising from the said manor, whenever and wherever I shall be advised and commanded to do so. And I shall serve the same well and faithfully in all matters relating to the same service, as far as in me lies.'[1]

The office of reeve (*prepositus*) on the Canterbury estates was of servile origin.[2] The reeve gradually rose in status and became largely assimilated to the serjeant or bailiff. In the fourteenth century he rendered an account and behaved in every respect as the *alter ego* of the serjeant. The rest of the manorial *famuli* need not detain us here, as they will be fully considered in the next chapter.

We have seen that the four monk-wardens stood at the apex of the elaborate hierarchy of manorial officials. They were the linchpins on which the whole edifice rested. For 200 years and more the manorial structure remained unaltered in its main lines and contours. Only at the end of the fourteenth century did it tremble for a while, before finding a new basis on which to rest.

---

[1] Trin. Coll. Camb. MS. O. 9/26, fo. 91.

[2] Nichols, *op. cit.* p. 150. Cf. H. S. Bennett, 'The Reeve and the Manor in the Fourteenth Century' in *Eng. Hist. Rev.* XLI, pp. 361 *et seq.*

## Chapter Eight

### RENT AND LABOUR

Nothing is known of the relationship of the Christ Church *familia* with the tenants on their estates in the Saxon period. It can, however, be said with certainty that '... even at the Conquest manorial economy in Kent was characterized... by reliance in the main on money rents'.[1] The Domesday Monachorum, studied with full knowledge of Maitland's warning that renders in kind were sometimes 'appreciated',[2] leaves no doubt as to the validity of this conclusion. It shows that the tenants of the priory—in Kent in particular, but also in other counties—were accustomed to paying considerable money-rents, and that these rents had risen sharply in the last half of the eleventh century.[3]

The hypothesis of a gradual evolution of English agriculture from a system of 'natural economy' to one of 'money economy' has fallen into wide disrepute in recent years.[4] Examples of a purely 'natural' economy have been hard to discover and evidence accumulates of the very early prevalence of money rents on estates in many different parts of the country. One historian has gone so far as to observe that, even before the Conquest, 'there was a universal practice of leasing out individual properties to other landowners or to professional stewards or bailiffs, who paid either in kind or in money, usually the latter, an agreed annual rent considerably less than the potential value of the estate. This was the farm-system which was ubiquitous throughout the eleventh and twelfth centuries.'[5] We know that this system of indirect

[1] *V.C.H. Kent*, III, p. 342.

[2] *Domesday Book and Beyond* (1907), pp. 57–58.

[3] See Miss N. Neilson's remarkable discussion of the Domesday Monachorum in *V.C.H. Kent*, III, pp. 185–86. The text of the Survey is given *ibid.* III, pp. 261–64.

[4] It is probably true to say that the death-blow was dealt to the hypothesis by Professor M. M. Postan in his article on 'The Chronology of Labour Services' in *Trans. Royal Hist. Soc.* (1937), Fourth Series, XX, pp. 169–93.

[5] Dom Knowles, *The Monastic Order in England*, 943–1216, p. 442.

exploitation certainly obtained on the Canterbury estates at the time of the Domesday survey.[1]

In the latter half of the twelfth century the monks of Christ Church adopted a quite different method of exploiting their estates. Instead of leasing out whole manors to *firmarii*, in return for the render of a lump sum in cash and certain food-rents, the monks now let out part or whole of the demesne (*dominium*) of a manor to the dependent tenantry. A great number of extant Canterbury leases for the period 1157–1222 show that the demesnes were let out to these small tenants at a fairly uniform rate of 1*s.* per acre, to be held *jure hereditario* or *in perpetuum*.[2] This crumbling of the demesne into the hands of the tenants was a widespread phenomenon in this country in the later twelfth century, especially on great ecclesiastical estates. The age was one of rapid manorial disintegration. In 1179 Pope Alexander III strongly condemned the disintegrating tendencies that were already apparent on the Christ Church estates,[3] and Urban III followed suit in 1187.[4] Neither pope, however, was able to arrest the breakdown of the manorial system or to apply a check to the rapidly spreading system of fee-farms (*feodifirmae*). It required the stimulus of powerful economic forces, of which the rise in the prices of corn and stock was the most potent, to persuade the monks that higher profits could be won by a personal exploitation of their demesne-lands. By 1225 most of the leases, except those on the remote estates in Essex and East Anglia, had fallen in, and the monks were already entering upon that epoch of 'high farming' which reached its apogee in the priorate of Henry of Eastry (1285–1331).

Two sources of indubitable veracity, the exchequer survey of 1211[5] and the *Assisa Scaccarii* of 1225,[6] make it quite clear that money rent largely predominated in the income of the priory at

[1] *V.C.H. Kent*, III, pp. 185–86.

[2] *Ibid.* III, pp. 342–43.

[3] 'Statuimus etiam, ut maneria vestra ulterius ad perpetuam firmam alicui non tradantur': *Papsturkunden in England*, II, p. 374.

[4] *Ibid.* II, p. 444.

[5] Dr Nichols has summarized this survey for the Essex custody in *Custodia Essexae*, pp. 166–68.

[6] Cant. MS. M 13, xix, mem. 3.

this period, as in the previous centuries. Services and rents in kind were never onerous on the Canterbury estates in Kent, although Dr Nichols' study of the Essex custody shows that they were quite heavy on this group of Christ Church manors. The chronology of money-rents and labour-services on medieval estates has in recent years been set in an entirely fresh perspective.[1] In this revaluation of the older views the Kentish estates have not, however, been so far considered. This is partly to be attributed to the lack of easily available evidence in the shape of account-rolls and partly, no doubt, to the peculiar difficulty experienced in relating the Kentish economy to the general agrarian development of this country. For the Kentish manorial system, in which the elements of primitive folkright persisted stubbornly in the centuries following the Norman Conquest, is to be clearly distinguished from that obtaining in the Midlands and the rest of the south-east of England. If the celebrated passage in the Year Book of Edward I denying the existence of villeinage in Kent cannot be accepted without qualification, it at least remains true that the Kent of the middle ages was 'a foreign makeshift, its manorial superstructure thrown up hastily and setting clumsily to the native foundations',[2] with a peasantry which enjoyed an altogether exceptional measure of personal freedom. In the light of these abnormal conditions, long recognized by historians, it is proposed to investigate the question of rent and labour and their relationship on the Kentish estates of Christ Church, Canterbury, deliberately ignoring the very different conditions on the Essex manors, which have been fully described by Dr Nichols.[3] How did this great undying landowning corporation of Benedictine monks fit into, and react upon, an agrarian structure impregnated with pre-feudal elements?

In one essential respect a comparison may be drawn between

[1] See E. A. Kosminsky, 'Services and Money Rents in the Thirteenth Century' in Econ. Hist. Rev. (1935), V, pp. 24–45 and Postan, loc. cit.

[2] J. E. A. Jolliffe, Pre-Feudal England. The Jutes (Oxford, 1933), p. 3. It was the proud boast of Lambard in the reign of Elizabeth that 'there were never Bondmen or villaines, as the law calleth them, in Kent': A Perambulation of Kent (1656 ed.), p. 9.

[3] Nichols, op. cit. pp. 237–66.

the Kentish estates and the fully manorialized part of England in the thirteenth century. Money-rents played a predominant part in the revenue of most of the manors in both areas. The *gabulum* or *gafol*, a money-rent, had been paid in Kent from time immemorial,[1] and by the latter half of the thirteenth century the *mala*, paid in commutation of ancient services and dues,[2] formed an appreciable part of the total income of Christ Church. *Gafol* and *mala* were condensed by the manorial serjeants into *redditus assisae*, which usually featured as the principal item of receipt in their annual accounts. The perpetual fixed rents called fee-farms (*feodifirmae*) were chiefly derived from the remote estates of the priory after c. 1220[3] and are of negligible importance from the Kentish viewpoint. Although the system of receiving food-farms from the manorial demesne-lands was maintained by the priory executive throughout the later middle ages, the food-rents of the tenants were early commuted for money payments and represented a separate item on the credit side of the account.[4] Commercial agriculture had made great headway in this part of England and the Romney and East Kent manors of Christ Church, in particular, derived a considerable income from the sale of corn and stock.[5] This revenue from market-profits seconded but rarely equalled the revenue from money-rents.

A study of the custumals and rentals compiled during Henry of Eastry's priorate (1285–1331) and of the magnificent series of treasurers' and serjeants' accounts, supplemented by information from other sources, shows us how the monks added to their rent-roll in the late thirteenth and early fourteenth centuries. In the first place, they made astute investments in land, which they purchased or took up on lease at a low rate as a preliminary to leasing much of it out again to their tenants at a higher rate. Secondly, the monks greatly developed the system of competitive leasehold

---

[1] N. Neilson, *Customary Rents* (Oxford, 1910), p. 42.

[2] *Ibid.* pp. 42–3.

[3] In particular, from the estates in the Essex custody (Essex, Suffolk, and Norfolk).

[4] The words *galline* and *ova*, accompanied by monetary equivalents, denote these commuted food-rents.

[5] See Chapter Nine.

rents for tenants of newly embanked land on their marsh manors. The rent per acre of leasehold land was vastly in excess of the *gafol* and *mala* arising from the ancient arable and pasture lands of the priory. Thirdly, certain labour-services of tenants were permanently commuted for money-rents and at once incorporated within the *redditus assisae* of the manor. Lastly, a number of labour-services were placed *ad denarios*, that is, rendered liable to be commuted at the will of the prior. Each of these four measures will be considered in turn, as they mark a consistent policy on the part of the monks to restore the financial solvency of the priory by accretions to its rent-roll. The success or failure of this policy can then be estimated.

The vast burden of debt notwithstanding, considerable sums of money were invested in purchasing and leasing land in the first thirty years of the priorate.[1] The peak year was 1291, when £122. 6s. 3¾d. were set aside for this purpose, but rarely did a year pass without some £30 or so being devoted to purchases of this character. Some of this land was cultivated as the demesne of the priory, but most of it seems to have been leased out to the dependent tenantry at a high rent per acre relative to the old standard. A rent of 1s. an acre was commonly imposed in the fertile corn-growing lands of East Kent,[2] although the demands were somewhat less exacting in the western part of the county. When this is compared with the average *gafol* of 1d. per acre and *mala* of 3d. per acre, it will be seen that the monks must have substantially increased their revenue by this policy of astute investment.[3]

The system of leasehold was greatly extended by a quite different line of policy, namely, by letting out newly embanked land. The manor of Cliffe in North Kent affords far the best example. Much labour was spent in reclaiming and embanking land endangered

---

[1] The purchases and leases of land for the years 1285–1333 are entered in detail in Cant. MS. D iv, fos. 134–47 v. The total cost *per annum* is entered in the treasurers' accounts: Cant. MSS. F ii and F iii.

[2] This was the case at Ickham throughout the period.

[3] Prior Eastry gives an account of the land purchased in the first thirty-seven years of his rule (1285–1331) in his private memorandum book (B.M. Cott. MS. Galba E iv, fo. 109).

I

by the floods of the Thames estuary during Eastry's early years. As soon as the land was reclaimed, it was let out at a competitive leasehold rent. Leasehold rents in the marshes of Cliffe already amounted to £119. 0s. 1½d. in 1291,[1] which shows that embankment and drainage had probably taken place here for a very long period, but these rents had risen to £139. 13s. 8d. in 1328[2] as a result of Eastry's vigorous policy of embanking and leasing new land. The other marsh manors tell a similar tale. At Appledore in 1294 a sum of £10. 5s. 1d. was derived from the leasing of reclaimed pasture-lands. Just over twenty years later the income from leases had risen to £19. 0s. 2d. The monastic officials could demand a high price for the rent of this rich pasture-land, for which there must have been much competition. Thus, 55 acres and 2 dayworks of the marsh of Scherle (*mora de Scherle*) in this manor were let out on lease for the sum of £7. 2s. 6d. at the rate of 2s. 7d. an acre, and 27 acres of the same marsh were leased for £2. 0s. 6d., that is, for 1s. 6d. an acre.[3] On the neighbouring manor of Ebony a plot of land called *Prioratus* was 'inned' and embanked in the early years of the priorate and then leased in 1301 for an annual rent of £2, which had increased to £3 in 1317.[4] The marsh manor of Lyden in East Kent has a similar tale to tell.[5] Leasehold rents were clearly superseding customary rents in these manors, since the competitive element which distinguished the former made them a most lucrative source of income at a period when peasants were hungry for land.[6]

[1] Cant. MS. F ii.
[2] Cant. MS. F iii. None of the marsh land at Cliffe was cultivated as demesne by the priory officials.
[3] Appledore, serjeant's account, 1315–16.
[4] R. A. L. Smith, 'Marsh Embankment and Sea Defence in Medieval Kent' in *Econ. Hist. Rev.* (1940), p. 30.
[5] Leases of pasture at Lyden amounted to £6. 18s. 2d. in 1291–92, to £9. 19s. 1½d. in 1304–5, and to £12. 6s. 0d. in 1317–18.
[6] See the general discussion of this question of the peasant land market by E. Miller in *St Albans and Herts. Architectural and Archaeological Soc. Trans.* (1938), pp. 287–89. Dr Nichols has shown how at Bocking in Essex, in the years between 1248 and 1271, the monks of Christ Church were 'steadily converting customary holdings into small parcels of land to be relet as several holdings': *Custodia Essexae*, p. 305.

The two other expedients which the monks devised for the increase of their rent-roll were the total remission or yearly commutation of certain labour-services for a fixed money-rent. The general character of labour-services in medieval Kent has been made sufficiently familiar to us by the work of modern historians. 'The most striking feature of the rural arrangements of Kent, aside from the denns and from the small partitioned holdings resulting from gavelkind, was the absence of week-work. It is clear that long established partibility of tenement almost necessarily prohibited the co-operative action necessary for the ploughing and other forms of agriculture on the demesne and in the open fields found in the usual type of English medieval village.'[1] It is true that the primitive customs of the free Germanic stocks retained their hold on Kent as on no other county, and that compulsory labour was never of a very onerous nature. It was, however, heavier on the ecclesiastical estates than elsewhere[2] and especially in respect of carrying-services, which were necessary for transporting food both to the priory and to the local markets.

On the Kentish estates of Christ Church the performance of labour-services depended to some extent upon the food-farm obligations of individual manors. In 1288 the senior monks at the exchequer issued an ordinance which revised the statutes of Lanfranc and limited the render of the food-farm to certain large Kentish manors.[3] It was found more convenient for the distant manors to sell their corn locally and to remit cash to the priory, so that adequate food supplies could be bought for the monks in the neighbourhood of Canterbury.[4] In this way heavy travelling costs were eliminated. It followed that those manors which were no longer saddled with a food-farm, and consequently owed no carrying-services for this purpose, were in a position to have these services commuted or substantially reduced.

[1] *The Cartulary and Terrier of the Priory of Bilsington, Kent*, ed. N. Neilson (British Academy Records, 1927, VII), p. 26.

[2] Jolliffe, *op. cit.* pp. 32–34. This was almost universally the case in medieval England; see Kosminsky, *op. cit.* p. 42.     [3] See Appendix I.

[4] See the letter of Prior Eastry to the Constable of Dover on this subject in 1323, printed in *Lit. Cant.* ed. J. B. Sheppard (1887), I, pp. 112–31. The subject is fully discussed in Chapter Nine.

The manor of Meopham in north-west Kent answered to this description. In 1306 the prior and chapter of Christ Church entered into an agreement with the tenants of Meopham, by which, for the payment of an annual rent of £2. 17s. 3½d. on the feast of St Peter and St Paul (29 June), certain services were totally remitted.[1] A distinction is made, here as elsewhere in Kent, between the services imposed on the tenantry of the outland, or *gavellond*, the traditional area of an immemorially free peasantry, and those imposed on the tenantry of the inland (*inlaunde*), which lay within the land right of the church of Canterbury and therefore corresponded to the *terra villanorum* of the typical manor.[2] The services of carrying 36 cartloads of hay from Cliffe to Meopham, of performing certain other *averagia*, and of erecting enclosures around the cornfields and *curia*, all of which were owed by the tenants of 18 yokes (*juga*)[3] of outland, were permanently commuted for an annual rent of £1. 13s. 2¼d. Similarly, the tenants of 6½ yokes of inland, who were obliged to thrash and winnow 35 quarters of wheat and 17½ seams of oats and to perform sundry works such as hoeing, stacking corn in autumn, making hurdles, roofing granges, catering for the prior on his visits, and assisting the tenants of the outland in the erection of enclosures, had these services remitted for an annual payment of £1. 4s. 1¼d. The tenants of Meopham differed from those of other Kentish manors of Christ Church that have been studied in that their commuted services were at once added to the *redditus assisae* and never formed a separate item in the serjeant's annual account.[4]

---

[1] The prior and chapter 'remiserunt et relaxaverunt hominibus et tenentibus suis de Mepham quasdam consuetudines et servicia pro annuo redditu quinquaginta septem solidorum, trium denariorum et unius oboli eisdem priori et capitulo in predicto manerio suo de Mepham in festo Apostolorum Petri et Pauli annuatim solvendo': Camb. Univ. Lib. MS. Ee. v, 31, fo. 121.

[2] On this distinction, see Jolliffe, *op. cit.* pp. 7, 18–19.

[3] The rectangular holding or field, which characterized the Kentish agrarian economy. See H. L. Gray, *English Field Systems* (Harvard Historical Studies, XXII, Cambridge, Mass. 1915), p. 286.

[4] As a consequence of this addition the *redditus assisae* of Meopham rose from £15. 15s. 2d. in 1300–1 to £18. 12s. 5½d. in 1312–13.

The more common method employed by the monks was, however, that of placing certain services *ad denarios*. This simply implied that they were liable to be commuted at the will of the prior. Certain manors already had some of their services placed *ad denarios* at the time of Henry of Eastry's accession. These lay in Kent, to the west of Canterbury.[1] Although mostly burdened with a food-farm, they were not so heavily charged in this respect as the great East Kent manors, none of which had any services made liable to optional commutation at this date. Early in the fourteenth century[2] four custumals and a number of rentals were drawn up for the Kentish manors, in which certain services, hitherto compulsory, were placed on the optional list of the prior. It is proposed to examine three of these custumals,[3] all of East Kent manors, and with the comparative material of account-rolls to give some indication of the interplay between money-rents and labour-services at this period.

The three manors which fall under review are Ickham, Eastry, and Monkton, all situated in that rich fertile region of East Kent, which is so well endowed with both arable and pasture land. They were the main bulwarks of the food-farm system, as well as being the source of high market-profits. The tenants of outland and inland on these manors were called upon to perform approximately the same services, lighter by far than those of the Midlands, at this period. Thus at Ickham the tenants of 4 sulings of outland and the cottars who occupied 80 acres of inland (here called *cotland*) performed carrying services and harvest and boon works of the same general character.[4] At Eastry and Monkton the same

[1] The neighbouring manors of Chartham and Godmersham fell into this category.

[2] In the case of the manor of Monkton, it is clear that the custumal was drawn up some time after 1305–6, as reaping was valued at $11\frac{1}{4}d.$ an acre, whereas in the custumal the commutation fee is $1s.$ an acre. This latter rate appears in the account-roll of 1307–8.

[3] I omit the manor of Adesham, the account-rolls of which are in a very bad condition.

[4] In the Ickham custumal (B.M. Add. MS. 6159, fos. 30–32) there is mention of a free tenement from which $2d.$ an acre is payable 'pro omni servicio' and of *wenlond*. There were also a number of freehold tenements at Eastry.

state of affairs obtained. Tenants of both inland and outland performed light services which were principally confined to the carriage of food and boon-services at harvest, although a little ploughing[1] and the washing and shearing of sheep[2] were sometimes demanded of them.

There was thus a wide diffusion of light labour-services over the tenants of the East Kent manors, whether holders of inland or outland. This was also the case in the other Kentish manors, as the example of Meopham has shown. The monks of Christ Church adopted the policy of placing most of these services *ad denarios*. The standard rate of commutation for ploughing or reaping corn varied between 10*d*. and 1*s*. an acre,[3] and the payment in *lieu* of carrying-services naturally varied with the distance of a manor from the priory. The custumals recite all the services liable to be commuted and state that 'ista servicia facientur vel dabuntur precio, si domino placet', or words to that effect. The serjeants of the manors accordingly recited the services liable to be commuted on the credit side of their accounts, with a cash total, and then on the debit side stated whatever services (if any) had been performed in a particular year, with their cash equivalents and the remark 'quia servicium factum fuit'.

When most of the labour-services of the Kentish manors had been placed *ad denarios*, which had certainly occurred by the year 1306, it was chiefly the carrying-services that continued to be performed. The monks could least of all afford to dispense with that essential service, which brought food to their household and served the local markets. The evidence of the account-rolls of Ickham, Eastry, and Chartham is very clear on this point. At Eastry, for example, the hitherto slight but compulsory labour-

---

[1] Thus, at Monkton, the ploughing of one acre of *averherde* was exacted from each ploughland (*caruca*): B.M. Add. MS. 6159, fo. 26 v.

[2] The cottars of Monkton were obliged to perform this service: *ibid.* fo. 27. The term *custumarii* was sometimes applied to the tenants who performed these services. Thus in 1326–27 the serjeant of Ickham recorded payments for bread made 'pro familia et custumariis in autumpno'.

[3] At Eastry, Godmersham and Chartham the rate was 1*s*. an acre, whereas at Monkton ploughing was assessed at 10*d*. an acre and reaping at 8*d*. in 1300–1. Subsequently the cost of reaping rose to 1*s*.

services of stacking corn, mowing, and ploughing, were commuted nearly every year for money-rents, but the carrying-
services seem to have been invariably performed.[1] Again, at
Chartham, a money-rent was usually paid for some of the
ploughing and reaping services which had been placed *ad denarios*,
but not for the carrying-services which were usually rendered in
their entirety.

The impressive increase in the rent-roll of the priory, which is
to be partly attributed to the movements described, is shown in
the central accounts of the treasurers. The figures selected to
exemplify this point must necessarily fall within the years 1306
(when most of the services on all the manors had been placed
*ad denarios*) and 1314–16, the period of the great famine and
agricultural depression during which the development of the rural
economy of the priory was grievously retarded. In 1285, the
year of Prior Eastry's accession, the treasurers received £1034.
6s. 2¾d. from the manors.[2] In 1312 the sum had risen to £1406.
5s. 8¾d., and in 1314–15 to £1653. 14s. 3¾d.[3] The development
of leasehold rents and the remission, or yearly commutation, of
certain labour-services were factors which, together with the
prudent economy of the prior and his capable administrative staff
and the big increase in commercial agriculture, restored the priory
of Christ Church to financial solvency. Although borrowing and
lending took place on an extensive scale, the turn of the century
saw the priory free of all large debts, a position it maintained for
the next twenty years.

One problem has so far been deliberately neglected in this
analysis, that of wage-labour. In a county where week-work was

[1] I have examined the Eastry accounts for the years 1307–8, 1319–20,
1322–24, 1325–27. Each year the full carrying-services were performed.

[2] Cant. MS. F ii.

[3] Cant. MS. F iii. These figures represent the sum of the liveries (*liberationes*) paid each year to the treasurers by the serjeants of all the Canterbury
manors within and without the county of Kent. As the amount of the livery
would be determined by the increase of market-profits as well as of money-
rents, too much must not be read into them for our present purpose. Nevertheless they remain significant when read in conjunction with the evidence
from individual manors.

never performed, the demesne-lands of the priory could not have been regularly cultivated by the compulsory labour of the tenantry. It has been shown that this labour was largely confined to the carriage of food and the performance of boon-services (*precaria*) at harvest-time. Sometimes, indeed, tenants were paid wages for performing services that exceeded their customary obligations. For example, at Eastry in the year 1319–20 a cottar was paid 3*s.* 10½*d.* for carrying 31 seams of wheat more than his allotted share (*ultra certum suum*), and four years later a cottar on the same manor was paid 8¼*d.* for the carriage of an additional 5½ seams of wheat.[1] But the paid labour of the tenantry was negligible in comparison with that of the permanent staff of the prior, the *famuli*, who were housed on the estates under the supervision of the serjeants and performed all the major agricultural operations. The importance of this class of permanent wage-labourers cannot possibly be exaggerated.[2] Wherever one turns on the Kentish estates, they are present in large numbers. At Monkton, for example, in 1307 there were no less than seventeen ploughmen or carters (*carucarii*), who were paid a wage of 3*s.* a year and given their food and a gift of gloves; four shepherds, two cowherds, and a swineherd, who received the same; a harrower, employed full-time, who received 3*s.*, and another employed part-time for 1*s.* 6*d.*; three stackers (*tassatores*) and three drovers (*furcarii*) who were paid at the same rate as the others; and a lambherd employed for 2*s.*, a sower for 4*s.*, and a cheesemaker for 3*s.* That makes a total of 35 *famuli* and does not, of course, include the serjeant, beadle, and hayward (*messor*), who were paid £2. 14*s.* 10*d.*, 13*s.* 4*d.*, and £1. 14*s.* 1*d.* respectively for supervising the *famuli* in the performance of their duties.

Again, consider the manor of Hollingbourne in the year 1290. Eight ploughmen were employed, a shepherd, a swineherd, an oxherd, a cowherd, a goatherd, and a dairymaid. Their wages

---

[1] Cf. Hollingbourne serjeant's account, 1323–24, 'In expensis custumariorum extrahencium fymum de consuetudine: ii sol.'

[2] The same remark might be made of the *famuli* on the Crowland Abbey estates. See F. M. Page, *The Estates of Crowland Abbey* (Cambridge, 1934), pp. 104–5.

were more than twice as high as those of the *famuli* of Monkton, four of the ploughmen receiving a wage of 8*s.*, as well as food and gloves, a standard which was still being maintained in the year 1323–24. On the marsh manors of Ebony and Orgarswick-and-Agney in south-west Kent and of Lyden in the east of the county, *famuli* must have performed nearly all of the work, as there were hardly any rent-paying tenants. The large numbers of *famuli* were not, as might be expected, introduced by Prior Eastry and his administrative staff as part of an economy campaign in which the money-rents paid for commuted services might exceed the low wages paid for hired labour, for there were numerous *famuli* on the Canterbury estates at Eastry's accession. At Meopham, for example, in 1287 there were eleven ploughmen and a large company of shepherds, cowherds, swineherds, and other servants. The number of *famuli* on the manors appears to have remained fairly constant throughout the priorate. One must argue, therefore, in the absence of any direct evidence, that the *famuli* were called upon to do more than their accustomed share of work, especially at harvest-time, when the boon-services and other minor dues of the tenants were until 1314 increasingly commuted for money-rents. They must have always been the solid basis of the labour-force of Christ Church and have borne the brunt of the heavier work, but it is not until Eastry's priorate that they assumed for a time the sole charge of almost every agricultural operation except the carrying of food supplies, still largely performed by the tenantry, and the shearing and washing of sheep, which was often performed by casual hired labour.[1]

Thus by the year 1314 the economy of the Kentish estates of Christ Church rested almost entirely upon a money-rent and wage-labour basis. Then came those three years of floods and famine and acute agricultural depression[2] which arrested and reversed the processes which have been described. The Christ

[1] For example, a sum of 2*s.* 4½*d.* was paid to labourers hired to shear and wash 286 sheep and lambs at Meopham in 1324–25, and at Hollingbourne in 1323–24 a sum of 1*s.* 2*d.* was paid for the same object.

[2] See C. E. Britton, *A Meteorological Chronology to* A.D. 1485 (H.M. Stationery Office, 1937), pp. 132–33, and H. S. Lucas, 'The Great European Famine of 1315–16, and 1317' in *Speculum* (1930), V, pp. 343–77.

Church executive was forced, willy nilly, into a policy of demanding the performance of those labour-services which had been yearly commuted for money-rent in the halcyon days before 1314. For example, commuted services at Godmersham yielded an annual revenue of £6. 10s. 3¼d. in the period of prosperity. In the two years 1325–27 certain ploughing and reaping services were reimposed, so that the money-rents derived from this source fell to £2. 19s. 1¼d. in the first year and to £2. 7s. 11½d. in the second. On the manors of Chartham, Monkton, Eastry, and Ickham a slight diminution also took place in the services commuted.[1] The great drought of 1325–26 and the severe pestilence of the following year[2] served to accelerate the return to compulsory labour. The decline in the money-rent derived from commuted labour on each manor may seem trivial in itself, but the cumulative effect of an all-round decrease on the Canterbury estates was far from inconsiderable and is reflected, to some degree, in the treasurers' accounts. The income from the manors, which had attained the figure of £1653. 14s. 3¼d. in 1315, had dropped by nearly £200 to £1459. 3s. 8d. in 1331—a testimony to the decline of both money-rents and market-profits in the period of agricultural depression.

The years 1330–50 marked a turning-point in English agrarian history. During this period changes in population and prices took place which severely jeopardized the prosperity of demesne-farming and commercial agriculture. In the fully manorialized part of England the great landowners met this crisis by leasing certain of their demesne-lands, commuting labour-services, and generally striving by all means in their power to increase their rent-roll. On the Kentish estates of Christ Church a very different course of events is to be observed. Instead of commuting services,

---

[1] The income from commuted services fell at Chartham from £2. 12s. 3¼d. in 1309–10 to £1. 8s. 9d. in 1317–18; at Monkton from 3s. 9d. in 1305–6 to nothing in 1317–18; at Eastry from £2. 9s. 11½d. in 1307–8 to £2. 6s. 5¾d. in 1326–27; and at Ickham from 4s. 0½d. in 1317–18 to nothing in 1327–28: serjeants' accounts.

[2] Britton, op. cit. p. 135. See the stark account of the large number of animals killed by pestilence on the Canterbury estates in Lit. Cant. I, pp. 243–46.

the monks strove to exploit to the full their resources of compulsory labour. The account-rolls of all the manors which have been studied show that in the years between 1340 and 1390 full labour-services were performed. The record is always the same: 'Omnia predicta servicia facta fuerunt.'[1] So the tendency on the Kentish estates of Christ Church at this period was the very reverse of that observable in the region of the classical manor. The shortage of labour in the half-century after the Black Death, which enabled the *famuli* to exact a great increase in wages,[2] was no doubt a decisive influence in prompting the return to compulsory labour. In 1390 the compulsory labour-services on the Kentish estates of Christ Church were far heavier than in 1314. Powerful external forces had checked and reversed that movement towards complete commutation which was so plainly discernible in the middle years of Henry of Eastry's priorate. It must, however, be once more emphasized that this compulsory labour, even when exacted in full, represented but a small fraction of the total labour-power of the priory. At all times the *famuli* bore the brunt of the agricultural operations on the Kentish estates of Christ Church.

[1] Thus at Chartham in 1346 the full complement of labour-services was performed. The last serjeant's account, that of 1391, shows that all the services still 'capta fuerunt in maneriis'. Again, the records of Ickham, which are abundant for this period, tell a similar tale.

[2] For example, at Monkton in 1307-8 *famuli* had received wages varying between 2s. and 4s. a year. In 1411 the lowest wage was 13s. 4d. and most of the *famuli* received £1 a year.

# Chapter Nine

## ARABLE FARMING

Two factors principally influenced the character of the agricultural operations on the Christ Church estates. As a Saxon Benedictine foundation, the monastery acquired most of its lands in the ancient arable south-east of the country. In contrast to the Cistercians, who developed vast sheep-runs while creating their arable granges, the Canterbury monks followed other Benedictine houses in devoting their main attention to cereal farming. Corngrowing always remained their staple agricultural industry, and it was only at a comparatively late period in their history that they took part in other agrarian pursuits on an appreciable scale. Secondly, it is important to recall the close proximity of the Canterbury estates, especially the rich arable lands of East Kent, to the Continent as well as to London and a number of other flourishing markets and sea-ports. A study of cereal cultivation and stock-farming in the medieval period will show how these two factors shaped the whole economy of the Canterbury estates.

The early history of monastic arable farming is bound up with a complex system of food-farms. It has been shown that 'in most, perhaps in all, great groups of manors belonging to churches there was a highly elaborated system according to which certain manors sent up in regular rotation once, twice, thrice, even seven times a year, a specified supply of food'.[1] 'These "farms" were not due primarily, if at all, from the tenants of the abbey. They were chargeable on the constituent units, whether manor or vill, of the estate as a whole.'[2] It was, therefore, the demesne-land which bore the brunt of this obligation. The food-farm was

---

[1] N. Neilson, *Customary Rents* (1910), pp. 16–19. For the system of food-farms at Ramsey Abbey, see *Cartularium Monasterii de Rameseia*, ed. W. de G. Birch (R.S. 1884–93), III, pp. 160 *et seq.*, 230 *et seq.* The 'Ordo Maneriorum, quomodo firmas facere debent' of Rochester cathedral priory is to be found in *Custumale Roffense*, ed. J. Thorpe (London, 1788), pp. 12, 35.

[2] Neilson, *op. cit.* p. 18.

essentially a primitive institution;[1] it represented the earliest
known method of supplying the monks with the necessities
of existence and is implicit in the Domesday survey with its
careful division of the Canterbury estates into manors *de cibo
monachorum* and *de vestitu monachorum*.[2] Lanfranc made detailed
provision during his archiepiscopate (1070–89) for the *firmae*
during the fifty-two weeks of the year, and his statutory enactment[3] formed the basis of all subsequent calculations. He carefully recited the *firma* that the monks could lawfully receive in
one week, in three weeks, and in one month. Thus the word
*ebdomadae* soon became attached to a system of provisioning
estimated in terms of weeks.

Lanfranc's enactment shows that on some of the manors cash
was already being sent to the priory in lieu of food.[4] Most of the
manors owed an annual supply of both corn and stock, but in
some cases the serjeant enjoyed the option of sending either stock
or a lump sum of money.[5] The early development of commuted
food-rents on the royal estates and in south-east England lends
substance to the conjecture that renders of stock probably ceased
to be made on the Canterbury estates at a very early date. In the
first half of the thirteenth century, when the records of the priory
become abundant, evidence of stock being sent to the monks
from their demesne-lands in the guise of a food-farm is altogether
lacking. Indeed the earliest extant serjeants' accounts show the
cellarer buying stock from the manors of the priory, and we know

[1] L. Levillain has shown in his edition of 'Les Statuts d'Adalhard' in
*Le Moyen Age* (1900), p. 352 *et seq.*, how a fully organized system of food-
farms obtained on the estates of the abbey of Corbie in the first half of the
ninth century.

[2] *Monasticon*, pp. 100–3.

[3] 'Hec sunt firme monachorum Sancte Trinitatis Cantuariensis quas bone
memorie Lanfrancus archiepiscopus sic constituit et ordinavit': Lambeth MS.
1212, fos. 344–45. These arrangements replaced the *institutio antiqua* of the
Saxon period; see *ibid.* fo. 346.

[4] Thus it is stated that Appledore 'non aliter firmat nisi tantum dat xv libras
et iii uncias auri et iii bindas anguillarum' and Little Chart 'reddit x libras
pro firma vii dierum': Lambeth MS. 1212, fo. 344.

[5] Hollingbourne was one of these manors, where 'hoc est in electione
prepositi utrum porcos an predictum precium velit accipere': *ibid.*

that Pecham expressly forbade the obedientiaries in 1282 to follow any other course.[1] From the beginning of the thirteenth century, then, and probably earlier, the food-farm consisted mainly, though not entirely, of corn; cheeses were rendered from some of the marsh-manors[2] and honey figures occasionally in the accounts.[3]

The annual *Assisa Scaccarii* recorded the delivery of the food-farms in great detail. The words 'fecit plenum' were used of an accountant who had made a full render but, in cases of default, the ominous words 'de tota firma est in arreragio' were accompanied by a monetary estimate of the 'farm' still owing to the priory. One manor sometimes helped another to fulfil its obligations. We find the serjeant of Ickham in 1225 contributing to the food-farm of Monkton from the resources of his manor.[4] The system remained a flexible one. An increase in the acreage under cultivation on any manor spelt an increase in the *firma*,[5] and the *antiqua firma* of Lanfranc was sometimes modified to meet new conditions and exceptional circumstances.[6]

At a very early period in Christ Church history the surplus corn of the manors was marketed. In 1207 Canterbury corn was being shipped abroad,[7] and it is impossible to say when this practice began. The earliest serjeants' accounts show us that a system of decentralized corn sales obtained everywhere on the estates. The individual serjeants accounted for the sales as part of the gross receipts of their manors. So, at least as early as the

---

[1] '...et nihil capiant in maneriis nisi emptum': *Reg. Epist. J.P.* I, pp. 341–48.

[2] See Chapter Ten.

[3] The price of a vessel of honey (*stoppa mellis*) was included in the annual *Assisa Scaccarii*.

[4] Cant. MS. M 13, xix, mem. 1.

[5] The serjeant of Ickham made record of sixteen acres of corn sown with oats in 1225 and observed that 'respondebit supra firmam horum maneriorum de profectu harum acrarum qui pro tempore habet custodiam maneriorum': *ibid.*

[6] The senior monks were satisfied in 1225 that the serjeant of Monkton 'fecit quod promisit' and yet 'desunt de antiqua firma cc summe et ligna': *ibid.* The costs of sea-defence at Monkton were very burdensome at this period.

[7] N. S. B. Gras, *The Evolution of the English Corn Market* (1915), p. 22.

beginning of the thirteenth century, 'the network of corn currents' to the priory 'was crossed by another network of currents evolving out of the growth of a territorial marketing system'.[1] In the year 1230–31 the sale of corn at Monkton realized no less than £74. 6s. 0d. and at Adesham yielded a sum of £50. 9s. 3d.[2] As both these manors were burdened with a food-farm of four weeks, it will be seen that corn production in East Kent was in an advanced stage of development, a fact which may be attributed to the richness and fertility of the soil no less than to the very favourable geographical situation of these estates.[3]

In the latter half of the thirteenth century a drastic reorganization of the food-farm system was made so as to enable the monks to swell their already considerable revenue from market sales. The age was one of rising prices,[4] and the bait of high market-profits acted as a powerful stimulus to a great increase in corn production. About the year 1285 a comprehensive list of priory estates entitled 'Adhuc de maneriis monachorum que firmant, non firmant' was composed.[5] The manors were divided into two classes, 'farm' manors and 'revenue' manors; the one rendering primarily corn, the other exclusively cash, to the priory. The obligation of rendering a *firma* was now confined to most of the manors of the two Kentish custodies, and the statement of the number of weeks (*ebdomadae*) was accompanied by a recital of the cash equivalent. At the foot of the list of 'farm' manors was

---

[1] N. S. B. Gras, *The Evolution of the English Corn Market* (1915), p. 22.

[2] Cant. MS. M 13, xix, mem. 3.

[3] Ickham, another manor in this district, derived a revenue of £30. 10s. 0d. from corn sales in the same year, and the manor of Appledore in south-west Kent was not far behind with a revenue of £24. 0s. 4d. from this source: *ibid.*

[4] See the decennial averages of the price of corn given by Thorold Rogers in *The History of Agriculture and Prices*, I, p. 245. I am aware that Rogers' figures have been severely criticized in the past (e.g. by H. L. Lutz in *Quarterly Journal of Economics*, XXIII, pp. 38–39, 350–58), but I use them here with confidence, seeing that Sir William Beveridge and his fellow-contributors to the history of *Prices and Wages in England* (1939– ) deliberately affirm that 'while many criticisms of detail can be made upon Thorold Rogers, the value of most of his early results, at least, seems likely to remain unshaken and, indeed, confirmed by the new enquiry' (*ibid.* I, p. xxvii).

[5] Lambeth MS. 1212, fo. 363.

added a memorandum to the effect that 'summa istarum pre-
dictarum ebdomadarum amuntat MCC libras, qualibet ebdomada
computatur pro xxx libris'. In 1288 the senior monks issued an
ordinance *ad scaccarium*[1] which gave in terms of produce the
statutory number of *ebdomadae* in which food-farms should be
rendered. Their calculation was based on the manorial returns of
that year, and they appended the word *defectus* and the number
of seams in default to any render that fell short of the full quota.
The carrying-services on certain manors owing an annual *firma*
were defined at this same period.[2]

   The main result of this reorganization of the food-farm, which
was one of several measures adopted by the monks to increase
the production of corn on their estates, was concisely stated by
Prior Henry of Eastry in a letter to the constable of Dover in 1323.
'Know, Sir,' wrote the prior, 'that one half of our estates lie so
far away from us outside of this country in the direction of
Oxfordshire and Devonshire, and elsewhere, that hence it behoves us to sell our corn in those parts and to purchase other in
this district. And know, sir, that all the corn that we possess
beyond the seed corn for our lands, between Sandwich and
Rochester, does not by any means suffice for the maintenance of
our convent and our household beyond Whitsuntide, and therefore we are obliged to buy a thousand quarters of corn and even
more, every year, in this department.'[3] As far as it went the
statement of the prior was true, but it was not the whole truth.
For some reason the prior was unwilling to sell wheat and barley
to the constable of Dover, so he carefully concealed the all-
important fact that the monks were selling large quantities of corn
on the home manors as well as making considerable purchases.
The letter is nevertheless instructive as showing the main feature
of the priory's corn policy, the calculated balance of sale and
purchase.

   By the end of the thirteenth century a point had been reached
when the monks preferred to receive a diminished food-farm
rather than forgo the chance of high market-profits. So on many

[1] See Appendix I.           [2] See *ibid.*
[3] *Lit. Cant.* I, pp. 112–13.

manors a continual default in the full *firma* went hand in hand
with large sales of corn. The manor of Ickham, one of the
richest corn-growing lands in East Kent, is a case in point.
Burdened with a huge annual *firma* of 534 seams, 3 bushels, the
serjeant of Ickham succeeded in rendering 461 seams in 1293–94
and reached the 500 mark in 1319–20, but I have found no instance
of its tenants delivering the full farm. Indeed the quantity of
produce rendered fell from 348 seams in 1321–22 to 330 seams,
3 bushels in 1326–27, and as low as 284 seams in 1327–28.[1] At
the same time large profits were accruing to the manor from the
sale of its corn.[2] It should nevertheless be observed that corn
was sometimes bought by the manorial serjeants to remedy deficiencies in the food-farm.[3] The immediate needs of the priory
household must have determined the policy pursued from year
to year.

The organization of the manors for marketing, which entailed
sweeping reforms in the corn-supply system of the priory, also
prompted a drive to increase the yield of seed per quarter and of
land per acre as well as the total acreage under crops. In the
seeding of cereals two distinct movements may be discerned.
A policy of sowing seed more intensively was adopted on some
manors. At Monkton 6½ bushels of oats were normally sown per
acre until the year 1302, when 7 bushels henceforth became the
rule. Similarly, at Barksore an acre of wheat was sown with 3½
bushels until the second decade of the fourteenth century, when
the common allowance became 4 bushels. Many other instances
could be cited of an intensified sowing of seed during that peak
period of demesne-farming which roughly coincided with the long
priorate of Henry of Eastry (1285–1331).[4] It may be observed

[1] Ickham, serjeants' accounts.

[2] For example, corn sales amounted to £15. 8s. 10d. in 1293–94 and to
£27. 16s. 2d. in 1321–22: *ibid.*

[3] Thus, in 1323–24 the serjeant of Hollingbourne sold 10 seams of oats
for £2. 5s. 0d. 'pro ordeo emendo ad mittendum domui'. Two years later
the serjeant of Eastry bought 17 seams, 6 bushels of barley, and the serjeant
of Godmersham 5 bushels 'ad mittendum domui'.

[4] For example, an increase from 4 bushels to 5 bushels per acre in the
seeding of peas took place at Godmersham and Chartham in the first two

that 4 bushels of wheat and 6 bushels of barley and oats were commonly sown on an acre towards the end of Eastry's priorate, when the system of seeding on the Kentish manors had become stabilized. The seed of peas was usually sown at the rate of 5 bushels an acre and the two other leguminous crops, beans and vetches, observed an average seeding of 4 bushels an acre.[1]

At the same time as seed-corn was sown more intensively on the acre, a movement was afoot to increase the efficacy of the seed itself. The advice of Walter of Henley, whose treatise on *Husbandry* the monks enrolled so carefully in a number of their registers,[2] may have suggested the method. 'Change your seed every year at Michaelmas,' writes this agricultural specialist, 'for seed grown on other ground will bring more profit than that which is grown on your own. Will you see this? Plough two selions at the same time, and sow the one with seed which is bought and the other with corn which you have grown; in August you will see that I speak truly.'[3] The purchase of seed-corn occurs very frequently in the serjeants' accounts of Eastry's priorate[4] and is noticeably absent in previous accounts. The seed of barley and of the leguminous crops, peas, beans, and vetches, was most commonly purchased from outside. The seed-corn of oats was bought somewhat less frequently and that of wheat but rarely.[5] Often the serjeant of one Canterbury manor purchased

decades of the fourteenth century. It should, however, be noticed that on more than one manor the seed of certain cereal crops was sown less intensively during this very same period. Thus at Monkton 7 bushels of barley-seed per acre were sown until the year 1314, when only 6½ bushels were used.

[1] Sir William Beveridge has remarked that 'the seed used per acre in the Middle Ages is for wheat and oats much the same, though slightly less, than the modern estimate of the Ministry of Agriculture. For barley it is considerably more': *Economic History* (a Supplement to *The Economic Journal*, 1929), p. 158.

[2] Four MSS. which belonged to Canterbury cathedral priory contain Walter of Henley's 'Treatise on Husbandry': *Walter of Henley's Husbandry*, ed. E. Lamond (1890), p. xxv.                                    [3] *Ibid.* p. 19.

[4] The accounts of the manors of Eastry and Chartham are particularly rich in this respect.

[5] I have come across only two instances of the seed of wheat being purchased from outside the manors. At Cliffe, in 1294–95, 4 seams of wheat were bought *ad semen* and at Monkton, in 1300–1, 5 seams were bought.

seed-corn from the serjeant of another manor of the priory.[1] On occasion the policy of selling corn to buy seed was even adopted. For example, at Eastry in 1325–26, 28 seams of barley were sold *ad emendum semen.* There is abundant evidence in the account-rolls of the century following Henry of Eastry's accession of the greatest attention being paid to all questions relating to the seeding of crops. It may seem surprising, in the light of these circumstances, that the yield of seed per quarter was not greater, for we know that these yields on the Canterbury estates generally fell far below Walter of Henley's expectations.[2] The wheat yield rarely answered to the fourth grain, averaging between 3 and 3·5, and barley yields were seldom higher.[3] The monk-warden constantly had to report that the seed was *nimis debile.*[4] There was, it is true, a definite increase in the productivity of barley-seed when it was purchased from outside, but the increase was not as appreciable as might be expected.[5]

Another expedient resorted to by the monks, in their great effort to increase the productivity of the soil and secure higher market-profits, was that of applying manure, marl, and lime to the land. The oldest and simplest method was that of spreading farmyard manure over the land before sowing. The use of the sheepfold for purposes of manure was also a familiar device.[6]

[1] Thus the serjeant of Chartham purchased seed-corn from Ickham and Brook in 1322–23.

[2] Walter of Henley categorically asserts that 'Barley ought to yield to the eighth grain, that is to say, a quarter sown should yield eight quarters... wheat ought to yield to the fifth grain' (*Husbandry*, p. 71). On the whole question of corn-yields, see Sir William Beveridge, *loc. cit.* and M. K. Bennett, 'British Wheat Yield Per Acre for Seven Centuries' in *Economic History* (a Supplement to *The Economic Journal*), 1937, pp. 12–29.

[3] For example, at Eastry in 1323 the seed of wheat yielded an increase per quarter of 3·2 and at Godmersham in 1326 a yield of 3·4 was recorded. Figures for barley yields in the same years are 3·1 and 3·5.

[4] Thus the serjeant of Godmersham stated in 1327 that the barley-seed was 'nimis debile per testimonium custodis'.

[5] Sir William Beveridge shows that the average yield per quarter of wheat in the later middle ages was 3·89, of barley 3·82, of oats 2·43. He observes that 'A threefold increase in the productivity of seed seems to measure broadly the difference between mediaeval and modern times': *loc. cit.* p. 159.

[6] E. H. Carrier, *The Pastoral Heritage of Britain* (1936), pp. 69–71.

Henry of Eastry calculated c. 1322 that the dung of sheep in all
the manors was worth no less than £91. 6s. 8d.; that of 100 sheep
was worth £1. 12s. od.[1] The presence of doves on most of the
manors indicates that guano was also used as a soil fertilizer.

In the sixteenth century William Lambard commented upon
the 'pits of fat marle' which were to be so often seen in Kent.[2]
There is evidence that the Canterbury lands were marled at an
early date. At first the expenses were very high. In 1225 the cost
of buying marl and applying it to 5 acres of land at Ickham came
to no less than £6. 10s. od., and at Monkton the marling of 8 acres
involved an expenditure of £4. In Essex, however, 20 acres were
marled for £4.[3] By the middle of the century marling was a less
expensive luxury and 11 acres at Monkton were marled in 1252
at a cost of 19s. 6d.[4] The realization that 'marl lasts longer than
manure'[5] and was therefore an essential instrument in his campaign for increasing corn production probably induced Prior
Eastry and his senior monks to issue the ordinance *De terra
marlanda* at the beginning of the fourteenth century. They enjoined that, on all manors where marl was easily accessible, marlers
(*marlatores*) should be employed in spreading the fertilizer over
as wide an area as possible during the summer months. The
monk-wardens, and not the serjeants, were to bear the expense
of these operations.[6]

A calcareous clay which is put on land chiefly for the sake of
the lime it brings with it, marl was used especially on newly
embanked and reclaimed land. It reduced the acid content of the
soil and infused it with nitrates. The manor of Ebony in the Isle
of Oxney may be taken as an example. The last two decades of
the thirteenth century had seen an extensive 'inning' and reclamation of land at Ebony. So, at the beginning of the next century,
marl was secured from neighbouring pits and horses and carts were

[1] B.M. Cott. MS. Galba E iv, fo. 177.
[2] *The Perambulation of Kent* (1656 ed.), p. 6.
[3] Cant. MS. M 13, xix, mem. 1.
[4] *Ibid.* mem. 7.
[5] *Husbandry*, p. 21.
[6] See Appendix I.

specially hired for the marling operations.[1] In 1302–3 a sum of
£3. 6s. 5d. was spent on treating 5 acres, 6 dayworks of land
with marl, and in the following year the same area was treated
not with marl but lime (*slycatura*),[2] while a further 8 acres of
land were dressed with marl at a total cost of £6. 7s. 1d. 150 heaps
(*cumuli*) of farmyard manure were spread on 4½ acres of soil. In
1304–5 the area marled increased to 16 acres and 9 dayworks,
whereas dressings of lime were applied to 4 acres, 12 dayworks.
Dung was spread in large quantities. The total expenditure
amounted to £11. 6s. 11d. The next year saw 12 acres and 13 dayworks of land dressed with marl, and lime was applied to 4 acres
at a total cost of £11. 14s. 6d. In 1306–7 the acreage marled and
limed decreased somewhat and the expenditure only amounted
to £6. 7s. 5d.

The grange accounts of the manor leave us in no doubt as to
the purpose and results of this dressing of reclaimed and embanked marsh-lands. The means employed for the reduction of
the acidity of the land and its infusion with nitrogenous properties had as their primary end the extension of the acreage under
wheat, the chief cash-crop of the manor. The cereal grown most
extensively at Ebony, as in the case of most marsh manors,[3] was
oats. The much higher prices which wheat fetched in the market
were, however, an irresistible attraction, and so marl, lime, and
dung were used as agencies to increase the wheat acreage.
Wherever these dressings were applied, wheat was sown. Sometimes the land was fertilized in its fallow stage; at other times,
when wheat had already been sown.

The increase in the yield of wheat as the result of these dressings
was often appreciable. For example, in the year 1305–6, 5 acres

---

[1] See, for example, the entry in the Ebony serjeant's account for the year
1302–3: 'In solutione carectario Karianti marlam xxii sol. ix den. In dicta
marla spergenda iv sol. viii den. In ii equis locatis ad dictam terram marlan-
dam per v dies—ii sol.... In marlatura (*sic*) fodienda ad v acras et vi deyworcs
terre—xxxii sol. vi d., pro acra v sol. vi d.'

[2] John Boys observed at the end of the eighteenth century that lime from
the chalk hills was used by the farmers of West Kent: *A General View of the
Agriculture of the County of Kent* (1796), p. 142.

[3] See Chapter Eleven.

and 6 dayworks of land were dressed with lime and sown with wheat at the rate of 4 bushels an acre. They gave a yield of 10 quarters, 2 bushels; that is, of 2 quarters, 2 bushels from each acre sown. Now in the same year undressed land in the same part of the manor was sown with wheat. The yield per acre (sown also with four bushels) here amounted to only 1½ quarters. The application of lime had therefore caused a 33 per cent increase in the yield per acre.[1] The extension of the total acreage under wheat, made possible by the deliberate policy of dressing the land thus sown, is well illustrated by the grange accounts. In 1303 only 16 acres were under wheat; then manuring, marling, and liming began, and the wheat area increased to 28 acres in 1305, reaching the figure of 43 acres by the autumn of 1317. Then, for some reason, the dressings ceased and the area under wheat decreased from 42 acres in 1318 to 27 in 1319 and 6 in 1328. Probably the storms and floods of this period made the further cultivation of wheat at Ebony an impossibility. But on the manors of Monkton and Agney-and-Orgarswick—to give only two examples of Kentish manors, widely apart from each other—a policy of dressing the land was consistently pursued in the first half of the fourteenth century. We know that in the first thirty-seven years of his priorate Henry of Eastry spent £111. 5s. on marl alone.[2] These experiments in seeding corn and dressing land were greatly facilitated on the Kentish estates of Christ Church by the fact that the demesne was largely held in severalty within an enclosed area.[3] Greater scope was thereby afforded to initiative in all departments of agriculture.

The campaign of the monks to increase the yield of corn per acre was paralleled by attempts to extend the total area under cereal crops. One way of doing this was to convert pasture-land

---

[1] Sir William Beveridge has declared that the average medieval yield per acre for wheat was 1·17 quarters or 9·36 bushels: *loc. cit.* p. 159.

[2] B.M. Cott. MS. Galba E iv, fo. 109.

[3] H. L. Gray, *English Field Systems* (1915), pp. 272–73. There are no surviving extents for the Kentish manors of the priory, but the serjeants' accounts supply copious evidence of enclosed corn-fields and pastures. See Chapter Eleven for a description of enclosures on the marshland manors of the priory.

into arable. Some of the richest soil in Kent was at Ickham and, in 1225, 46 acres were ploughed and sown with oats. In the Essex custody a sum of £3 was spent in the same year on sowing land *preter solitam*—probably pasture-land.[1] The reclamation of marshland was attempted on an ambitious scale in order to increase the acreage under crops.[2] Finally, a great increase in the cultivation of legumes occurred in the late thirteenth and fourteenth centuries. It has been shown that 'a partial legume rotation...was undoubtedly beginning to appear in many parts of England between 1275 and 1350',[3] and the figures about to be cited will show that this was certainly the case on the Canterbury estates.[4] The measures described brought about an all-round increase in the acreage under cereal crops. At Monkton in Thanet, for example, the wheat area steadily increased in the first quarter of the fourteenth century, and the grange accounts of the manor of Merstham in Surrey tell the same story.[5] Dr J. F. Nichols has shown that on the manors of the Essex custody of Christ Church there was both an extension of the area cultivated and an increased yield in the years c. 1285–1305. 'There can be little doubt', he says, 'that this was the result of the reforming zeal and efficient management'[6] of Prior Henry of Eastry.

In 1322, after he had been prior for thirty-seven years, Henry of Eastry summed up his many and varied achievements for the benefit of posterity and included in the recital of his good deeds a survey of the total acreage under corn and legumes on each manor.[7] This survey is so interesting and valuable that it seems

[1] Cant. MS. M 13, xix, mem. 1.

[2] See Chapter Eleven.

[3] T. A. M. Bishop, 'The Rotation of Crops on the Manor of Westerham' in *Econ. Hist. Rev.* (1938), p. 44.

[4] Peas and beans were used as forage for cattle and horses and in making pottage (*potagium*) and mixed corn (*mixtura*) for the *famuli* of the manors. Vetches were simply used as forage.

[5] At Merstham the acreage under wheat rose from 46 in 1288 to 83 in 1296, and became stabilized in the fourteenth century at a figure not lower than 73 or above 100.

[6] *Custodia Essexae*, p. 183.

[7] B.M. Cott. MS. Galba E iv, fos. 76–78.

appropriate to give the figures for the two Kentish custodies in full:

### CUSTODY OF EAST KENT

| Manor | Wheat | Rye | Barley | Oats | Legumes | Total acreage |
|---|---|---|---|---|---|---|
| Monkton | 70 | — | 90 | 50 | 80 ⎫ | |
| Brokesend | 14 | — | 60 | 40 | 40 ⎭ | 444 |
| Lyden | 6 | 8 | 8 | 12 | 16 | 50 |
| Eastry | 90 | — | 110 | 25 | 100 | 325 |
| Adesham | 110 | — | 130 | 60 | 100 | 400 |
| Ickham | 120 | — | 120 | — | 100 ⎫ | |
| Brambling | 60 | — | 60 | 30 | 60 ⎭ | 550 |
| Barton | 62 | 15 | 50 | 12 | 45 | 184 |
| Chartham | 56 | — | 60 | 16 | 60 | 192 |
| Godmersham | 70 | — | 60 | 20 | 60 | 210 |
| Brook | 16 | — | 15 | 30 | 10 | 71 |
| TOTAL | 674 | 23 | 763 | 295 | 671 | 2426 |

### CUSTODY OF THE WEALD AND MARSHES

| Manor | Wheat | Rye | Barley | Oats | Legumes | Total acreage |
|---|---|---|---|---|---|---|
| Mersham | 42 | — | 17 | 30 | 36 | 125 |
| Rocking | 6 | 2 | 4 | 80 | 13 | 105 |
| Agney-and-Orgarswick | 26 | — | 14 | 46 | 50 | 136 |
| Appledore | 24 | 5 | 5 | 60 | 10 | 104 |
| Ebony | 14 | — | — | 130 | 3 | 147 |
| Great Chart | 70 | — | 8 | 54 | 50 | 182 |
| Little Chart | 46 | — | 6 | 40 | 20 | 112 |
| Welles | 80 | — | 36 | 100 | 60 | 276 |
| Hollingbourne | 30 | — | 40 | 100 | 60 | 230 |
| Loose | 30 | 4 | 5 | 30 | 30 | 99 |
| East Farleigh | 60 | 10 | 10 | 80 | 50 | 210 |
| West Farleigh | 60 | 6 | 6 | 82 | 55 | 209 |
| Peckham | 30 | 3 | 5 | 36 | 20 | 94 |
| Barksore | 20 | — | 10 | 20 | 12 | 62 |
| Leisdon | 13 | — | — | 10 | 12 | 35 |
| Eilwarton | 18 | — | 16 | 2 | 20 | 56 |
| Ham | 4 | — | 6 | 8 | 8 | 26 |
| Copton | 65 | — | 30 | 20 | 30 | 145 |
| TOTAL | 638 | 30 | 218 | 928 | 539 | 2353 |

The figures of the total acreage sown with cereals in the two other custodies, those of Surrey and Essex, are as follows:

| | Wheat | Rye | Barley | Oats | Legumes | Total acreage |
|---|---|---|---|---|---|---|
| Surrey | 708 | 112 | 257 | 522 | 172 | 1771 |
| Essex | 657 | 202 | 196 | 640 | 128 | 1823 |

So, if the four custodies are taken together, the number of acres sown with different crops at this peak period of monastic farming was:

| Crop | Acres sown |
|---|---|
| Wheat | 2677 |
| Rye | 367 |
| Barley | 1434 |
| Oats | 2385 |
| Legumes | 1510 |

which means that, in all, no less than 8373 acres were under crops.

It has already been observed how extensively legumes were sown, especially in the East Kent custody, where they covered only three acres less than the wheat crop. The prevalence of oats on the marsh manors will also be noticed. Sir William Ashley has commented upon the fact that in the two Kentish custodies very little rye was sown 'but in the manors of the *custodia* of Essex the acreage under rye was a third of that under wheat—202 as compared with 657; and in the *custodia* of Surrey more than one-seventh—112 as compared with 708'.[1]

This huge acreage under corn was, as we have seen, largely brought about by the compelling attraction of high market-profits in an age of rising prices. The figures of corn sales on the individual manors will speak for themselves. At Agney-and-Orgarswick the yield from sales rose from £10. 6s. 7d. in 1280–81 to £17. 10s. 8d. in 1285–86, and reached a summit of £49. 1s. 10d. in 1315–16. At Merstham, in Surrey, a steady rise from £9. 10s. 2d. in 1288–89 to £20. 11s. 9d. in 1317–18 took place. Again, at

---

[1] *The Bread of Our Forefathers* (Oxford, 1928), p. 87. Sir William also points out that at Walworth the acreage under rye and wheat was almost equal, 40 of rye and 42 of wheat (*ibid.*). This is interesting in view of the proximity of Peckham Rye to Walworth.

Ickham a sum of £15. 8s. 10d. was derived from corn sales in 1285–86, and in 1322–23 the yield totalled £27. 16s. 2d. In short, the estates of Christ Church resembled other large estates of the period by being a capitalist concern, a 'federated grain factory, producing largely for cash'.[1]

No information is vouchsafed as to where most of this corn was sold. Sometimes the words *in patria*—in the neighbourhood— are appended to the figures of sale, but in most cases the simple heading *Bladum Venditum* is all that we are told. One thing appears to be certain. Most of the corn, besides that which was shipped abroad, was sold in the local markets. We know that a differential price level tended to obtain in any given marketing area.[2] It is extremely unlikely, for example, that corn produced on the manors of Christ Church in Essex, a consuming area, was ever sent for sale at Canterbury, which lay in a producing area.[3] All the evidence goes to show that a system of decentralized grain sales had been established on the Canterbury estates at least as early as the first quarter of the thirteenth century, and continued in being throughout the middle ages. In a number of their manors the monks enjoyed the commercial monopoly of markets and fairs,[4] which must have greatly facilitated the sale of corn, stock, and produce of all kinds. At Canterbury there were im-

---

[1] M. M. Postan, 'The Fifteenth Century' in *Econ. Hist. Rev.* IX (1939), p. 162.

[2] Gras, *op. cit.* p. 42.  [3] *Ibid.* p. 64.

[4] In 1279 the monks asserted their right to hold a market at Westwell and fairs at Great Chart, Appledore, Rocking and Godmersham. The claim was allowed by the royal justices (Trin. Coll. Camb. MS. O. 9/26, fo. 88). In 1235 Henry III had granted them a yearly fair at Barksore (*Cal. Charter Rolls*, 19 Henry III, p. 202). Edward III made the grant of a weekly market and annual fair at Merstham in 1338 (*ibid.* 12 Edward III, p. 445) and, twenty years later, he granted the same privilege to the monks at Appledore (*ibid.* 32 Edward III, p. 157). Godmersham followed with like privileges in 1364 (*ibid.* 38 Edward III, p. 190). In 1383, at the instance of Archbishop William Courtenay, the monks were given the right of holding four annual fairs within the *curia*, each of ten days' duration (*ibid.* 38 Edward III, p. 190). Finally, in 1447 Henry VI granted the priory a weekly market and annual fair at Hollingbourne, Eastry, Monkton, and Meopham (*ibid.* 25–26 Henry VI, pp. 79–80).

portant markets for wheat[1] and oats,[2] at which the produce of some of the home manors was probably marketed. The fact that the large and scattered estates of the priory fell within several distinct market areas with sharply varying price levels[3] is a sufficient explanation for the decentralized corn sales, which stand out in contrast to the centralized wool sales of the same period.[4]

. . . . . .

The peak period for the marketing of both corn and stock on the Canterbury estates occurred in the middle years of Henry of Eastry's priorate. The years 1306–24 were the 'high farming' period *par excellence*. Of the fifteen Canterbury manors (omitting those in the Essex custody) for which there is evidence sufficient to warrant reliable conclusions,[5] ten registered their highest sales during these years. Three of the manors did so between the years 1285–90, before the great floods and tempests at the end of the century administered a temporary set-back to the progress of demesne economy. Only one manor, Hollingbourne, has been found to achieve its highest profits from sales of corn and stock in the 1290–1306 period,[6] and Godmersham (at which sales were so slight as to be hardly significant) is the sole example of a Canterbury manor which achieved its highest sales in the years subsequent to 1324.[7]

[1] A very ancient wheat-market stood without Burgate in the parish of St Paul's (D. Gardiner, 'Merchants of Canterbury in the Middle Ages' in *The Parents' Review*, 1925, XXXVI, p. 6). In 1365 this market was moved into the centre of the city (*Cal. Let. Pat.* 39 Edward III, p. 203).

[2] The oat-market stood on Oaten Hill at the south-east of the city, outside the walls. See C. Cotton, *The Greyfriars of Canterbury* (1926 ed.), p. 4.

[3] Thus the manors in Oxfordshire and Buckinghamshire fell within the low-price marketing area of the Upper Thames (Gras, *op. cit.* p. 48). Kent 'stood about midway between the lowest and the highest price district' (*ibid.* p. 51). The manors in Surrey lay within a marketing area characterized by a high price level (*ibid.* p. 53), and so did those in east Essex (*ibid.* p. 53). The Canterbury estates thus lay scattered in areas marked by greatly varying price levels.

[4] See Chapter Ten.

[5] Merstham, Walworth, Eastry, Ickham, Monkton, Lyden, Godmersham, Chartham, Agney-and-Orgarswick, Ebony, Appledore, Barksore, Cliffe, Meopham, and Hollingbourne.

[6] In the year 1293–94.

[7] In 1326–27.

The causes of the decline of demesne-farming, which began in the third decade of the fourteenth century and gathered increasing momentum as the century advanced, are still somewhat obscure. It seems highly probable that movements of population and prices—a topic that awaits full investigation[1]—lay at the root of the agricultural changes of this period. The abnormal weather conditions which afflicted the Kentish estates with peculiar severity[2] were no doubt a factor of some importance in this decline, nor must we neglect to consider the effect on Canterbury farming of the death of the energetic Prior Eastry in 1331. The shrinkage in market-profits had made much headway before the Black Death and merely accelerated its progress after that disaster.[3] The Great Plague of 1348–49 therefore had no decisive influence on the fortunes of the Christ Church economy.

Although corn-marketing rapidly dwindled in the latter part of the fourteenth century, the system of food-farms was still maintained. The accounts of the garnerer and bartoner show that large supplies of corn continued to be sent to the priory year by year. For this reason more corn was bought than sold on a number of Kentish manors in the last two-thirds of the cen-

[1] The problem has been stated by Professor E. Levett in *The Black Death on the Estates of the See of Winchester* (1916) and by Professor M. M. Postan in his article on 'The Fifteenth Century' in *Econ. Hist. Rev.* IX, pp. 160–67.

[2] See C. E. Britton, *Meteorological Chronology*, pp. 134–35, and *Lit. Cant.* I, pp. 243–46.

[3] The immediate effect of the Black Death on the Canterbury estates was calamitous, if a substantial measure of truth is contained in the letter which the monks addressed to the pope in 1350. They claimed that 'terre siquidem plurime ipsius ecclesie jacuerunt, et adhuc jacent, pro defectu cultorum inculte; item, plura edificia decidebant, et que nunc remanent, cum non sint qui ea inhabitarent, manifestam minantur ruinam; ac, deficientibus tenentibus, non supersunt qui de redditibus potuerint respondere. Terre insuper annis proximis, culte laboribus et sumptibus excessivis, nullos quasi fructus reddentes pejus quam steriles remanserunt': *H.M.C.* App. to VIIIth Report, p. 341. After this recovery was rapid, but there was a further increase in the already considerable purchases of corn and stock on the manors and a further diminution in sales. For example, at Ickham in 1350–51 a sum of £37. 11s. 0d. was spent on buying corn and none was sold. Similarly, at Chartham in 1348–49, £5. 8s. 6d. was spent on buying corn and £2. 11s. 7d. was realized from its sale. Little stock was bought or sold on either manor.

tury.[1] Even when the demesnes of the manors were let out on lease
at the end of the century, statutory food-farms were still exacted
from a number of them. This final phase in the arable farming
of Christ Church will, however, be fully discussed on a later page.

[1] Thus in 1345 the garnerer received 843 seams, 1 bushel of wheat from
the custody of East Kent (Cant. MS. M 13, iii, mem. 32). At Ickham, in the
same year, £6. 12s. 5d. was spent on the purchase of corn and a sum of
£1. 10s. 10d. was derived from sales. At Chartham purchases came to
£4. 12s. 11d. and sales to £1. 18s. 1d. Serjeants' accounts.

## Chapter Ten

### PASTURE FARMING

All the principal animals denoted by the inclusive term *staurum* were reared on the Canterbury estates in the middle ages. Cows, oxen, horses, sheep, pigs, and poultry could be found at an early date on nearly all the manors. We have seen that by 1225 stock had ceased to be rendered as a food-farm and was bought from the serjeant by monks who happened to be residing on the manors or passing through them on their travels. Each year the monks sent their purveyor to the manorial serjeants, who were instructed to 'set down in writing how many beasts, what kind of beasts, and the price of each beast, that you have delivered to our cellarers for our larder during this year'.[1] In most cases the cellarer purchased pigs. The necessity of using salted meat during the winter months made it imperative for the monks to secure a large supply of pigs, 'since no meat it appears takes salt more readily, or preserves its natural properties after curing, so fully as pork'.[2] The serjeants of Monkton, Ickham, and Eastry, the three East Kent manors, were particularly lavish in selling pigs to the monastic cellarer.[3]

Just as the tempting bait of high market profits stimulated a great increase in corn production in the thirteenth and early fourteenth centuries, so did the same influence powerfully react upon the development of Canterbury stock-farming. In the early thirteenth century a deliberate policy of increasing the stock on the manors was adopted. Thus in 1225 the monk warden of the

[1] *Lit. Cant.* II, p. 37.

[2] J. E. T. Rogers, *The History of Agriculture and Prices*, I, p. 326. See also C. S. and C. S. Orwin, *The Open Fields*, p. 52.

[3] To take Monkton alone, 28 pigs were sold to the cellarer in 1300–1 for £3. 9s. 4d., 40 pigs in 1302–3 for £4. 13s. 4d., 16 in 1305–6 for £1. 12s. od., and 18 in 1307–8 for £2. 8s. od.

Wealden custody supplied the manor of Orgarswick-and-Agney
with a large quantity of stock,[1] and a sum of £3. 11s. 10d. was
spent on buying stock at Lyden. In the Essex custody 435 sheep,
157 rams, and 242 lambs were bought in the same year. So in this
single year the total investment of monastic capital in stock came
to £42. 3s. 0d.[2] No general study has yet been made of the
evolution of the English stock market, and it is therefore impossible to say when stock sales became a regular feature of
manorial economy. In the earliest Canterbury serjeants' accounts
there is no evidence at all of stock being sold. Plainly in Kent,
the county which was probably in the most advanced stage of
agrarian development, stock-marketing came into being at a much
later date than corn-marketing, which was well organized in the
first quarter of the thirteenth century. The general movement
upward of prices[3] was doubtless the determining factor which led
the monks in the middle and latter half of the thirteenth century
to organize certain manors especially for stock-marketing, as well
as to rear stock on a small scale for the market on a number of
other manors. The monks of Crowland Abbey were pursuing a
very similar policy at the same time.[4] At the zenith of this movement on the Canterbury estates c. 1320 there were 767 cows on
the manors[5] and unnumbered quantities of other stock.

It might, perhaps, be supposed that the manors burdened with
a food-farm of corn were least likely to go in for stock-farming on
a large scale. Some animals would, of course, always be required
for draught purposes and for manuring the soil, but normally the
lack of adequate pasture of good quality would severely limit
their numbers.[6] On certain East Kent manors, however, the

---

[1] 'Notandum quod Dominus R. dedit conventui ad instauracionem de
Hagn' xiv vaccas et i taurum et c oves et iv equos ad aratrum': Cant. MS.
M 13, xix, mem. 1.

[2] *Ibid.*                    [3] Rogers, *op. cit.* I, pp. 361–62.

[4] See M. Wretts-Smith, 'Organization of Farming at Crowland Abbey'
in *Journal of Econ. and Business History* (1932), IV, pp. 168 *et seq.*

[5] B.M. Cott. MS. Galba E iv, fo. 177.

[6] See the remarkable review by R. H. Tawney of N. Riches' 'The Agricultural Revolution in Norfolk' in *History* (1940), XXIV, pp. 346–49, for a
discussion of the problems of mixed husbandry.

peculiar richness of the soil and the vast expanse of pasture and salty marsh land, together with the favourable geographical situation, made mixed husbandry both desirable and profitable. The manor of Monkton in the Isle of Thanet was the scene of sheep-breeding and cattle-rearing and also of extensive corn-growing. Eastry, near Sandwich, was another manor which combined arable and pasture farming with much success. As it will not be possible to embark upon an exhaustive study of every branch of Canterbury stock-farming, attention may be directed to the two most important and lucrative pursuits on the Kentish estates, namely, wool production and dairy-farming.

It is by now a commonplace that 'Large-scale sheep-farming was introduced into Britain by the monks, especially those of the Cistercian Order'.[1] So far, however, attention has been largely concentrated on the Cistercians, and no considerable literature has yet arisen on the subject of Benedictine sheep-farming.[2] This is probably because the Benedictines undertook sheep-farming on a less spectacular scale than the Cistercians and as a pursuit ancillary to their main occupation of arable farming. Nevertheless the practice of pasture farming on the great Benedictine estates is worthy of the closest study, and some attempt must be made to describe the contribution of the monks of Christ Church to 'the pastoral heritage of Britain'.

It is not until the first half of the thirteenth century that we learn anything of Canterbury sheep-farming. At that time the sale of the wool, for which sheep were primarily bred and reared throughout the middle ages, yielded quite considerable sums on a number of the Canterbury manors. In 1231, for example, the sale of wool and dairy produce realized an income of £11. 17s. 3d. at Barksore, £7. 1s. 1d. at Appledore, £2. 11s. 4d. at Great Chart,

---

[1] E. H. Carrier, *The Pastoral Heritage of Britain*, p. 204.

[2] Miss F. M. Page has described the sheep-farming on the Crowland Abbey estates in her article 'Bidentes Hoylandie' in *Economic History*, I, pp. 603 *et seq*. The definitive work on medieval sheep-farming and wool production in this country by the late Professor Eileen Power, to be published by her literary executors, is foreshadowed by her Ford Lectures on *The Wool Trade in English Mediaeval History* (1941).

and £1. 13s. 6d. at Ickham.[1] Wool sales continued to take place on the individual manors of the priory until the year 1288, when Henry of Eastry centralized the sale of the wool of the two Kentish custodies at Canterbury.[2] Henceforth the treasurers became responsible for the sale of the Kentish wool and enrolled the total proceeds in their annual account. Although the wool of Kentish wethers and ewes was always sent to Canterbury in the century after the reorganization of 1288, lambs' wool was still often sold on the manors,[3] as the cost of transport could hardly have been justified by the slender profits accruing from such sales. On the manors remote from Canterbury, in the Surrey and Essex custodies, the sheep and their wool were either let out on lease and a lump sum of cash sent to Canterbury,[4] or the wool clip was sent to London for sale.[5]

Most of the Kentish wool in the late thirteenth and early fourteenth centuries appears to have been bought by Italian merchants. The normal procedure at this period was for the merchants to give credit to the seller and to buy the wool in advance while it was still on the backs of the sheep.[6] A *littera obligatoria* of the priory for the year 1285 shows that such a system obtained at Christ Church. The monks declared that they 'are held in bond to Wlpus and Duckus Pitycan in person as well to their other fellows and associates, citizens and merchants of Florence, for (the

[1] Cant. MS. M 13, xix, mem. 3. The sale of wool and dairy produce, much of which was made from ewes' milk, was included under one total in the early Assisae Scaccarii accounts.

[2] Cant. MS. F ii.

[3] Thus the wool of the lambs at Ickham and Godmersham was sold locally, while at Monkton a part of the lambs' wool was sold in the locality and a part sent to Canterbury with the main wool crop. At Chartham, the manor nearest to the priory, the lambs' wool was always sent to the treasurers.

[4] Thus at Monks Eleigh in Suffolk and at Bocking in Essex the sheep and their wool were leased out to farmers during the greater part of Henry of Eastry's priorate. At Milton Hall in Essex, however, the wool was sold in the locality, as in the early thirteenth century.

[5] In 1287 the 'profectus de lana missa London" in the Surrey custody amounted to £31. 12s. 2d.: Cant. MS. M 13, xiv, mem. 3.

[6] See R. J. Whitwell, 'English Monasteries and the Wool Trade in the Thirteenth Century' in *Vierteljahrschrift für Social- und Wirtschaftes-geschichte* (Leipzig, 1904), II, pp. 1–33.

L

payment of) 17 sacks and 25 pounds of wool; that is, of wool of our house dried and weighed in accordance with the custom of our house, as the remainder of that load of 100 sacks of wool which we owe to the same John and his associates'. They contracted to deliver this final payment to the merchants at Pentecost 1286.[1] Sandwich was the port within easiest access of Canterbury and the most flourishing on the Kentish coast.[2] All the evidence points to the conclusion that the bulk of the Canterbury wool was shipped abroad from here.[3]

The priorate of Henry of Eastry (1285–1331) saw a great expansion of sheep-farming, as of other branches of demesne economy. The flocks of the priory were increasingly concentrated in two main areas, the Isle of Thanet and the Romney marshes. Monkton in Thanet became an important sheep-breeding centre in the first half of the fourteenth century. Large flocks were drafted there from the neighbouring manors.[4] Thus in 1307–8, 57 ewes from Chartham and 35 from Godmersham were driven to Monkton. Altogether in this year there were 478 ewes in the manor, 111 wethers, and no less than 8 rams. In 1315 the number of sheep at Monkton had increased to 847, including 689 ewes. The land of the Romney marsh manors was undergoing reclamation and embankment at this time and did not see such large flocks of sheep as Monkton. Nevertheless the manor of Orgarswick-and-Agney had a flock of 289 sheep—178 ewes and 111 wethers—in 1281 and remained an important place for fattening

---

[1] Camb. Univ. Lib. MS. Ee. v, 31, fo. 10. See the numerous *litterae obligatoriae* enrolled by the monks in this register. Curiously the wool from the Kentish estates of Christ Church receives no mention in the list drawn up by Pegolotti (ed. Evans, p. 268), although 8 sacks of 'Canterbury' wool are said to come from the district of Stafford and Nottingham. It is not easy to interpret this reference, as I have no knowledge of property owned by Canterbury monks in either county.

[2] See R. A. Pelham, 'Some Aspects of the East Kent Wool Trade in the Thirteenth Century' in *Arch. Cant.* XLIV, pp. 218–28.

[3] The cost 'pro cariagio lane ad Sandwycum' came to 3s. 6d. in 1286: Lambeth MS. 242, fo. 92. The monks of Christ Church are constantly found transporting their wool by river to this port.

[4] It is impossible to say whether cross-breeding took place at Monkton in this period, as the particular breed of sheep is never specified in the accounts.

sheep throughout the fourteenth century. Normally the Romney marshes were used solely for fattening sheep and the breeding took place in the rich pasture-lands of Thanet and East Kent, but sheep were also bred on a small scale in some Kentish manors which were primarily valued for their arable land.[1]

The technique of Canterbury sheep-farming appears to have differed little from that of other estates. On each sheep farm there was a shepherd (*bercarius*) and sometimes a keeper of the lambs (*custos agnorum*). There was never an *instaurator* or a master shepherd. If the chapter ordinance of 1305 was obeyed, the culling of sheep and other farm animals took place between Easter and Whitsun[2] and 'the old or feeble sheep or crones, whose teeth were too worn for them to be able to feed any longer on the pastures, were given a better food so that they could be fattened for sale about St John's Day, to be finished off for Michaelmas slaughter and salting for winter consumption'.[3] The washing and shearing of sheep occurred about midsummer, usually by means of hired labour but sometimes as part of the compulsory service of the tenants.[4] The flocks were then 'raddled' with a red stone (*rubra petra*) so as to be distinguished from other sheep quartered upon the pastures of the priory.[5] Butter and tar were applied to the fleeces as a safeguard against the scourge of murrain.

Fortunately we possess a full account of the numbers of sheep on the Canterbury estates c. 1322.[6] This, coupled with a recital of the wool sales enrolled on the treasurers' accounts, will give a clear picture of the extent of sheep-farming and wool production on the Christ Church manors at this 'boom' period in English

[1] E.g. at Chartham and Godmersham.
[2] See Chapter Nine.
[3] Carrier, *op. cit.* p. 72.
[4] See Chapter Eight.
[5] The item 'pastura vendita' is very common in the serjeants' accounts of the East Kent manors. At Lyden, in particular, a considerable profit accrued from this annual lease of pasture.
[6] The document is entitled 'Agistamentum vaccarum et ovium per totum annum in omnibus maneriis Prioratus Cantuariensis': B.M. Cott. MS. Galba E iv, fo. 177.

agrarian history. The sheep are grouped under the four custodies thus:

### CUSTODY OF EAST KENT

| Manor | Number of sheep |
| --- | --- |
| Barton | 400 |
| Monkton | 2000 |
| Eastry and Lyden [1] | 2000 |
| Adesham and Knowldon | 600 |
| Ickham and Brambling | 400 |
| Chartham | 300 |
| Godmersham | 300 |
| Brook | None |
| TOTAL | 6000 |

### CUSTODY OF THE WEALD AND MARSHES

| Manor | Number of sheep |
| --- | --- |
| Mersham | 200 |
| Rocking | None |
| Fairfield | None |
| Agney | 300 |
| Orgarswick | 100 |
| Appledore | 250 |
| Ebony | 300 |
| Great Chart | None |
| Little Chart | None |
| Welles | 600 |
| Hollingbourne | 300 |
| Loose | 100 |
| East Farleigh | 300 |
| West Farleigh | 250 |
| Peckham | None |
| Leisdon | 100 |
| Barksore | 600 |
| Eilwarton | None [2] |
| Ham | 600 [3] |
| Copton | None |
| TOTAL | 4000 |

[1] The pastures of Eastry and Lyden were shared in common. Thus in the 1319–20 serjeant's account of Eastry we read 'De herbagio yemali, nihil, quia oves de Lydene pasturabantur apud Eastry illo tempore'.

[2] 'qui stant apud Hame'.          [3] 'cum Eylwarton'.

### CUSTODY OF SURREY AND OXFORD

| Manor | Number of sheep |
|---|---|
| Meopham | 300 |
| Orpington | 350 |
| Walworth | 200 |
| Chayham | 300 |
| Merstham | 200 |
| Woodtown | —[1] |
| Horley | 300 |
| Newington | 250 |
| Britwell | 300 |
| Risborough | 200 |
| Halton | 200 |
| TOTAL | 2600 |

### CUSTODY OF ESSEX AND SUFFOLK[2]

| Manor | Number of sheep |
|---|---|
| Cliffe | 120 |
| Milton Hall | 140 |
| Lalling | 140 |
| Bocking | 120 |
| Mersey | 150 |
| Monks Eleigh | 120 |
| Hadleigh | 100 |
| Deopham | 120 |
| Borley | 120 |
| TOTAL | 1130 |

It will be observed that, out of a total number of 13,730 sheep, no less than 10,000 were agisted on the Kentish manors.[3] It was estimated that all these sheep yielded 50 sacks of wool a year which, on the basis of £6 for a sack, spelt an annual revenue of £300. In addition, the manure of the sheep was valued at £91. 6s. 8d. a year and the milk of 6000 ewes at £96. The lambs were said to be worth £150 and their wool £50 at 2d. a fleece.[4]

[1] No figure is given.          [2] 'cum Clyve et Borle'.

[3] The figures are, of course, round numbers and slight exaggeration may well have crept into some of the estimates. But Dr Nichols has shown (*Custodia Essexae*, pp. 190–91) that the figures are substantially reliable for the Essex custody, and I have no reason to suspect the contrary of those for the Kentish manors.

[4] B.M. Cott. MS. Galba E iv, fo. 177.

The wool sales enrolled on the treasurers' accounts are not representative of the total sales, as they only include the manors incorporated in the centralized system of wool-marketing. Nevertheless these Kentish manors contained well over two-thirds of the total number of Christ Church sheep and the money derived from the centralized sales cannot, therefore, have fallen very far short of the total yield.[1] The figures[2] have been chosen for the period of Henry of Eastry's priorate, beginning in the year 1288 when the centralized system was first established.

| | Sale of sheep's wool | | | Sale of lambs' wool | | | Total profit | | |
|---|---|---|---|---|---|---|---|---|---|
| Year | Sacks | Weys | Great pounds | Sacks | Weys | Great pounds | £ | s. | d. |
| 1288 | — | — | — | — | — | — | 48 | 10 | 0 |
| 1289 | — | — | — | — | — | — | 62 | 13 | 0 |
| 1289–90[3] | — | — | — | — | — | — | 84 | 11 | 4 |
| 1290–91 | — | — | — | — | — | — | 91 | 8 | 6 |
| 1291–92 | — | — | — | — | — | — | 96 | 0 | 0 |
| 1292–93 | 18 | 0 | 0 | — | — | — | 90 | 0 | 0 |
| 1293–94 | — | — | — | — | — | — | None | | |
| 1294–95 | — | — | — | — | — | — | None | | |
| 1295–96 | — | — | — | — | — | — | 9 | 10 | 10[4] |
| 1296–97 | — | — | — | — | — | — | 143 | 7 | 0 |
| 1297–98 | 14 | 0 | 0 | 1 | 1 | 13 | 95 | 9 | 0 |
| 1298–99 | 19 | 1 | 22 | 1 | 1 | 13 | 135 | 16 | 1 |
| 1299–1300 | 16 | 0 | 21 | — | 1 | 20 | 96 | 0 | 0 |

[1] It should also be recalled that the sheep on some Essex manors were leased out to farmers.

[2] The wool was estimated in terms of sacks, weys, and great pounds. The relation of the three measures was stated in the 1299–1300 treasurers' accounts thus: 'Memorandum quod due pense lane faciunt saccum; pensa vero continet xxvi libras magnas, quarum quelibet continet vii libras parvas et quelibet parva libra ponderat xxv sterlingos' (B.M. Add. MS. 6160, fo. 85). The record 'Item, pro lana ponderanda—vi sol. viii den.' occurs in Lambeth MS. 242, fo. 147.

[3] From 1289 onwards the treasurers' accounts ran from Michaelmas to Michaelmas. Previous to this the single year only was given at the head of the account.

[4] The disastrous collapse of wool production in these three years 1293–96 may be attributed to the violent floods and tempests. See C. E. Britton, *A Meteorological Chronology*, pp. 128–30.

| Year | Sale of sheep's wool | | | Sale of lambs' wool | | | Total profit £ s. d. | | |
|---|---|---|---|---|---|---|---|---|---|
| | Sacks | Weys | Great pounds | Sacks | Weys | Great pounds | | | |
| 1300–1 | 14 | 1 | 0 | 1 | 1 | 20 | 96 | 0 | 0 |
| 1301–2 | 11 | 1 | 8 | 1 | 0 | 1 | 81 | 0 | 0 |
| 1302–3 | 15 | 1 | 0 | 1 | 0 | 24 | 99 | 16 | 0 |
| 1303–4 | 17 | 0 | 18 | 1 | 1 | 0 | 105 | 0 | 0 |
| 1304–5 | 11 | 1 | 0 | — | — | 17 | 70 | 10 | 0 |
| 1305–6 | 11 | 1 | 0 | — | — | 16 | 78 | 3 | 4 |
| 1306–7 | 14 | 0 | 13 | — | 1 | 16 | 98 | 10 | 4 |
| 1307–8 | 16 | 0 | 13 | — | — | — | 124 | 10 | 0 |
| 1308–9 | 21 | 0 | 13 | 2 | 0 | 0 | 173 | 17 | 0 |
| 1309–10 | 18 | 1 | 0 | 1 | 0 | 2 | 137 | 15 | 0 |
| 1310–11 | 20 | 0 | 18 | 1 | 0 | 0 | 119 | 19 | 8 |
| 1311–12 | 22 | 1 | 0 | — | — | 22 | 101 | 5 | 8 |
| 1312–13 | 16 | 0 | 13 | — | — | 17 | 80 | 12 | 0 |
| 1313–14 | 20[1] | 0 | 0 | — | — | — | 113 | 6 | 8 |
| 1314–15 | 20 | 0 | 0 | 2 | 0 | 0 | 116 | 13 | 4 |
| 1315–16 | 11 | 0 | 13 | — | 1 | 13 | 71 | 0 | 0 |
| 1316–17 | 14 | 1 | 19½ | 1 | 0 | 12½ | 90 | 0 | 2½ |
| 1317–18 | 15 | 0 | 0 | 1 | 1 | 13 | 98 | 3 | 4 |
| 1318–19 | 15 | 0 | 0 | 1 | 0 | 19 | 106 | 7 | 8 |
| 1319–20 | 18 | 0 | 0 | 1 | 1 | 0 | 146 | 0 | 0 |
| 1320–21 | 18 | 1 | 0 | 1 | 0 | 12 | 157 | 0 | 0 |
| 1321–22 | 14[2] | 0 | 0 | — | 1 | 16 | 92 | 19 | 10 |
| 1322–23 | 13[3] | 0 | 0 | 1 | 0 | 13 | 74 | 13 | 4 |
| 1323–24 | 11[4] | 0 | 0 | 1 | 0 | 6 | 72 | 6 | 0 |
| 1324–25 | 13[5] | 0 | 0 | 1 | 0 | 0 | 92 | 13 | 4 |
| 1325–26 | 12[6] | 0 | 0 | 1 | 0 | 0 | 73 | 6 | 8 |
| 1326–27 | 13[7] | 0 | 13 | — | — | — | 81 | 14 | 2 |
| 1327–28 | 13[8] | 1 | 22 | — | — | — | 74 | 5 | 4 |
| 1328–29 | 14[9] | 1 | 0 | — | — | — | 77 | 6 | 8 |
| 1329–30 | 14[10] | 0 | 21 | — | — | — | 76 | 16 | 0 |
| 1330–31 | 16[11] | 1 | 6 | — | — | — | 88 | 12 | 0 |

|  |  | £ | s. | d. |  |  |  | £ | s. | d. |
|---|---|---|---|---|---|---|---|---|---|---|
| [1] Price of one sack = | | 5 | 13 | 4 | [7] Price of one sack = | | | 6 | 3 | 4 |
| [2] ,, ,, ,, | | 6 | 6 | 8 | [8] ,, ,, ,, | | | 5 | 6 | 8 |
| [3] ,, ,, ,, | | 5 | 6 | 8 | [9] ,, ,, ,, | | | 5 | 6 | 8 |
| [4] ,, ,, ,, | | 6 | 0 | 0 | [10] ,, ,, ,, | | | 5 | 6 | 8 |
| [5] ,, ,, ,, | | 6 | 13 | 4 | [11] ,, ,, ,, | | | 5 | 6 | 8 |
| [6] ,, ,, ,, | | 5 | 13 | 0 | | | | | | |

It will be noticed that, whereas the peak period of wool production occurred in the years 1319–21—the very time that Henry of Eastry compiled his statistics of agistment—there was a marked decline in the later 'twenties. The cause of this shrinkage was, beyond any doubt, the long drought and flooding of the sea during the years 1324–26, which combined to play havoc with the stock of the Christ Church manors and killed no less than 4585 sheep.[1] The Canterbury flocks, caught between the upper and nether millstones of pestilence and flood, never recovered from this mortal blow. As we have seen in the previous chapter, the numbers of stock markedly declined before the middle of the fourteenth century. The drop in the output of Canterbury wool production faithfully reflected the general decline in sheep-farming which took place in England at this period. Not only were the sheep decimated by a succession of severe pestilences,[2] but Edward III's war taxation and the quasi-monopoly of the wool trade by the Merchant Staplers also served to limit wool production and to discourage sheep-farming. Some of the finest of the Canterbury sheep marshes in Thanet became depopulated, and the manor of Lyden saw a gradual dwindling of the flock that grazed on its spacious pastures.[3] On the Romney marsh, however, the numbers of sheep were maintained and even increased,[4] largely owing to the heroic labours expended on embankment and sea-defence. Right until the time when the marsh manors were leased out to *firmarii*, in the last quarter of the fourteenth century, the Romney pastures were always well stocked with Canterbury sheep. And, even then, the system of stock-and-land leases prevented the Romney flocks from undergoing any serious diminution in numbers.

.    .    .    .    .    .

[1] *Lit. Cant.* I, pp. 243–46.

[2] See H. Harrod, 'Some Details of a Murrain of the Fourteenth Century' in *Archaeologia* (1867), XLI, pp. 1–14. The writer gives some account of the severe murrains of 1348, 1363, 1369, and 1386.

[3] The number of sheep at Lyden shrank from 722 in 1331 to 509 in 1345, to 324 in 1357, and to 221 in 1375.

[4] At Orgarswick-and-Agney the flock rose from 177 in 1328 to 247 in 1350. In the latter half of the century the number was stabilized at about 250.

Although wool production was the most important feature in the pastoral economy of Christ Church, dairy-farming was also well developed on certain manors. By the latter half of the thirteenth century the manors of Ebony and Orgarswick-and-Agney in the Romney area, and of Monkton and Lyden in East Kent, were burdened with an annual food-farm of cheese.[1] Large quantities of cheese continued to be sent regularly to Canterbury from these manors throughout the first half of the succeeding century.[2] On the other hand, dairy-farming was undertaken on some manors solely with a view to market profits. It was natural that this should largely occur in the two non-Kentish custodies. All the dairy produce was marketed and the profits were remitted to Canterbury as part of the annual livery of the manor. Considerable quantities of dairy produce were also marketed on the manors which owed the food-farm of cheese.

In the two systems of dairy-farming which have just been illustrated—the one undertaken to feed the monks, the other to supply the market—it was usual for the cows and ewes involved to be part of the stock of the manor. In medieval times dairy-farming was a lesser activity, usually subordinate to cattle-rearing and wool production. Indeed it was often a by-product of these two types of farming. Stock, bred and reared for its meat and wool, would be diverted at due times and seasons to swell the manorial revenues by the production of its milk. On some manors, however, there were no large quantities of stock. If milk was required and if butter and cheese were to be made, the manorial executive hired cows or ewes (or both) in the seasons when they were 'in milk'. This occurred, for example, at the manor of Barksore in 1297–98, when 9 cows and 167 ewes were hired for their yield of milk. On the other hand, nothing was easier on small or predominantly corn-growing manors, where dairy-farming could not be organized on an effective scale, than to

[1] There is no evidence of this food-farm being rendered before 1260.
[2] In 1285–86, 7 weys (*pensae*) of cheese were sent to the treasurers from Orgarswick-and-Agney, a number which had risen to 10 in 1291–92 and to 27¾ weys in 1315–16. A peak point was reached in 1323–24, when 33 weys of cheese were sent to Canterbury.

lease out the cows and ewes during the milking season to *firmarii* for a cash sum. This policy was initiated on a number of Canterbury manors during the priorate of Henry of Eastry (1285–1331) and was increasingly adopted as the century proceeded. Its evolution can be traced on the manor of Meopham. At the beginning of Prior Eastry's rule a sufficient number of cows were retained at Meopham to realize a small market profit by the sale of their milk and the butter and cheese made therefrom. At the same time one cow was leased to the manorial *famuli* during the milking season for the sum of 2s. In the next Meopham account which I have examined, that for the year 1300–1, all the cows and ewes of the manor are shown to be leased out to a *firmarius*. In 1312–13 they were all farmed out in like manner and continued to be so for the rest of the century.[1]

A good example of one of these milk leases may be taken from the 1307–8 account of the serjeant of Chartham. The financial side of the account simply states that a profit of £5. 5s. 0d. has accrued from the lease of the milk of 30 cows, without calf, until Michaelmas (29 September) at the rate of 3s. 6d. per cow. A memorandum on the *dorso* of the same account recalls the fact that the leasehold value of the cows in question, *with* calf, is 4s. 6d. per head until Michaelmas. It goes on to state that the leasehold value of cows between the feast of St Michael (29 September) and the feast of St Andrew (30 November), when the milk rapidly deteriorated both in quantity and quality, is only 6d. It is most instructive to compare this statement with that of the anonymous author of *Hosebonderie*, who agrees that the yield of a cow's milk is worth 3s. 6d. between May and Michaelmas, but states that 'for all the other season' the yield is worth 10d.[2] He is clearly thinking of the whole seven months between Michaelmas and May and is therefore more comprehensive than the writer of the Chartham serjeant's account, who does not go beyond the last day of November. Walter of Henley viewed the problem in terms

---

[1] The manors of Bocking and Lalling in Essex also had their cows and ewes 'dimissis ad profectum' for a fixed annual sum during Henry of Eastry's priorate.

[2] 'An Anonymous Husbandry' in *Walter of Henley's Husbandry*, ed. E. Lamond (1890), p. 77.

of cheeses and declared that between Easter and Michaelmas a cow was worth 3s.[1] He made no estimate for the rest of the year.

Dairy-farming chiefly flourished on the marsh manors of Canterbury cathedral priory. Here, as we have shown, there were vast stretches of good pasture-land where the cows and ewes could be quartered. Manors like Monkton and Lyden in East Kent and Ebony and Orgarswick-and-Agney in the south-west of the county happily combined the three pursuits of sheep-breeding, cattle-rearing, and dairy-farming. The production of milk, butter, and cheese—which is the particular province of dairy-farming—took place largely in the summer months of the year. It usually began on the Canterbury estates a week or so earlier than the time contemplated by the writers of the treatises on estate management, for the feast of St George (23 April) was the date on which regular milking commenced. Calves and lambs were weaned somewhat earlier in the south-east of England than elsewhere. On the estates of Battle Abbey, most of which were in Sussex but of which one large manor was at Wye in Kent, milking actually began in the first week of April, a date which 'would have horrified Tusser'.[2]

A distinction was always made in the Canterbury accounts between butter, milk, and cheese de Rewanne (or, alternatively, Rowen) and the same commodities produced in the period between 23 April and Michaelmas. The word Rowen[3] clearly denoted the period between the end of September and 23 April, when milk was not readily forthcoming. Dairy products de Rewanne were always negligible in comparison with the late spring and summer yields.

[1] *Walter of Henley's Husbandry*, ed. E. Lamond (1890), p. 27. The value of a cow per head would, of course, tend to vary with the price of milk and the physical condition of the animal. Thus at Barksore in 1329–30 the *precium capitis* of a cow was said to be as high as 5s. during the milking season. At Hollingbourne, in 1323–24, five cows were worth 3s. 9d. per head, while two heifers were worth only 1s. 10½d. each.

[2] A. M. M. Melville, *The Pastoral Custom and Local Wool Trade of Medieval Sussex*, 1085–1485 (an unpublished London M.A. thesis), p. 88.

[3] Now a somewhat archaic expression for the second crop of hay in a season.

It has been shown that ewes were milked as well as cows.[1] Henry of Eastry calculated in 1322 that the 6000 ewes on the Canterbury estates yielded milk worth £96 a year.[2] The comparative value of cows and ewes for dairy purposes was a fertile subject of speculation in medieval England. Walter of Henley was of the opinion that 30 ewes, provided they were well pastured, ought to yield as much butter and cheese as 3 cows.[3] This gives us a ratio of 10 to 1. Memoranda on this subject were frequently written at the foot of the *dorso* of Canterbury serjeants' accounts. Stephen atte Broke, the Ebony serjeant, appears to have been in cordial agreement with Walter of Henley when he observed at the foot of his 1300–1 account 'Memorandum quod respondet de v vaccis ii pense casei et de xxv matricibus 1 pensa. Et de ii pensis casei 1 pensa butire.' Although he expressed the problem in slightly different terms, it will be seen that he came to the same conclusion as Walter of Henley, postulating a ratio of 10 to 1 for the comparative yield of a cow and a ewe.[4]

On the other hand, memoranda enrolled by the serjeants of Lyden revised the ratio established by Walter of Henley and confirmed by the serjeants of Ebony. In 1305 the Lyden serjeant wrote a 'memorandum quod debet respondere de v vaccis ii pense casei et de xxx matricibus 1 pensa. Et de iii pensis casei i pensa de butira.' This increased the ratio of cow to ewe from 10 to 1 to 12 to 1. The value of the two yields was made still more disproportionate when the serjeant of Lyden enrolled in 1319 a 'memorandum quod respondet de ii vaccis de Lyden i pensa et de xxv matricibus 1 pensa'. This gives a ratio of 12½ to 1. The serjeant went on to observe 'et de v vaccis de Estry, ii pense', a statement which, assuming that the yield from ewes was the same on both these neighbouring East Kent manors, affirmed for Eastry

---

[1] As a general practice 'ewe-milking ceased in autumn in order that the sheep might be in as good a condition as possible to meet the hardships of winter': Carrier, *op. cit.* p. 72.

[2] B.M. Cott. MS. Galba E iv, fo. 177.

[3] *Husbandry*, p. 27.

[4] This ratio was more than once re-affirmed by Ebony serjeants in their accounts of cheese production (e.g. in the 1319–20 account).

that ratio of 10 to 1 which was common to Walter of Henley
and the serjeants of Ebony.[1]

It should be emphasized that a ratio of the comparative yield
of cows and ewes varying from $12\frac{1}{2}$ to 10 to 1 was only applicable
to the best dairy-farms on the Canterbury estates, namely, those
in the pasture-lands of the south-west and east of Kent. For the
manor of Barksore, in the north-west of Kent, there was a very
different set of figures. In 1329–30 a sum of £4 was realized from
the milk yield of 16 cows on this manor. The commercial value
of each cow in milk was thus 5s. a year, an appreciably higher
figure than the 4s. 4d. postulated by the anonymous author of
'Husbandry'. On the other hand, 20 ewes in milk were only
worth $3\frac{1}{2}d.$ a head. This fixes the ratio of cows to ewes on the
manor of Barksore at just over 17 to 1. One is left with the conclusion that the ewes produced about a third less milk on manors
like Barksore than they did on the rich pasture-lands in other
parts of the county.

The dairies on the Canterbury estates were of a simple and
uniform kind; little more, perhaps, than rough wooden sheds.
The purchase of salt for the butter and cheese was the most common item of expenditure.[2] It was usually bought at the rate of
a bushel a year at Ebony. Presses (*pressurae*) for the cheese and
canvas (*canvenacium*) 'ad caseum imprimendum' were constantly
purchased, and churns, tins, spoons, and other utensils occur with
the frequency that one might expect. The overhead expenses incurred in running a dairy were never large; no elaborate technique
was employed.

The dairies were staffed by dairymen or dairymaids (*dayes*),

---

[1] Sometimes the serjeants of the Canterbury manors appended these
general calculations to the financial side of their accounts without writing
any memoranda on the *dorso*. Thus at Ebony, in 1319, the serjeant made
record of 'xiv pensis factis hoc anno, scilicet, de ii vaccis i pensa et de xxv
matricibus i pensa'. The summer was an unusually dry one and it may cause
no surprise that the serjeant had recourse to the $12\frac{1}{2}$ to 1 ratio which obtained
at Lyden. In the next year the normal ratio was restored, and the serjeant
accordingly accounted for $7\frac{1}{4}$ *pense* of cheese 'factis de lactagio vi vaccarum,
cxxix matricum, scilicet, de v vaccis ii pense et de xxv matricibus i pensa'.
In the next year the same ratio was observed with 8 cows and 133 ewes.

[2] A distinction was often made between *sal grossum* and *sal album*.

one or more in number, and on the more important manors a professional cheesemaker (*caseator*) was employed. On manors where dairy-farming was conducted on a more modest scale, like Barksore, there were no specialized officials, if the list of *solidata* given to farm-servants is a fair indication. No doubt the *vaccarius*, *bercarius*, or *custos agnorum* on this manor would do the milking and assist in the cheese production.

As a marketable commodity cheese quite eclipsed butter and milk in importance. The sale of butter and milk was never conducted on a large scale, but cheeses were often sold in great quantities. The Essex manors lay in an important area for cheese production,[1] and the records of the Kentish manors also yield some very interesting results. A description of cheese production on the Kentish estates during Henry of Eastry's priorate will illustrate this branch of dairy-farming at its most flourishing period.

A little cheese was sometimes made in the autumn and winter (*caseum de Rewanne*), but the manufacture was largely confined to the 160 days stretching between the feast of St George on 23 April and the feast of St Michael on 29 September.[2] The manor of Ebony normally achieved a rate of production of one cheese a day during these late spring and summer months.[3] Between 1291 and 1306 the serjeants of this manor always recorded the production of exactly 160 cheeses. After 1306 they based their statistics on the weight of the cheeses and thus concealed the numbers produced. The manor of Orgarswick-and-Agney always seems to have produced a larger number of cheeses than Ebony,[4] while at Monkton no less than 985 cheeses were made in the year 1314–15. The two East Kent manors of Monkton and Lyden accounted between them for a very large number.

Figures based purely on the number of cheeses produced are, however, somewhat deceptive. Cheeses varied in size, and it is

---

[1] See Nichols, *op. cit.* p. 209.

[2] At Ebony in the years 1301–2 and 1302–3 the serjeant explicitly distinguished between butter, milk, and cheese *de Rewanne* and *in estate*.

[3] Some cheese was sometimes made out of the *colostrum*, the milk yielded by the cow directly after calving. .

[4] 196 cheeses were produced in this manor in 1285–86, 301 in 1291–92, and 350 in 1298–99. After this date the cheeses were calculated by weight.

therefore more useful to calculate the total weight of the output. The standard of measurement used on the Canterbury estates was the wey (*pensa*), which represented 32 great pounds *secundum pondus Lanfranci*.[1] On this basis the 985 cheeses of Monkton were said to weigh 66 weys, while at Orgarswick-and-Agney, in 1315–16 and 1323–24, weights of 36 and 39 weys were attained. These figures give us some indication of the important part played by cheese production on the large dairy-farms of Kent.

It is impossible to speak with precision of the character of the cheeses. We are told that, in the middle ages, 'cheese was made either of skimmed milk, or at least a portion of the butter was abstracted'.[2] There is much evidence that rennet (*rennet* or *coagula*) was used on the Canterbury dairy-farms for cheese production. It was usually purchased from outside the manor. ' The common practice', says Rogers, 'was to make up the curd into small cheeses, described as largest, middle, and least shape',[3] a statement which is fully substantiated by the Canterbury evidence. Thus at Ebony, in 1318–19, 48 cheeses of the largest size (*majoris forme*) were made,. of which 10 weighed one wey. 77 cheeses of the middle size (*medie forme*), of which 14 weighed one wey, were made, and 36 of the smallest size of cheese (*caseum minoris forme*), of which 18 made a wey, were also produced.

In East Kent cheeses of much smaller size were made. At Monkton, for example, in 1302–3 the largest size weighed $\frac{1}{16}$th, the middle size $\frac{1}{24}$th, and the smallest size only $\frac{1}{36}$th, of a wey. The smallest type of cheese was the one most frequently made at Monkton, and this is the very reverse of what occurred in the manors of the Romney area. Similarly, the cheeses made on the East Kent manor of Lyden were much smaller than those produced in the Romney and Walland district.[4] This marked difference in

---

[1] Canterbury Register B, fo. 423 v. By the royal standard of measurement, used for the Canterbury wool, the wey represented only 26 great pounds.

[2] Thorold Rogers, *The History of Agriculture and Prices*, I, p. 403.

[3] *Ibid.*

[4] Thus in 1304–5 the largest type of Lyden cheese weighed only $\frac{1}{24}$th of a wey, a cheese of the middle size weighed $\frac{1}{26}$th of a wey (it was the type of cheese most often produced this year) and one of the smallest size weighed $\frac{1}{32}$nd of a wey.

the size of the cheeses must always be borne in mind when the relative cheese production of the two regions of Kent is in question.[1]

At Lyden cows were hired from the neighbouring manor of Eastry for the specific purpose of yielding milk for cheese. In 1317–18, 22 weys of cheese were made at Lyden between 23 April and Michaelmas from the milk yield of 32 cows and 120 ewes belonging to the manor, and from the yield of 18 cows hired from Eastry during the milking season. In the next year 13 cows were hired from Eastry and 5 from elsewhere for summer milking.[2] It would seem that this practice of hiring cows and ewes for the limited purpose of cheese production was common on the neighbouring Christ Church manors.[3]

The disposal of the cheeses depended primarily, of course, on whether the manor on which they were produced owed a food-farm to the priory or was free to remit a lump sum of cash to the treasurers. If a manor fell into the first category, the largest cheeses were sent to the prior's household, while others were carried to the cellarer for consumption in the monastic household. On every manor which has been studied some cheeses were sold. At Monkton, for example, 22 out of 23 weys were sold in 1307–8, and in 1314–15 no less than 32 out of 34 weys were marketed.[4]

---

[1] The cheeses made at Orgarswick-and-Agney in the Romney Marsh were even larger than those of Ebony. Thus in 1292–93, 91 cheeses were sent to the cellarer weighing 11 weys (i.e. a single of these cheeses weighed nearly $\frac{1}{8}$th of a wey). 14 cheeses were sent to the prior weighing $2\frac{1}{2}$ weys. Each one of these therefore weighed between $\frac{1}{5}$th and $\frac{1}{6}$th of a wey. 110 cheeses weighing $11\frac{1}{2}$ weys were sold. Each one of this type must have weighed between $\frac{1}{9}$th and $\frac{1}{10}$th of a wey.

[2] '...et de xiii vaccis de Eastry et de v vaccis alienis conductis ad lactandum in estate'—serjeant's account, Lyden, 1318–19.

[3] Thus there was a constant transfer of cows from Appledore to the neighbouring manor of Ebony, in the Isle of Oxney, during the milking season.

[4] Again, at Lyden in 1298–99, 349 cheeses weighing $28\frac{3}{4}$ weys were manufactured. 16 of these cheeses weighing 2 weys (each, therefore, weighing $\frac{1}{8}$th of a wey) were sent to the prior and 304 cheeses weighing 24 weys (nearly $\frac{1}{13}$th of a wey each) were directed to the cellarer. Cheeses weighing $2\frac{1}{2}$ weys (about $\frac{1}{12}$th of a wey each) were sold.

It is to be observed that on most manors less cheeses were sent
to the prior and cellarer and more were marketed as the priorate
of Henry of Eastry proceeded. In the last years of his rule nearly
all the cheeses were marketed. This noticeable change in the
course of cheese currents may be attributed partly to the fact
that 'during the years 1311–1330 the price of cheese is exceptionally high',[1] and partly to the growth of local markets for this
commodity.

At Monkton the increase in the sales of dairy produce during
Henry of Eastry's priorate is very noticeable. In 1306 the profits
came to £8. 4s. 0d., in 1308 to £12. 3s. 0d., and in 1315 to
£20. 16s. 0d. This denoted over a 100 per cent increase in profits
in eight years. The figures for the manor of Lyden are equally
arresting.[2] But after the great pestilence of 1327, some four years
before Henry of Eastry's death, dairy-farming participated in that
general decline of stock-farming which took place on the Canterbury estates and throughout the country at large. By the middle
of the century dairy profits had shrunk to half their former size
and rapidly dwindled,[3] until they ceased altogether with the
advent of the leasehold system in the last decade of the century.

[1] Rogers, op. cit. p. 405.
[2] Dairy profits rose at Lyden from £4. 2s. 8d. in 1291–92 to £10. 17s. 6d.
in 1304–5 and £14. 0s. 1d. in 1317–18.
[3] For example, at Lyden there was a steady decline in dairy profits from
£13. 6s. 4d. in 1344–45 to £6. 7s. 6d. in 1374–75.

M

## Chapter Eleven

### MARSH EMBANKMENT, LAND DRAINAGE, AND SEA DEFENCE

No account of the monks of Christ Church as landowners would be at all complete without some estimate of their achievements, sustained and often remarkable, in embanking marshes and defending the coast against the inundation of the sea. It will be necessary, first of all, to give some description of that *lex marisci*, or body of marsh laws and customs, which acted as the administrative framework within which individual enterprise was conducted. There is abundant evidence that marsh embankment on the Canterbury estates goes back as an organized and regularized activity, subject to precise conditions, to a very early date. It can certainly be traced to the first half of the twelfth century when, in the reign of Henry I (1100–35), grants of land at Appledore were made by the prior of Christ Church on the condition that the tenants 'engage to maintain the walls and sewers against the salt and fresh water, and as often as there should be need, to repair and strengthen them, according to the law of the marsh'.[1] The earliest account-rolls show the monks fulfilling these obligations on their individual manors in accordance with that local custom which already had the binding force of law.[2] By the middle of the thirteenth century there had crystallized a comprehensive *consuetudo marisci*, built up on an empirical basis from many scattered sources and having the status of *antiquae et approbatae*

---

[1] M. Teichman Derville, *The Level and the Liberty of Romney Marsh*, p. 5, who quotes as his evidence land-grants enrolled in Registers A and B in the Dean and Chapter Library, Canterbury. See, also, E. Hasted, *The History of Kent*, VIII, p. 467.

[2] Thus in 1225 a sum of £1. 10s. 2½d. was spent at Appledore, and £2. 7s. 4½d. at Ebony, on the upkeep of walls and sewers: Cant. MS. M 13, xix, mem. 1.

*consuetudines.*[1] Marsh tenements and marsh lands were clearly distinguished from other land in a given village or manor by the customary division of land into upland and marshland, the former being called *terra montana* and *terra susanna* or *suseyne.*[2]

The severe storms which in the middle and latter half of the thirteenth century wrought havoc on the Kentish coastline and the movement towards governmental centralization, which is another feature of the period, now combined to give further clarity and definition to the *lex marisci.* Royal statute and royal ordinance gradually replaced local and regional custom. The initial step was taken in 1252. In that year Henry III granted a charter to the twenty-four lawful and sworn men of Romney Marsh in confirmation of the privilege which they had enjoyed from time immemorial of levying a proportionate contribution upon all holding lands and tenements in the marsh, to be applied to the maintenance of the walls and watercourses. The king also confirmed the exemption of the men of the marsh from the sheriff of the county and the royal bailiff; appeal was to be made to the king's court or to justices appointed by the king's 'especial mandate'.[3]

Six years later, on hearing that some marsh-dwellers had resisted the execution of repairs assigned to them, Henry III appointed his justiciar, Henry of Bath, to hear complaints and see to the necessary repairs of walls and watercourses. At a representative assembly of the men of the marsh at Romney, at which the sheriff of Kent was present, Henry of Bath drew up those ordinances which are the fundamental source for the history of marsh administration. Having ordered the election of twelve lawful men

---

[1] For a detailed discussion of the growth and evolution of the *consuetudo et lex marisci,* with special reference to the estates of Bilsington Priory, which held land in and about Romney Marsh, see N. Neilson, *The Cartulary and Terrier of the Priory of Bilsington, Kent* (British Academy), pp. 39–56.

[2] *Ibid.* p. 55.

[3] The charter is printed in full in *The Charters of Romney Marsh, or the Laws and Customs of Romney Marsh* (1846 ed., English only) 1, and (in Latin and English) in M. Teichman Derville, *op. cit.* pp. 73–74. Its *inspeximus* and confirmation by Edward II in 1313 is contained in *Cal. Let. Pat.* 7 Edward II, pp. 75–76.

to measure old and new walls and land as yet unembanked by the standard marsh rod of 20 feet, the royal justiciar confirmed the jurisdiction of the twenty-four elected and sworn men, whose right it was to levy proportionate contributions from all land-holders in the marsh for the upkeep of the embankment and drainage system. The common bailiff of the marsh was to act as the executive of the *jurati*, and those who failed to render the proportion assigned to them were to be forced to pay *duplum*, that is, double costs.[1]

The royal authority delegated in this manner to Henry of Bath was 'in essence a commission of sewers' and 'may be regarded as beginning the regular series of commissions of sewers'.[2] The floods and heavy storms on the coast of Kent soon called for further commissions and ordinances. In 1285 the marshes of East Kent received a similar organization to that of Romney Marsh.[3] The ferocious storms of the year 1287–88, which changed the course of the river Rother, destroyed all the walls, and flooded nearly all the lands between the great wall of Appledore and Winchelsea,[4] served to complete the administrative organization of the Kentish marshes. In the years 1288–90 the Walland and Denge and other marshes stretching between the Romney Marsh and the county of Sussex, the marshes in south-east Kent in the hundreds of Eastry and Cornilo, the marshes in the Isle of Thanet, and those on the banks of the Thames in the north of the county, all received their separate organization by the way of royal com-mission and ordinances.[5] Those common features, which found full expression in the ordinances of Henry of Bath and which may well have represented the growth of centuries,[6] were applied in

[1] B.M. Cott. MS. Galba E iv, fo. 148.

[2] H. G. Richardson, 'The Early History of Commissions of Sewers' in *Eng. Hist. Rev.* XXXIV, p. 391.

[3] Sir William Dugdale, *History of the Imbanking and Draining of divers Fens and Marshes, both in foreign parts and in this Kingdom, and of the Improvements thereby* (1772 ed.), pp. 36–38.

[4] Gervase, *Opera*, II, p. 293.

[5] B.M. Cott. MS. Galba E iv, fos. 148–52, summarized by H. G. Richardson, *op. cit.* pp. 390–91.

[6] Miss Neilson suggests (*op. cit.* p. 44) that all these royal ordinances were in the main 'affirming local custom'.

each case to the marsh area under consideration. The elected and sworn men (*jurati*), the common bailiff, the system of proportionate contribution, and the threat of *duplum* (double costs), obtained everywhere in the marsh districts of Kent and, indeed, served as the pattern which the whole kingdom would eventually adopt.[1]

Thus by 1290, five years after Henry of Eastry's accession, all the Kentish estates of Christ Church which lay in marshland districts were forced into a common administrative system. Before studying the embanking and draining operations on the Canterbury manors, it is therefore necessary to give some short account of the working of this administrative system and its relation to private enterprise in the areas which it covered.

There is ample evidence to show that the royal ordinances were in the main effectively executed in the reigns of Edward I and Edward II. Offenders against the marsh laws and the decrees of the *jurati* were regularly prosecuted.[2] Henry of Eastry was once so prosecuted, in the year 1312, for diverting a watercourse,[3] and commissions *de walliis et fossatis* were issued with increasing frequency.[4] We also have evidence that lands were measured for assessment,[5] the accounts of the collectors of contributions have survived in at least one instance,[6] and record remains of the common meeting or last of the officials and commonalty of Romney Marsh. The meeting of the last of Romney Marsh at Snargate in 1287 is so instructive in its detail that its deliberations may be briefly summarized. The twenty-four *jurati*, the landholders of the marsh (*domini feodorum*), and their representatives, decreed that a new wall should be built at Holewest where once a jetty

---

[1] Thus William Lambard was able to write in 1570 (in his *Perambulation of Kent*, pp. 180–81) that the ordinances of Henry of Bath had 'now become a paterne and exemplar to all the like places of the whole Realme whereby to be governed'.

[2] See the cases listed in Dugdale, *op. cit. passim.*

[3] *Ibid.* p. 41.      [4] *Ibid. passim.*

[5] For example, the measurement of land in the south-east marshes of Kent and of the Canterbury estates in the Romney Marsh are contained in B.M. Cott. MS. Galba E iv, fos. 151 v.–152.

[6] B.M. Cott. MS. Cleopatra C vii, fo. 43.

(*geteya*) had been erected. They gave their opinion that the land could not otherwise be saved from flooding unless such a wall be built 12 feet high and of a given length and breadth. The work should begin on the Monday in the octave of the feast of the Purification and after a month the wall should have reached the height of 6 feet. It should be finished before Easter. The archbishop and prior of Canterbury were made responsible for the east side of the wall, the rest of the cost was to be borne by other marsh lords.[1]

These details should leave no doubt as to the translation into practice of the principles of marsh administration set forth in Henry of Bath's ordinances. They appear to have been universally enforced throughout the marsh districts of Kent during the period of Eastry's priorate. In the light of this knowledge it would seem tempting to suppose that private enterprise and private initiative in land drainage and sea defence were largely or entirely superseded by this all-embracing system of public control. Indeed Miss Neilson has lent her great authority to the statement that 'with the organization of royal control of the marshes the lord's private actions in recovery of land from the sea were necessarily limited and superseded'.[2]

Now there is one class of documents which should prove conclusive in this respect: the serjeant's accounts, which detail the annual financial receipts and expenditure of single manors. For the estates of Christ Church, Canterbury, five of the manors fall within the marsh area and have numerous accounts extant. The five manors in question are Ebony, Appledore, and Orgarswick-and-Agney in the West Kent and Romney Marsh area, and Monkton and Lyden in the East Kent marshes. The collective witness which their accounts afford is quite conclusive. The common contribution (or common scot, as it is called) invariably and without exception coexisted with private expenditure on embankment, drainage, and sea defence on the part of the serjeant of the manor. Moreover, the private expenditure nearly always entailed a greater outlay than the common scot. In some years no

[1] B.M. Cott. MS. Cleopatra C vii, fo. 36.
[2] Neilson, *op. cit.* p. 52.

scot was paid at all, although large sums were expended on private embankment. One is forced to the conclusion that the common scot was only levied for severely limited purposes and that the greatest scope was given to landholders who wished to reclaim land and to erect embankments and drain lands on their own initiative. The examples of Appledore and Orgarswick-and-Agney, two Romney Marsh manors, should clinch the argument. The Appledore wall, which consisted of a *magna wallia* and *parva wallia*, was at this time the principal sea-defence work in the Romney Marsh area.[1] An early fourteenth-century document in the Chapter Library, Canterbury, tells us exactly which lands of the priory owe scot to this wall; 21½ acres in Appledore, 185½ acres in Rocking, 77 acres in Benequik, and 137½ acres in Orgarswick are so burdened, making a total of 421½ acres.[2] When we turn to the serjeants' accounts of Appledore and Orgarswick for our period, we see that scot is also levied for certain other defence works (e.g. the wall of Scherle at Appledore and certain watercourses at Orgarswick) but in every case for which we have evidence the scot is only a very small part of the total annual outlay on embankment. Thus at Appledore in 1315–16 the scots for the wall and the new dyke near the jetty amounted to £1. 1s. 5d., only a small fraction of the £8. 4s. 10d. which the serjeant thought fit to expend in his private capacity. Again, in the year 1321–22, the scots at Appledore amounted to only 6s. in a total outlay of £8. 3s. 2d. The manor of Orgarswick tells a similar story. In 1291–92 scots came to 10s. 11d. in an expenditure of £4. 9s. 11d. and in 1301–2 totalled 14s. 8d. in an outlay of £3. 13s. 2d.

To sum up the first part of our enquiry. The marsh manors of Canterbury cathedral priory were subject to the *consuetudo et lex marisci*, crystallized by royal statute and ordinance. They were allotted their share in the common burdens of marsh embankment, drainage, and sea defence, and were assessed for common scot. The widest scope was, however, given to private enterprise

---

[1] M. Teichman Derville, *op. cit.* pp. 7–8. See also A. J. Burrows, 'Romney Marsh, Past and Present' in *Trans. of the Surveyors' Institution* (1885), XVII, pp. 335–76.     [2] Canterbury MS. M 169.

and initiative and it seems quite certain that the priors of Canterbury were in no way limited or superseded in their private actions for the recovery, embankment, and drainage of land.

As a complete description of embanking operations on the Canterbury estates in the later middle ages is clearly impracticable, a study of the Kentish marsh manors during the priorate of Henry of Eastry, 1285–1331, that high-water mark of Christ Church economy, will give some indication of the work that was performed. The marsh manors fall conveniently into three groups; those in the Romney Marsh and south-west Kent area, namely Ebony, Appledore, and Orgarswick-and-Agney; Lyden and Monkton in East Kent; and the manors of Seasalter and Cliffe in the north of the shire.

The church of Canterbury had made its influence felt at an early date in the marshes of south-west Kent. The Walland marsh, lying to the west of the Romney Marsh, was systematically reclaimed by the archbishops in the twelfth and thirteenth centuries when a series of 'innings' or land reclamations took place, which were associated with the names of Archbishops Becket, Baldwin, Boniface, and Pecham.[1] When in the later thirteenth century the total acreage of land in the Romney Marsh belonging to the Barony and the Liberty of the church of Canterbury was measured and assessed, the following return was made. In the whole marsh lying between the great wall of Appledore and Hythe there were 17,300 acres; of which the church of Canterbury owned no less than 7140 acres, that is between $\frac{1}{3}$ and $\frac{1}{2}$ of the total area. 5450 acres belonged to the archbishop, leaving the cathedral priory with 1690 acres, of which 433 were held in demesne and 1257 in the hands of the tenants.[2] When we add to this Romney Marsh estate the lands of the archbishop in the Walland and Denge marshes and the possessions of the priory on the Isle of Oxney and at Appledore, some idea may be gained of the most powerful territorial interest which the two lords of Canterbury, archbishop and prior, had in the improvement of the south-west marshes of Kent.

[1] R. Furley, *A History of the Weald of Kent*, II, pt. 2, pp. 767–68.
[2] B.M. Cott. MS. Galba E iv, fo. 152.

But it is with the priory we are concerned and so, leaving the archbishop and the improvement of his estates on one side, let us begin by considering the priory's manor of Ebony. The greater part of this manor lay on the Isle of Oxney beyond the north-west boundary of the Romney Marsh. It was bounded on the north and east by the river Rother and chiefly consisted of very low-lying, wet, and swampy marshes.[1] There appears to have been no rent-paying tenantry resident in the manor during Henry of Eastry's lifetime. Hired servants or *famuli* performed the necessary agricultural and embanking operations, and no less than 87 per cent of the revenue was derived from the sale of corn, stock, and dairy produce. Thus the amount of capital available for embanking operations in any given year depended to a large extent on the state of the market. It must, however, be noticed (and this observation applies to all the Canterbury manors here studied) that the farms and cash sums paid annually to the central treasury at Canterbury remained flexible in their nature and varied greatly from year to year. In a bad year, therefore, the 'farm' (in this case, cheese and wool) and the money payment could be severely curtailed in such a way as to enable the manor to maintain its financial stability.

The extent of market profits and the demands of the food-farm were two of the three principal factors determining capital invest-ment on embankment; the third was, of course, the influence of meteorological conditions which is, in its turn, linked intimately to the first two factors. In years of great floods and storms invest-ment in embankment and drainage had to be made, even if it ruined the annual balance-sheet. The most glaring instance may be taken from the neighbouring manor of Appledore at the time of the great floods in the early 'nineties of the thirteenth century. In 1293–94 it was found necessary to run up a bill of £128. 14s. 9d. for banking operations on this manor in spite of the fact that the revenue only amounted to £74. 3s. 0d. The common scot was another external demand made on the revenue of the manor but was, as we have seen, of secondary importance, being usually trivial in amount.

[1] E. Hasted, *The History of Kent*, VIII, pp. 493–94.

The principal conditions governing the supply of capital having been briefly stated, we may now ask ourselves the question: on what was it invested? What processes were undertaken? On the manor of Ebony there were several occasions when land was inned (*intrare*), that is, reclaimed and rendered fit for cultivation and grazing, during Eastry's priorate. Take, for example, the strip of land going by the name of *Prioratus*.[1] An embankment known as the *vetus walla* was already in existence here on Eastry's accession, and 80 perches of it were strengthened in 1286–87. In the following year 28 acres of land were inned at a cost of £3. 10s. 0d. and a new embankment (*nova walla*) was erected at the same time as the old one continued to be strengthened. In 1289–90 the *nova walla* was raised in height and given greater solidity while the strengthening of the *vetus walla* still proceeded. By the year 1301 it was possible for this newly 'inned' strip of land to be leased for an annual rent of £2, which had increased to £3 in 1317.

Or again, consider the piece of land called *Ovenhamme*. As in the previous example, some kind of embankment already existed here at Eastry's accession, 32 perches of which were strengthened in 1286–87. In the year 1287–88, £6. 5s. 0d. was spent on 'inning' this land and in the next three years the new embankments were given greater height and strength. New ditches or dykes were made as the necessary complement to the wall defence. After the year 1301 we hear no more of expenditure on the land called *Ovenhamme*; it appears to have been successfully reclaimed.

It will be noticed that the 'inning' of these two pieces of land coincided with the great storms and floods of the end of the thirteenth century. A somewhat later instance may be taken from the year 1304–5, when a section of expenditure in the serjeant's account is grouped under the significant heading of *Custos novi marisci*. The 'inning' of marsh land here demanded the erection of a wooden wall. Timber was therefore cut down and some indication of the magnitude of the operation is given by the

---

[1] I have examined the 1840 Tithe Maps in the custody of the Tithe Redemption Commission and find that it is impossible to reconstruct the field-systems of the manors here studied. Very few of the thirteenth- and fourteenth-century field-names have survived.

record that fifty-four carts as well as a boat were hired for transporting it to the site of the *nova walla*. Dykes were made, the
land was levelled, and the total cost of the intake in this year
amounted to £4. 18s. 6d.

After 1305 there is no evidence of marsh land being reclaimed
on the manor of Ebony to any appreciable extent. There are,
however, several other interesting features. The effect of the
gradual drying of reclaimed land is to lower the surface by some
2 or 3 feet. The land, therefore, becomes more liable to inundation
after reclamation than before. This fact seems to explain the
constant efforts made on the manor of Ebony to guard and maintain the new embankments and dykes and to prevent the re-
flooding of the land. Take as an example the area of land called
*le Neulonde* or *Nova Terra*. In all the Ebony serjeants' accounts—
twenty in number—which I have examined for Eastry's priorate,
this piece of land occurs in no less than twelve different years in
connection with banking and ditching operations. The bank was
constantly faced, strengthened, and topped, a hedge was erected
to give additional strength, and stones and sand were introduced
into the fabric. The total cost of embanking *le Neulonde* in the
twelve years noticed amounted to £7. 8s. 8d.

The land which lay around the Reading ferry (*passagium de
Redynge*) on the north side of the manor also required constant
attention. The Reading sewer (as it is now called) was a major
watercourse and the siding and topping of its embankments was
accompanied by the application of quantities of straw. Three
dams were made here in 1317–18 (presumably of wooden piles,
if the analogy of other parts of the manor is valid) and the embankment figures prominently in 50 per cent of the accounts that have
been studied. A careful distinction was made between the embankment *ex parte occidentali* and *ex parte orientali* of the Reading ferry
and equal attention appears to have been bestowed on both sides.

The problem of the materials used in these embanking operations admits of no easy solution. Timber, as we have seen, was
used for the wall defence of newly reclaimed land. Straw and
stones were also employed for consolidating existing defence
works which, I suspect, largely consisted of clay. The manor is

characterized by a clayey soil (as are nearly all marsh districts) and clay is the material most commonly employed in embankment where it is obtainable. The fact that the costs of labour are always given in the accounts, while on the contrary the costs of materials are only occasionally cited, would seem in itself to suggest that the thick clayey soil of the neighbourhood was the staple embanking material. It may also be conjectured with high probability that turf and peat-moss and other kindred material were frequently employed. Let it be noticed also that the facing, strengthening, topping, and siding of embankments, which went on constantly in our period, would necessarily call for the application of material which was local and easily obtainable. Lastly, the fact that the raising and strengthening of embankments and the making and clearing of ditches commonly proceeded at the same time in the same stretches of land (thus facilitating the transfer of material from the one to the other) would seem to be proof conclusive that clay, turf, and the native marsh soils were the staple and primary banking materials.

The erection and maintenance of embankments, together with the reclamation of new land, went hand in hand with other processes appropriate to a marsh manor. Levelling and enclosure were two of these operations. The year 1287–88 affords us the interesting statement '*in terra coequanda ad novam breccam—iis. iid.*' Plainly land, after reclamation, required to be levelled before cultivation was possible, and here we have a capital instance of the process in question. The study of enclosure on the manor raises several interesting problems. What type of enclosure obtained there, and what was the main purpose of such closures? Enclosure proceeded in two principal ways, by hedges and by a system of cross-dykes, and seems to have had at least two and probably three objectives, namely, to strengthen embankments, to exclude cattle from certain parts of the manor and, alternately, to confine cattle and sheep within certain well-defined areas.

That hedges were employed as a form of supplementary embankment may be illustrated from the statement in the serjeant's account of 1303–4 to the effect that 1s. 6d. was spent *in sepe facta contra Wallam de Newelonde*. Or again, in the year 1305–6 there is record of three hedges made *in nova terra*. But the system of enclosure by cross-dykes was more common than the erection of hedges. Indeed the heading *Fossatura et Clausura* frequently occurs in the serjeants' accounts. Many examples might be given. In 1303–4, 47 perches of land were dug and enclosed *circa Goldwode et Forstal*. In 1317–18, 1 furlong, 37 perches of land were dug and enclosed between the two sections named *le Drove* and *Shepetegh* and in the following year the 2½ furlongs between these plots of land and neighbouring territory were also ditched and enclosed. As the land enclosed was usually cultivated (witness the grange accounts) the enclosures would seem to have served the twin purposes of embanking land and excluding cattle.

A system of cross-dykes was also employed for the purpose of confining cattle within certain areas. For example, embankment and enclosure takes place *contra pasturam vaccarum* and the land called *Shepetegh*, a subject of enclosure both in 1305–6 and in the years 1317–19, was almost certainly a sheep-pasture.

There is no direct evidence of enclosure on the manor of Ebony before 1302, but after that year the use of the word *clausura* and the description of the process become a commonplace. The absence of a manorial tenantry would certainly make the problem of enclosure simpler and more convenient than elsewhere.

The drainage system of the manor seems to have been efficiently maintained during our period. The Reading sewer served as a natural marsh-dyke or water-fence for the outlet of water from the subsidiary drains and cross-dykes. Communicating sluices were established, as may be seen from the expenditure *in sulcis aquaticis aperiendis* for the year 1320–21. Dams were erected both in the Reading sewer[1] and the manorial dykes[2] and appear to have consisted largely of wooden piles.

It was never possible to grow wheat on a large scale on the manor of Ebony in Eastry's priorate. Most of the land, newly embanked and sodden, was certainly on the economic margin

---

[1] In the year 1317–18, three dams were erected *juxta passagium de Redynge* at a cost of 9s.

[2] In 1305–6, 5s. was spent *in dammys et gutteris reparandis et emendandis per loca*.

of cultivation and oats was always the staple crop. Figures taken
for the whole of the period show us that 75·6 per cent of the
cultivated area of the manor was under oats, 15·6 per cent under
wheat, 6·6 per cent under legumes (i.e. beans and vetches) and
2·2 per cent under rye. The crop rotations and field-systems were
appropriate to a marsh district where oats was the predominant
cereal crop. Attention has been drawn to the very small size of
the *campi* or fields in marsh districts,[1] and the manor of Ebony
exemplifies this truth. Here are some typical rotations taken from
the years 1317–20. *Opperhassoke,* a field of 5 acres, followed the
sequence oats, fallow, oats. *Opper Appletone,* 3 acres in extent,
was fallowed the first year and then sown with oats for two successive seasons. *Magna Palstre,* a field of 10 acres, held to a
sequence of wheat, fallow and vetches. *Magna Donne,* a 17-acre
field, was sown with wheat in its first year, half of it was then
fallowed and the other half sown with beans, and in the third year
the whole area was again sown with wheat. The field-systems
display the greatest diversity in rotation and sequence, ringing
the changes on oats, wheat, legumes, fallow and semi-fallow in
many different ways.[2] The serjeants certainly showed no lack
of experimental zeal in this respect.

Some general conclusions on the economy of the manor of
Ebony during the period of Eastry's priorate may now be stated.
In the first fifteen years or so of that *régime* considerable sums were
expended on the embankment and reclamation of land. In 1287–88,
the year of the great floods and storms, no less than 60 per cent
of the revenue was spent on 'inning' and embankment, and
39 per cent of the revenue was devoted to these objects in 1289–90.
Such high figures as these do not occur again; the 26 per cent of
the revenue expended on embanking operations in 1329–30 was
the next highest proportion and that is exceptional for the latter
two-thirds of the priorate. A general view of the whole priorate
shows that on average 14·2 per cent of the annual revenue of the
manor was devoted to embankment and drainage.

[1] N. Neilson, *op. cit.* p. 62.
[2] Oats appear to have been nearly always the initial crop sown on newly
reclaimed land.

In spite of all this activity little or no permanent increase of the area under cultivation was made. In 1286, there were 141 acres of land under cultivation and that number had only increased to 148 at the time of Henry of Eastry's death in 1331. It is true that in the middle of the priorate the acreage did make a considerable increase, reaching a maximum figure of 197 in 1319. This was largely the result of the increase in the area under wheat which was made possible by the assiduous dressing of the soil with dung, marl, and lime. When the dressing was abandoned, however, the area under cultivation shrank in proportion as the acreage under wheat declined. Only 114 acres were cultivated in 1330, 27 less than at the beginning of the priorate. When marl was again applied in the last year of Eastry's rule, 34 more acres were brought under cultivation, but the final acreage figures mark only a very small advance on the initial figures. Thus it is necessary to conclude that, in spite of the large expense devoted to reclaiming, embanking, draining, and dressing the land, no adequate return was made for the capital invested. Even the number of sheep and cattle pastured made no appreciable increase. There were 60 cows on the manor in 1286 and only 27 in the last two years of the priorate; the 137 ewes pastured in 1286 had only increased in number to 166 at the time of Eastry's death. The natural poverty of the soil, the recurrence of floods,[1] the presence of famine, all have to be taken into account as militating against the success of the embanking operations pursued so indefatigably on the manor of Ebony during Henry of Eastry's priorate.

The case of Ebony, so rich in extant serjeants' accounts for our period, has been considered at some length. It is proposed to treat more briefly of the other Kentish manors, none of which has a comparable series of serjeants' accounts. The manor of Appledore lies immediately to the east of the Isle of Oxney and has a wide belt of marshland on its southern side. When Henry of Eastry was prior of Canterbury the great wall of Appledore was the main defence work of Romney Marsh, and dwellers in the region paid common scot for the upkeep of that structure. The change in the

---

[1] For example, land sown with rye was flooded in 1320–21 and pasture was flooded in 1323–24.

course of the river Rother in 1287 and the fierce storms which destroyed the great wall of Appledore and other embankments in 1288 certainly had a catastrophic effect on the manor of Appledore. Five years later the serjeant of the manor found it necessary to incur embanking costs to the extent of £128. 14s. 9d. in spite of the fact that his revenue only amounted to £74. 3s. 0d. Against the record of expenditure he appended the cryptic remark *non alocantur* [*sic*], evidence that the floods and geological changes had caused him grievous financial embarrassment. However the financial equilibrium of the manor was restored at least by the second decade of the fourteenth century and a vigorous policy of reclamation and embankment was pursued.

In contrast to Ebony there was at Appledore a considerable body of rent-paying tenants, who at the time we are considering paid annual rents amounting collectively to over £32. The manor resembled Ebony, however, in having most of the embanking work performed by hired labour. It is interesting to notice that considerable sections of the marshland were let out on lease.

The reclamation and embankment of land appear to have proceeded here on a most elaborate scale. Consider first the 'inning' operations of 1293–94. The very large expenditure detailed under the heading *Novus introitus* for that year shows a number of technical processes to which the neighbouring manor affords no parallel. Timber was cut down in large quantities and borne in boats to the *nova walla*, there to be converted into poles (*poles*) and scaffolding (*weytrowes*) by a carpenter. Beams on rails (*juga*) were then fastened to these poles, forming a solid framework for an embankment. 1075 hurdles (*clays*) were requisitioned and the enveloping of these wooden structures in sand gave thickness and security to the entrenchment. No less than £53 was devoted to *dyriwerk*, that is, a strengthening and buttressing of the embankment that was calculated to render it impregnable. A crest (*kere*), whose principal ingredient appears to have been peat-moss (*mora*), served to crown the elaborate edifice.

The large reclamation of land in 1293–94 was undertaken in exceptional circumstances. Normally, however, much attention

was given to strengthening and maintaining existing entrench-
ments and fortifications. If the great wall of Appledore appears
largely to have been maintained out of the proceeds of the common scot, other subsidiary embankments demanded constant
attention. This was, of course, particularly the case with newly
reclaimed land. 50 perches of the embankment called *Nova Terra*
underwent refacing, strengthening, and topping in 1293–94. The
next account examined, that for 1315–16, shows 1 furlong, 10
perches of this same wall being treated with straw, and in 1320–21
layers of gutter-tiles (*hwelf*) and earth (*terra*) were thrown thereon.
Three other embankments within the manor, the walls of *Ussestall*
and *Scherle* and the little wall of Snargate (*parva walla de Snergate*)
were also faced, strengthened, sided, and topped in these years.
The manor was distinguished by a system of protective outworks
known as groynes (*groynes*) and jetties (*geteyes*). The inrush of
the sea at the time of storms and spring-tides and the devastating
floods must have necessitated the construction of these breakwaters. Thus, in 1321–22 groynes were made to protect the *Nova
Terra* (*Newelonde*) and the land in the region of the Reading ferry
(*passagium*). A system of pile-driving by means of rams was used
to erect these bulwarks.

In addition to its elaborate fortifications the manor of Appledore
possessed a thorough system of land drainage. The digging of
cross-dykes, by which drainage and enclosure were effected
simultaneously, was a common practice. For example, in 1315–16,
3 furlongs of land were dug and enclosed *circa Mellefeld et peciam
ante portam*, 15 perches *inter gardinium et Mellefeld* and 36 perches
*inter Ovineularum et Mellefeld*. *Mellefeld* was therefore enclosed
on all sides in the one year. The other form of enclosure, that is,
enclosure by hedges, also obtained on the manor in our period
and in close conjunction with existing embankments. Thus, in
1321–22 material was brought *ad sepem claudendam inter dictam
wallam* (i.e. the wall of Scherle).

The chief cereal crop grown on the manor of Appledore was,
as might be expected, oats. Oats absorbed over 78 per cent of the
cultivated area, wheat 10 per cent, legumes (i.e. beans and vetches)
9 per cent, and rye a little over 4 per cent of the area. The grange

accounts are much briefer here than at Ebony and no evidence has been found of any attempt to manure and dress the land.

If we discount the abnormal circumstances of the last decade or so of the thirteenth century, it would seem that the 10·1 per cent of the revenue spent on embankment in 1315–16 and the 11·1 per cent of 1321–22 probably represented the normal annual outlay for the greater part of Eastry's priorate. The evidence would lead us to conclude that the natural disasters of 1287–88, bringing in their train financial ruin to the manor, were succeeded after a period by a balanced accountancy and a vigorous initiative in preserving the land from the dangers of sea and flood.

The manor of Orgarswick-and-Agney, lying in the Romney Marsh immediately to the north of Dymchurch, is the next to be studied. Here, as at Ebony, there was no rent-paying tenantry. The professional staff of the manor ( *famuli* ) and hired labourers undertook all the necessary agricultural and embanking operations. The pull of the outside market was the determining factor in the manorial economy. In Henry of Eastry's priorate 84 per cent of the revenue was derived from the sale of corn, stock, and dairy produce. So here, as at Ebony and to a less extent at Appledore, investment on embanking operations was primarily determined by the yield and sale of crops and dairy produce and the disposal of cattle and sheep in any given year. Sales fluctuated and expenditure on embankment fluctuated accordingly but the latter never attained large figures. The outlay of £7. 2s. 4d. in 1298–99 is the highest figure that has been discovered, and in the years covered by the priorate an average annual expenditure of 6·7 per cent was devoted to marsh embankment, land drainage, and sea-defence.

The onslaught of the sea at Orgarswick-and-Agney was constantly giving cause for the erection of new defence works. Indeed, sea-defence was the single largest item in the serjeants' embanking programme. In 1298–99, 2 furlongs, 22 perches of wall were built *contra mare* at an expense of £3. 5s. 6d. and marine fortifications both on the southern side of the manor and on the west towards Romney required constant attention. The walls here were stiffened and strengthened and coated with layers of sand and earth at regular intervals.[1]

If the sea-walls were mainly protective in their nature, it may also be surmised that a policy of 'inning' and reclamation was judiciously combined with sea-defence. The 3 perches of wall that underwent repair in 1292–93 were *in nova terra* and two dams were built here in 1301–2 to regulate the course of the drainage. By the year 1315–16 the *nova terra* was cultivated land, having 5½ acres sown with oats and 4 with vetches.

The levelling of land was pursued at Orgarswick with remarkable vigour. The reference in 1291–92 to expenditure *in terra removenda et dispergenda* clearly shows that attempts were made to fill up hollows or 'pans' with material from the dykes and other sources. The simultaneous expenditure on levelling and ditching in certain parts of the manor strongly suggest that the two processes were always undertaken in conjunction. Indeed the serjeant stated his aims most clearly in 1292–93 when he used the words *in blado exaquando* (which we may translate as 'in ridding the corn of superfluous water') as the operative phrase in his annual account.

The attempt to extend the acreage under cultivation on the manor of Orgarswick met with some considerable success during Eastry's priorate. 108 acres were under corn in 1292, a number which rose to 163 in 1327. This increase, as at Ebony, was closely linked with an extension of the area under wheat. The wheat acreage jumped from 11 in 1315 to 42 in 1327, and the marling and manuring of the land which took place in the latter year—the only instance which we have for Orgarswick—was clearly preparatory to or contemporary with the wheat crop. It seems hardly necessary to add that oats was the largest single crop. The acreage it covered, 33·6 per cent of the whole, was however closely followed by the legume crops, beans and vetches, which occupied 31 per cent of the total area. The manor of Orgarswick-and-Agney may be said, therefore, to have reflected credit on its administrators and workmen during Eastry's priorate. Its sea-

---

[1] For example, in 1327–28 a sum of 7s. 4d. was expended on a sea-wall *de novo sadanda et terra supponenda*.

defences and embankments were carefully maintained and the cultivable area underwent an appreciable increase.

Now let us turn to the East Kent marshes and halt at the manor of Lyden,[1] closely connected with the adjacent manor of Eastry. One of the late thirteenth-century measurements of land states that the prior of Canterbury owned 405 acres at Lyden *sub periculo maris*—in danger of the sea.[2] Here, as at Appledore, he adopted the policy of letting out some of the marsh-lands on lease to tenants while keeping the greater part of it in his own hands. These leasehold tenants were few in number and of customary tenants there is no mention at all. Little land was under cultivation and the bulk of the manorial revenue was derived from the sale of stock and dairy produce. Altogether, such sales, together with the comparatively small sales of corn, amounted to 52 per cent of the revenue, the rest of which was derived from leases of marsh and pasture.

In the embanking operations undertaken here in our period sea-defence figured very prominently. At a site called *Kalblowesande* a wall was erected *contra mare* in 1317–18 and crowned with a triple crest. Wooden gutters were made to communicate with the sea and to direct the course of the small stream called *Gestlynge*. Indeed the building of walls and gutters is constantly detailed as one operation. For example, in 1317–18 two gutters were made next to the marsh of Thomas Edward; a wall was then erected between the marsh in question and the mill of Lyden and another wall of 1 furlong, 24 perches, consisting chiefly of turf, was built to border the same marsh.

Particularly interesting is the evidence we have for the general widening and deepening of ditches that took place in 1317–18. In that year 1 furlong, 24 perches of ditch from *Spitelemanshope* up to the northward corner of the field were widened by 16 feet and deepened by 2 feet. The ditch running from the same corner to the mill 30 perches distant, was increased 10 feet in width and 2 feet in depth. Similarly, the 114 perches of ditch between the cornfield (*Cornfeldes*) and the sheepfold (*Bercariam*) were made 8 feet wider and 2 feet deeper.

[1] Now Lidde Court in the parish of Worth near Sandwich.
[2] B.M. Cott. MS. Galba E iv, f. 151 v.

Wooden gutters were freely used to direct the manorial stream as well as to communicate with the sea. For example, in 1291–92, three new gutters were laid and the old gutter that skirted a main embankment (*extra wallam*) underwent repair. The damming of the streams required some skill. In 1317–18 two dams at the head of the stream (*ad capita fletorum*) were repaired and strengthened by the ramming of piles and the juxtaposition of hurdles. Ditching and enclosure here as elsewhere went hand in hand. Ditches round the field where cows were pastured were dug and cleaned in 1317–18 and the ditches and gutters round the cornfield (*Cornfelde*) were constantly scoured and cleaned. Indeed, the ditches that surrounded the arable and pasture land of the manor were an object of very special attention to the serjeant of Lyden, who was never tired of disbursing money on their behalf. The acreage under corn rose from 56 in 1305 to 77 in 1330 and, what is more important, the number of sheep agisted rose steadily from 214 in 1291 to 490 in 1330. The 13·9 per cent of the annual revenue which on average was spent on embankment in Eastry's priorate was, therefore, rewarded by an all-round expansion of the manorial economy.

The manor of Monkton, the next on our list, is situated in the Isle of Thanet off the north-east coast of Kent. It differed from all the other Kentish marsh manors of Canterbury cathedral priory in that, by the time of Henry of Eastry's accession, the greater part of its large area of rich arable land had been given over to the extensive cultivation of barley and oats. It rendered a large annual farm of corn to the priory and made large market profits each year out of the sale of corn, stock, and dairy produce. Again, in contrast to previous examples, the manorial tenantry was numerous, as the rent-roll clearly shows.

There was, however, a clearly defined marsh district in the manor of Monkton. This was measured in the presence of the royal justiciars in 1288 and found to comprise an area of 257½ acres, 61½ of which were held by the manorial tenantry.[1] By the year 1302 the marsh lands in the demesne land of the priory had risen to an area of 366 acres (i.e. had increased by just over

[1] B.M. Add. MS. 6159, fo. 27.

100 acres) while the land in the hands of tenants had dropped from 61½ to 53½ acres.[1] This remarkable increase in the marsh area of the manor of Monkton—land that would eventually evolve into rich grazing land or, after a course of manure, be converted into arable—is explained by the concentration on sea-defence, embankment, and drainage that characterized the period of Eastry's priorate and made the reclamation of new land an economic investment.

In the attempt to erect impregnable fortifications against the onrush of the sea the serjeants of Monkton showed the greatest resource. No year has been found in which some new and original attempt is not made to drive back the sea and to encroach on its preserves. Thus, in 1300–1, 1 furlong and 32 perches of earthen sea-wall were renovated and thatched with straw. In 1302–3 the siding, strengthening, and facing of the sea-wall was accompanied by the application of straw, 650 bundles of thatch, and the ramming of 24 hurdles and numerous piles. In 1307–8 the topping and strengthening of 39 perches of the sea-wall and the digging of an adjacent dyke occupied the serjeant's attention. Not content with this achievement, he had five groynes (*groynes*) made with poles and faggots as an added challenge to the onslaught of the waves. In 1314–15 two further groynes or breakwaters were made and the existing structures underwent repair.

Communicating with the sea was a series of gutters, the utility of which for draining the marshes of their flood water (*pro marisco exaquando*) was clearly expressed in the year 1300. The so-called East Gutter ran alongside the main sea-wall[2] and other gutters were laid and repaired as part of the normal manorial routine. The system of simultaneous ditching and enclosing was as characteristic of Monkton as of the other marsh estates. To take only one example, 32 perches of ditch encircling the cattle marsh (*circa mariscum boviculorum*) and the sheep pasture (*carthope*)[3] were dug and cleaned in 1302–3. The presence of gates in the

---

[1] Monkton, serjeant's account, 1302–3.

[2] *In Wallatura exaltanda juxta Estguteram*—3s.: Monkton, serjeant's account, 1314–15.

[3] The suffix *hope*, as Miss Neilson has shown (*op. cit.* p. 56), denotes a sheep pasture.

marsh area is additional evidence that enclosures for cattle and sheep were contemplated.[1]

For the years which we have examined, 3·5 per cent of the total manorial revenue represented the average annual expenditure on embanking operations at Monkton. It is clear that much capital must have been invested between 1288 and 1301, when the marsh area underwent such a remarkable increase; unfortunately there are no accounts extant to illustrate this fact.[2] Those which do survive tell of a remarkable increase of pasture and dairy farming in Eastry's priorate, which is almost certainly related to the increase in the marsh area under pasture. The 408 sheep pastured in 1302 had risen to 847 in 1314, and cheeses rose from 15½ *pensae* to 33 *pensae* and there was a 100 per cent increase in the sale of dairy produce.[3] In the same period the arable area of the manor actually declined[4]—a fact which makes it seem highly probable that the rich grazing value of the Isle of Thanet and the high profits to be drawn from such a practice were fully realized by Henry of Eastry and his manorial staff.

Finally, our journey has brought us to the two North Kent manors of Seasalter and Cliffe. The policy which Eastry, following his immediate predecessors, adopted to the marsh areas contained therein was definite and clear-cut. He let out the marshes on leasehold rents (*feodifirmae*) to tenants and confined himself to encouraging the work of others in embanking and reclaiming land. For example, he wrote a letter in 1325 to the archbishop of Canterbury in which he enclosed the petition of a principal tenant of the marshes of Seasalter and himself suggested that a rate should be levied on the landlords and tenants of the marshes to enable embanking operations to take place.[5]

---

[1] E.g. *In porta in marisco emenda*—12d.: Monkton, serjeant's account, 1307–8.

[2] The accounts listed in the *Bulletin of the Institute of Historical Research*, *loc. cit.* relate primarily to the lands of the almonry at Monkton, as distinct from those of the manor.

[3] The profits from the sale of dairy produce totalled £9. 1s. 0d. in 1302–3 and £20. 16s. 10d. in 1314–15.

[4] 430 acres were under arable in 1302 and 398 acres in 1314.

[5] *Lit. Cant.* (R.S.), I, 138–41.

The large manor of Cliffe, which is on the southern bank of the Thames estuary, was divided into two parts in the period we are studying; the first part was a rich arable and grazing area and lay in the demesne of the cathedral priory; the other part, that is the marsh district, was entirely occupied by leasehold tenants and had in 1292 a flourishing rent-roll of £71. 2s. 11d.[1] Thus, the policy of peopling marsh areas with leasehold tenants, of which we have already had some evidence at Appledore and Lyden, was carried to its logical extreme in the case of the North Kent marshes, which proved a steady and fertile source of revenue for the priory.

Some general conclusions may now be attempted as a result of the foregoing study. The importance of the records of marsh areas as a source for the study of the medieval enclosure movement need hardly be stressed. Enclosures seem to have taken place here with as great a frequency as they undoubtedly did on manors containing large assarts. Newly cleared land and newly reclaimed and embanked land are, it seems, the two types of land that were most frequently enclosed in the middle ages. Both were largely exempt from the rules of communal cultivation, a fact which made enclosure all the more easy and desirable. The great prominence of the oats crop on the Kentish marsh manors is also a matter of some general interest. The growing of oats in the middle ages has been associated with land on the economic margin of cultivation.[2] The land of the marsh manors under review certainly conformed to this description. Gallant attempts were made to increase the wheat acreage by manuring and dressing the land, but with little success, and oats always remained the largest cereal crop.

Finally, any attempt to estimate the success of capital investment on marsh embankment and its attendant processes must take the weather conditions of the time into full account. When he summed up the work of the first thirty-seven years of his priorate

---

[1] The serjeant's account of 1294 and the rent-roll headed *Redditus mariscorum de Clive in festo Sancti Michaelis anno regni Edwardi regis vicesimo* of 1292 illustrate these two aspects of the manorial economy of Cliffe.

[2] T. A. M. Bishop, *Economic History Review* (1938), p. 42.

in 1322 Henry of Eastry noted in his Memorandum Book that he had already spent £360. 7s. 0d. on inning land and protecting it from the sea.[1] His total expenditure on embanking and draining operations of every description must have reached a very high figure. The results achieved thereby, as evidenced by increase of arable and pasture, market profits and rents may, at first sight, seem a little disappointing. It is only when the great storms and floods and geological changes of 1287–93 are taken into consideration and when full weight is given to the floods of 1307, the famine years of 1314–16, and the prolonged drought of 1325–26,[2] that the achievement begins to fall into perspective, and to appear as a sustained attempt, in the face of natural disasters and much discouragement, to maintain the marsh manors in their fullest integrity and, as if by way of reprisal, to wrest new lands from the onslaught of the sea.

[1] *Pro terris intrandis et salvandis contra mare in diversis locis*—£360. 7s.: B.M. Cott. MS. Galba E iv, fo. 109.

[2] See C. E. Britton, *A Meteorological Chronology to* A.D. 1485 (H.M. Stationery Office), pp. 121–37.

# Chapter Twelve

## THE LAST 150 YEARS

The last decade of the fourteenth century saw the opening of a new era in the economy of Christ Church. The changes which took place in household organization and estate management were of the most comprehensive character. From an administrative standpoint, therefore, the last 150 years of monastic life at Canterbury must be sharply distinguished from the preceding age. Previously, symptoms had not been lacking of a coming change. Simon of Sudbury's injunctions to his cathedral priory in 1376 showed that all was not well with the monastic community. Among other abuses, the common seal was carelessly kept and there was a tendency for a number of monks to dwell in separate households.[1] The ordinance which the senior monks promulgated in the same year plainly revealed the beginning of a breakdown in the central financial system, for the chamberlain was instructed to receive his income from the shrine-keepers, almoner, and wardens of the manors, without recourse to the central office.[2] In 1384 the treasurers ceased to enrol their accounts in the white book for public scrutiny. Prior John Vynch (1377–91) was a man of small economic ability. We are told by an anonymous chronicler that he 'wisely depended more on the power of prayer and the care and worldly wisdom of his brother monks W. Woghope and T. Chillindenne than on his own good management'.[3] The inevitable result was that the treasurers tended more and more to take things into their own hands and to forget that their office was held as a trusteeship. Fortunately one of the treasurers, Thomas Chillenden, was a man of outstanding financial acumen, and it is impossible to raise a reproach of negligence against men who may with more justice be accused of setting an evil pre-

---

[1] Wilkins, *Concilia*, III, pp. 110–11.
[2] *Lit. Cant.* III, p. 6.
[3] *Arch. Cant.* (1911), XXIX, pp. 58–61.

cedent for the future. There is much evidence to show that the treasurers were active in the execution of their duties throughout the period.[1]

The year 1391 is crucial for our study. Accustomed to many years of autocratic action and with his head full of ambitious building schemes, the new prior Thomas Chillenden determined to retain his control over the finances of the monastery. So, on his accession to the priorate, he fused the more important functions of the central office with his own and assumed the role of a prior-treasurer. He it was who now received all the income from manors and oblations and who gave the obedientiaries sufficient revenue to meet the demands made on them.[2] The treasurers continued to be appointed—there were still three in number in 1407[3]—but their power had shrunk to shadowy proportions and their chief concern now lay with building repairs and estate management. The account of Prior Chillenden for the year 1396–97 *de omnibus proventibus prioratus ecclesie predicte*[4] shows that the administrative change was unaccompanied by any breach in the standardized forms of the central organization. The prior virtually stepped into the treasurers' shoes (which he had already worn for some considerable time) and retained those methods of classifying receipts and expenditure which centuries of experience had proved to be most profitable. In particular, the four mainstays of local finance, the monk-wardens, incurred no immediate diminution of their authority; the administrative framework was maintained in its entirety.

The revolution in the central system of accounting, which placed absolute power in the hands of the prior-treasurer, was

---

[1] Lambeth MS. 243, fos. 196, 203, 205 v., 215, 217, illustrates their multifarious activities. It also shows that the external expenditure of the treasurers was enrolled in the traditional manner until 1391, the year of Chillenden's accession to the priorate.

[2] The change-over is well exemplified in the chamberlain's accounts. In 1384 this obedientiary received all his income from the treasurers (Cant. MS. M 13, xiii, mem. 5) and in 1391 a sum of £150 'de domino Thoma Chillyndene priore' (*ibid.* mem. 6). The sacrist's accounts for 1385–86 and 1390–91 (*ibid.* xvi, mems. 8 and 10) tell the same story.

[3] Cant. MS. M 13, xiv.　　　　　　　　[4] *Ibid.* xvii, mem. 4.

quickly followed by changes of equal importance in the sphere
of estate management. Within a very short period nearly all the
manorial demesnes of the priory were let out on lease. The direct
exploitation of the estates was therefore almost universally
abandoned. In the century before Chillenden's accession the
leasehold system had made some little headway on the Christ
Church estates. We have seen that Prior Henry of Eastry bought
land for the express purpose of leasing it, and that newly embanked
land was often demised for a competitive leasehold rent.[1] Parcels
of demesne on some of the most important manors, like Monkton
and Ickham, were leased in like manner.[2] Such leases of small
parcels of demesne acquired increasing importance as the century
advanced.[3] In the 'seventies the practice of leasing out whole
demesnes was adopted on a number of East Kent manors.[4] The
accession of Chillenden in 1391 marked the decisive turning-point.
Faced with the costs of the reconstruction of the nave of the
cathedral and other expensive building projects, Chillenden sought
all means of swelling his rent-roll. The leasing of the manorial
demesnes was clearly the simplest solution. This policy was pursued with such thoroughness in the first years of the priorate
that by 1396 the leasehold system was established everywhere
on the Christ Church estates.[5] The most sweeping change in

[1] Chapter Eight.
[2] B.M. Add. MS. 6159, fos. 26 v.–27, 30.
[3] Thus at Walworth, in Surrey, the demesne was intact in 1319, but in
1324 80 acres, 1 rood were let out on lease for an annual rent of £11. 10s. 5d.
At Chartham in 1350 the leasehold system had made no headway, but in
1376 the lease of parcels of demesne and fulling-mills yielded an annual
revenue of £9. 4s.
[4] In 1374–75 the demesnes at Monkton, Eastry, Lyden, Godmersham, and
Brook were let out on lease (Cant. MS. D.E. 6) and in 1379–80 the demesnes
of the first four manors and that of Adesham were leased (ibid.).
[5] The accounts of manors all have a similar tale to tell. At Ickham the
demesne was still farmed by the monks in 1385, but in 1393 one John Stonestrete was the lessee of the manor. At Lyden in 1381–82 the demesne was
being farmed for the profit of the monks. In 1391 it was leased to William
Scott. At Merstham there was no lessee in 1389, but in 1398 Nicholas Stake
was in the fourth year of a ten-year lease. The prior's account of 1396–97
(Cant. MS. M 13, xvii, mem. 4) shows the presence of *firmarii* on all the Christ
Church manors.

the administration of the estates was therefore accomplished in almost the shortest possible period of time.

At first only the manorial demesnes were let out on lease, and beadles or rent-collectors were commissioned by the priory executive to collect the rents of the tenants and the profits of the manor-courts. The rent thus acquired a composite character. In the first place, there was the *firma annalis*, fixed by an indenture between the two contracting parties, the monks and the *firmarius*. Secondly, there were the *redditus assisae, perquisita curiarum*, and all the other miscellaneous dues not included in the terms of a stock-and-land lease. From these revenues the monks had to deduct all expenditure involved in the upkeep of the property on the manor. The first leases were for short terms varying from 3 to 10 years. The period of from 5 to 7 years seems to have been the most common.[1] On the corn-growing manors of Kent the *firmarii* rendered a fixed annual supply of wheat and barley to the priory as well as a money-rent. Thus at Monkton in 1391–96 the *firmarius*, Thomas Stefthy, paid an annual *firma* of £22, 40 quarters of wheat, and 80 quarters of barley.[2] Similarly at Ickham in 1393–96 the lessee, John Stonestrete, was burdened with a *firma annalis* of £10, 200 quarters of wheat, and 100 quarters of barley.[3] So the old food-farm system remained in force under a different guise.

There is much evidence to show that the *firmarii* were usually prosperous peasants and small landowners.[4] More often than not the serjeant of a manor took up the lease. To take only one example, Nicholas Stake was the serjeant of Merstham in 1389 and farmed the demesne on behalf of monks in return for a yearly wage. In 1395 he took up the lease of the manor for a term of ten years, paying an annual rent of £38.[5] The serjeants were chiefly recruited from the growing class of prosperous peasants and, on the basis of their past experience, were well equipped for

[1] This was the case on the manors of the Essex custody (Nichols, *op. cit.* p. 303). Lyden was demised for 5 years in 1391 and Monkton for 6 years in the same year.
[2] Serjeants' accounts.                    [3] *Ibid.*
[4] Nichols, *Custodia Essexae*, pp. 302–3.
[5] Merstham, serjeant's account.

'farming' the manor. Probably very little change took place in agricultural operations as a result of the general adoption of the leasehold system. With the same stock and often the same manager, though with a different title, the manors may well have enjoyed an uninterrupted continuity in administration. The wisdom of Chillenden's twin innovations—the prior-treasurer and the system of demesne leases—was severely tested during the twenty years of his priorate. Chillenden, that *flos priorum*, 'the greatest Builder of a Prior that ever was in Christes Churche', spent vast sums on building works in the cathedral church, the *curia*, and on the manors.[1] In the year of his accession, 1391, building expenses came to £520, in 1392 to £738. 19s. 10d., in the next year to £1872. 6s. 8d., and reached a summit in 1393–94 with a total outlay of £2522. 6s. 8d.[2] For the rest of his priorate the masons and carpenters were always busy, and it is to Chillenden that we chiefly owe the reconstruction and completion of that exquisitely delicate piece of work, the nave of Canterbury cathedral.[3] Although he necessarily had recourse to loans,[4] the prior-treasurer succeeded in meeting the bulk of this heavy expenditure. The income of the house reached its highest recorded level, £4100. 1s. 9d., in 1411,[5] the last year of the priorate, and Chillenden died leaving a debt of only £1043.[6] His financial resource and acumen had abundantly justified the experiment of a prior-treasurer, but a heavy responsibility rested upon his successors in the office.

John Woodnesburgh, the immediate successor of Chillenden, was a man of equal financial enterprise.[7] He appears, however,

[1] See the list of his works compiled in 1411 and printed in *Lit. Cant.* III, pp. 112–22.

[2] *Arch. Cant.* XXIX, pp. 61–79.

[3] The work had been begun nearly twenty years before Chillenden's accession, but little progress had been made.

[4] Thus in 1407 he borrowed £100 from Thomas Glyuyam, a citizen and draper of London (*Cal. Let. Close*, 8 Henry IV, p. 247), and in 1411 he stood indebted to a canon of St David's (*Arch. Cant.* XXIX, pp. 78–79).

[5] Cant. MS. M 13, xvii, mem. 2.     [6] *Arch. Cant.* XXIX, pp. 78–79.

[7] The chief aim of an anonymous fifteenth-century Canterbury chronicler was 'to utter a panegyric on the financial talents of John of Woodnesburgh': *ibid.* XXIX, p. 48.

to have had a different conception of the rôle of the treasury in his cathedral priory. Under his rule a revolution more radical than that of 1391 took place, and the treasury became a central reserve fund similar to that of Abingdon Abbey and certain other Benedictine monasteries.[1] The prior continued to receive the bulk of the conventual revenue, but he carefully allotted a large part to the treasurers as well as disbursing the usual income to the monastic departments. In 1415, for example, it was remarked at the annual audit that a sum of £313. 8s. 11½d. remained 'in the hands of the treasurers'[2] and monks without regular allocations (e.g. the chaplains of the prior) drew readily on this central reserve.[3] But the evil fruits of a policy that removed the treasury from responsible control were already manifest. Centrifugal tendencies in the financial system can be observed as early as 1411, the last year of Chillenden's life. In the chamberlain's account for that year a number of cross-payments from one obedientiary to another is clearly evidenced.[4] An increasing tendency on the part of the several obedientiaries to acquire separate endowments is also to be observed. In 1421 the sacrist still received the bulk of his income from the prior, but a sum of £3. 6s. 8d. was already 'officio sacristarie assignata' and a number of rents and leases acquired in the city of Canterbury further emphasized the growing independence of his office.[5] There was a general tendency at this time for financial affairs to become the exclusive concern of the prior and certain *seniores ecclesiae*, a logical result of the relegation of the treasury to the position of a central reserve fund. Sometime in the first year of Woodnesburgh's rule a schedule of priory debts was inspected *per seniores ecclesiae*,[6] and in 1414 it was the prior and the *seniores ecclesiae* who certified to the archbishop the freedom of the priory from all debt.[7] Too much can be read into

---

[1] See Chapter Two.

[2] *Arch. Cant.* XXIX, pp. 82–83.

[3] See the chaplain's accounts for 1423–24: Cant. MS. M 13, v.

[4] The chamberlain received £35 from the prior 'pro elemosinario' and direct payments were made to him by a shrine-keeper and a warden of the manors: Cant. MS. M 13, xiii, mem. 58.

[5] Cant. MS. M 13, xvi, mem. 21.

[6] *Arch. Cant.* XXIX, pp. 78–79.   [7] *Ibid.* XXIX, pp. 80–81.

this vague, rather elusive term *seniores*, but it seems likely that for a time a body of elder monks, versed in corporate action at the exchequer, exercised functions that had once belonged to the all-powerful treasurers.

The financial history of the last 100 years of Christ Church before the Dissolution is somewhat obscure on account of the decreasing number of original sources. Certain general tendencies may nevertheless be observed with some caution. In the first place, this period saw the rule of three very remarkable priors, Thomas Goldston I (1449–68), William Sellyng (1472–94), and Thomas Goldston II (1495–1517), all of whom showed energy and resourcefulness in temporal administration.[1] There seems, in consequence, to have been a very definite reaction against the centrifugal symptoms of Woodnesburgh's rule and the disposition of each obedientiary to become independent in his own department. Indeed the priors appear to have asserted their financial control with no uncertain emphasis. The first indication of such a reaction is afforded by the sacrist's account for 1449–50. Prior Goldston I reverted to the old expedient of the appropriation clause, and the sacrist was obliged to record the receipt of money for specific objects such as the purchase of wax and the payment of wages.[2] In 1474[3] and 1507[4] the sacrist was still following the same procedure; the independence of his department had been permanently curbed. The cellarer was subjected to the same discipline, and in the year 1484–85 received £583. 8s. 1½d. 'super providenciam victualium et aliorum omnium per diversas vices hoc anno',[5] from the hands of the prior. Clearly the obedientiaries were once more being compelled to toe the line.

In substance the policy of the three priors appears to have been a return to the system of Thomas Chillenden, opposed both to the centrifugal tendencies that had appeared in Woodnesburgh's priorate and to the centralization of finance under the treasurers

[1] For a brief account of these priorates, see Woodruff and Danks, *Memorials of Canterbury Cathedral*, pp. 202–15.

[2] Cant. MS. M 13, xvi, mem. 36. The formula 'de domino priore pro...' runs throughout the account.

[3] *Ibid.* mem. 57.          [4] *Ibid.* no membrane number.

[5] Cant. MS. M 13, ix, mem. 8.

that had obtained in the preceding century. The treasurers were kept in the position that Chillenden had allotted to them. They devoted their attention to building repairs[1] and *expensa forinseca*,[2] and there is no evidence to show that they were any longer in charge of a central reserve fund. Prior Chillenden left abundant evidence of his financial dealings, and it is perhaps not altogether wrong to suppose that the vision of his successful autocracy captivated his successors with the desire to behave in like manner.

The financial record of the priory for the thirty years or so after Chillenden's death was altogether exemplary. By 1415 Prior Woodnesburgh had cleared the house of all debt,[3] and his prudent economy helped to maintain the financial equilibrium of the priory for the rest of his life. His successor, William Molash (1428–38), of whom little is known, presented an account in 1437 showing a credit balance of £48. 12s. 8d.[4] The social and political unrest of the latter half of the century and the growing luxury and independence of monastic life were primarily responsible for the *bouleversement* of this happy state of affairs. In 1454 the monks owed £663. 13s. 5¼d. to their creditors;[5] two years later their debts had increased to £1158. 11s. 7d.[6] In 1468, however, the priory was only indebted to the extent of £661. 5s. 2½d.,[7] and in 1473 the monastic debts amounted to no more than £264. 13s. 0¾d.[8] The lack of prior's accounts after this date makes it impossible to reconstruct the financial history of the priory in the last half century of its existence. Probably, like most other houses at this time, it was in a state of continual indebtedness without ever incurring financial disaster.

In household administration the general tendency of the age in the larger monasteries was towards separatism, exclusiveness,

---

[1] The weekly bills of their building expenses for the years 1436–43 and from 1471 well on into the next century are preserved in the Dean and Chapter Library, Canterbury.

[2] The treasurers' account for the year 1512–13 (Cant. MS. M 13, xv) gives much space to this item.

[3] *Arch. Cant.* XXIX, pp. 82–83.

[4] Cant. MS. M 13, xvii, mem. 7.

[5] *Ibid.* mem. 9.

[6] *Ibid.* mem. 10.

[7] *Ibid.* mem. 11.

[8] *Ibid.* mem. 12.

and the growth of *proprietas*. The *Chronicle of John Stone*, 1415–71,[1] reveals the continuance of a large measure of corporate and liturgical life at Christ Church in the fifteenth century, but there is much incidental evidence to show that the Rule of St Benedict was being openly flouted by the monks. It is not only that there were particularly flagrant cases of individual *proprietarii*;[2] each member of the community was in the habit of receiving gifts of money[3] and of possessing his own *jocalia*.[4] The system of pittances became more and more elaborate. A long pittance-roll of 1464–65[5] recounts the wine, dates, almonds, spices, and other delicacies supplied to the monks at frequent intervals throughout the year. Each obedientiary paid part of his income into the *deportum* so that the pittance-fund might never be under-subscribed.[6] The monks in the infirmary had a particularly easy time, being regaled with sugar cordials, lozenges (*loʒyngs*), and a host of similar luxuries.[7] Large sums were constantly being spent on spices,[8] and the O's of Advent were an occasion for very special feasting.[9] One at least of the Christ Church monks at this period suffered some pangs of conscience, for he is the author of the lines:

> Resoun me bad, and redde me as for the best
> To ate and drynke in tyme and temprely.

---

[1] Ed. W. G. Searle, *Camb. Antiq. Soc. Publ.* (1902), XXXIV.

[2] See, for example, *H.M.C.* App. to IXth Report, p. 104.

[3] In 1451 a sum of £29 was paid by the prior to 87 monks on the day of the *regressio* of St Thomas (1 December). They received a further £7. 11s. 4d. on the obit-day of Bishop Buckingham of Lincoln. This same day a paltry sum of 8s. 4d. was given to the poor in alms: Cant. MS. E. vi.

[4] An inventory of the *jocalia* of the monks was drawn up in 1465; see *H.M.C.* App. to IXth Report, p. 105.

[5] Cant. MS. D.E. 25.

[6] The obedientiaries normally made these payments for 37 weeks of the year. Some attempt was still made, it seems, to observe the austerities of Advent and Lent.

[7] See the account of the expenses of the infirmary c. 1523: Cant. MS. D.E. 58.

[8] In 1451 the cellarer spent £10. 5s. 7½d. on spices (Cant. MS. E. vi) and as much as £21. 11s. 11d. in 1455–56: Cant. MS. M 13, ix, mem. 5.

[9] Each obedientiary, after the recital of his antiphonal O, was called upon to feast the convent. In 1455–56 the cost of the cellarer's O in wine and spices came to £1. 17s. 6d.: Cant. MS. M 13, ix, mem. 5.

But wylful routh nat obeye lest
Unto his red, he sette not therby;
He of hem both hathe take outrageously
And out of time, nat two or three,
But xx<sup>ti</sup> yeres passyd contynually.
Excesse at bord his knyff hath leyd wyth me.[1]

Luxury of diet was not the only remarkable feature in the life of the Canterbury monks, for their great retinues of servants were equally deserving of censure. The prior alone employed over forty servants in his private household,[2] and all the senior monks and obedientiaries, many of whom dwelt in separate chambers (*camerae*), had their own entourage.[3] All the monks seem to have been allowed to go on holiday at certain times in the year, for William Glastonbury, an inmate of Christ Church, included in his chronicle a list of the monks who were permitted to go for their holidays at the beginning of 1438.[4] The pernicious effect that such vacations might well have on monastic discipline and the whole conception of *stabilitas* need hardly be emphasized. The growing secularization of life at Christ Church is, indeed, evidenced in a great variety of ways. The constant presence of actors and minstrels at the priory is one more symptom of this general tendency. In 1451, for example, the players of the king, the duke of Buckingham, and the city of Canterbury, all gave performances in the priory at different times in the year and were liberally rewarded for their services.[5] The multiplication of chantries in the cathedral,[6] served by secular priests, and the presence of secular clergy in the infirmary,[7] must also have militated against the strict observance of monastic discipline.

As the life of the monks increased in luxury and ostentation the primary duties of hospitality and almsgiving fell more and

[1] *H.M.C.* App. to IXth Report, p. 108.
[2] Woodruff and Danks, *op. cit.* p. 226.
[3] Cant. MS. D.E. 29 is a list of the servants of the chief obedientiaries of the convent in the fifteenth century.
[4] *Arch. Cant.* (1925), XXXVII, p. 138.  [5] Cant. MS. E. vi.
[6] See the list of chantries in W. Woolnoth, *Canterbury Cathedral*, pp. 115–16.
[7] Woodruff and Danks, *op. cit.* p. 255.

more into the background. The erection of the famous Chequers of the Hope at the corner of Mercery Lane in 1395[1] is eloquent of·the change of outlook. Like so many other communities the monks passed on the burden of hospitality to others, saving themselves the trouble of receiving guests in person.[2] The Christ Church monks were at no period conspicuous for the liberality of their almsgiving, but in the fifteenth century their work in this direction nearly ceased altogether. In spite, however, of the paucity of their donations to the poor, they still maintained a large establishment of clerks and servants in the almonry. All the evidence goes to show that they cared but little for their obligation of charity to poor travellers and to the poor at the gate.

The leasehold system which Chillenden established persisted on the Christ Church estates until the Dissolution, but in the fifteenth century these leases acquired a somewhat different character. In the first place, whole manors, and not merely demesnes, were let out on lease. Secondly, the leases were made for much longer periods. The lease of the manor of Walworth for ninety years c. 1450[3] and of the Irish lands for sixty years[4] in 1472 are two typical examples. Thirdly, for a period most of the corn-rents were commuted for a money equivalent. Finally, on most manors the *firma annalis* underwent a gradual increase.[5] To these four distinct alterations in the original leasehold system must be added the innovation, first apparent in the second decade of the century, of keeping one important Kentish manor in demesne to be exploited directly for the benefit of the monks. In 1411 Monkton was the manor in question,[6] and in 1455 Ickham was alone held *in dominio*.[7]

---

[1] It was begun in 1391 and completed in 1395: *Arch. Cant.* XXIX, pp. 65–66, 69.

[2] See R. H. Snape, *English Monastic Finances*, p. 112. There is some evidence, however, to show that the Cellarer's Hall and Hog Hall were still used as guest-houses, although Maister Omers was usually leased out to distinguished residents.

[3] *Lit. Cant.* III, pp. 257–58.          [4] *Ibid.* III, p. 248.

[5] For example, at Monkton the *firma annalis* rose from £22 in 1406 to £26. 13s. 4d. in 1433: serjeants' accounts.

[6] Serjeant's account.          [7] Cant. MS. M 13, xvii, mem. 10.

In the second quarter of the fifteenth century there was a temporary breakdown in the food-farm system. The prior was obliged to purchase large quantities of corn in the markets, though he often simply effected a cash transaction with the *firmarii* of the manors instead of receiving the wheat and barley by way of farm.[1] After the middle of the century, however, the traditional food-farm system was restored and remained substantially in force until the Dissolution. The garnerer's accounts,[2] many of which have survived, conveniently illustrate this collapse and recovery.

| | Corn received as food-farm | | Corn purchased by prior | |
|---|---|---|---|---|
| Year | Quarters | Bushels | Quarters | Bushels |
| 1422–23 | 1572 | 6 | — | — |
| 1427–28 | 1342 | 6 | — | — |
| 1429–30 | 725 | 5½ | 20 | — |
| 1433–34 | 278 | 4 | 402 | 6½ |
| 1434–35 | 319 | — | 753 | 3½ |
| 1435–36 | 262 | — | 337 | — |
| 1440–41 | 270 | — | 801 | 4 |
| 1443–44 | 304 | — | 539 | 3 |
| 1444–45 | 226 | 2 | 532 | 6 |
| 1446–47 | 208 | 2 | 478 | 7 |
| 1449–50 | 621 | — | — | — |
| 1452–53 | 952 | 7 | — | — |
| 1463–64 | 483 | 5 | — | — |
| 1464–65 | 493 | 6 | — | — |
| 1504–5 | 686 | 5½ | 92 | 6 |

With the general prevalence of leases on the Canterbury estates, the functions of the wardens of the manors were naturally much reduced in importance. The monks were now *rentiers*, living on an expanding rent-roll, and the *custodes maneriorum* became rent-collectors on a large scale. Their numbers dropped from four to one. They still, however, had the responsibility of making leases

[1] The prior's account of 1436–37 (Cant. MS. M 13, xvii, mem. 7) shows large quantities of corn bought 'cum firmariis de' various Christ Church manors.

[2] Cant. MS. M 13, iii. At the beginning of each accounting year large stocks of corn usually rested in the granaries. These are not included in the figures about to be cited.

and of supervising the upkeep of manorial property. Thus it was
c. 1490 that Thomas Humfrey, the warden of the manors, wrote
to the prior, saying: 'Att Meopham we have delyveryd the ferme
ther to John Ov'ny with all such stor as ys conteynyd yn the
byll yndentyd of the stor delyveryd to W...except the store of
whete, barle, oatys, pesyn, and tarys. Also such stuff as was left
in the custody of Richard Dent, and was not appraised, as ytt
apperyd by an odyr byll that y had off your fadyrhede, y have
of them but...answers safe of a pott of brasse and of a few
shelvys. I have charged hym that he schall dressh and delyver
no graynys owt of the barnys ther unto the tyme ye be contentyd
of hys dewte. He ys agreabyll therto, and seyth that att my
nexte comyng hedyr yn thys progress he wyll fynd suffycyent
suerte.'[1]

The survival of two pocket notebooks of fifteenth-century
monk-wardens,[2] as well as of numerous travelling accounts,[3]
makes it easy to reconstruct their work in the last era of monasticism. As well as conducting the bi-annual progress, on which
they collected rents, made or renewed leases, and saw to the maintenance of property, they also paid certain pensions to scholars
and chantry-priests and settled the debts which the monks owed
to London tradesmen.[4] In other words, part of the money which
they collected was never received by the prior-treasurer but
passed directly to the creditors and pensioners of the monastery.
So, while losing their tight control over the internal mechanism
of manorial finance, the wardens were given tasks which they

[1] *Christ Church Letters*, ed. J. B. Sheppard (Camden Soc. 1877), p. 55.
Cf. *Lit. Cant.* III, p. 305.

[2] These note-books, which are now Cant. MS. R.E. 40 and 6, contain
accounts of the expenses of the wardens on their 'progresses' in the years
1447 and 1493.

[3] Cant. MS. R.E. 131 is a roll of the expenses of the 'progress' of Thomas
Humfrey c. 1490, and Cant. MS. D.E. 70 is a similar account for the year
1518. In Drawer 32 in the Dean and Chapter Library, Canterbury, there is
a series of accounts of 'progresses' for the years 1463–99.

[4] The accounts for the years 1463–99 show that the wardens regularly
paid pensions to the warden and fellows of Canterbury College and to the
priest of the chantry at Bocking, and settled the bills of London fishmongers
and grocers.

had not previously fulfilled. Nevertheless their power was but a pale shadow of that comprehensive authority which they had enjoyed in the age of demesne farming.

The growing of corn and the rearing of stock ceased to be a personal concern of the monks after the institution of the lease-hold system. Their interest was confined to receiving the food-farm and to seeing that the crops and stock were diminished neither in quantity nor quality when a lease expired or was ready for renewal. But in all questions involving the upkeep of the manorial property the monks continued to have a personal re-sponsibility. Embanking and draining operations were, of course, included in this responsibility, and the work they accomplished in this sphere in the fifteenth century is well worthy of comment. For the first time on the Kentish manors, as in the Fenland area at the same period,[1] large-scale embanking schemes were under-taken. The 'inning' of the Appledore marsh, which was attempted piecemeal in the early fourteenth century,[2] was begun in earnest c. 1400[3] and proceeded steadily throughout the century. Prior Thomas Goldston I (1449–68) spent no less than £1200 on this work,[4] and Prior William Petham (1471–72) laid out a further £300 for the reclamation of 600 acres of the marsh.[5] Before the Dissolution the Appledore marsh had been completely 'inned' and rendered fit for the grazing of sheep and cattle. The manor of Ebony suffered grievously from the great flood of 1436,[6] but the large 'inning' at Appledore must have done much to reduce this peril. At Monkton in Thanet sea-defence and land drainage

[1] H. C. Darby, *The Medieval Fenland*, pp. 167–68.

[2] See Chapter Eleven.

[3] *H.M.C.* App. to IXth Report, p. 108.

[4] E. Hasted, *The History of Canterbury*, p. 163.

[5] *H.M.C.* App. to IXth Report, p. 116. See the letter of Prior Sellyng to Archbishop Bourchier on the subject of the Appledore marsh in *Lit. Cant.* III, p. 274.

[6] Prior William Molash accounted in 1437 for a sum of £28. 1s. 6d. received 'de stauro manerii de Ebbene post inundacionis rabiem hoc anno contingentem mense Septembris, per quam inundacionem omnes marisci ejusdem manerii submersi existunt, qua de causa bestie et animalia ejusdem manerii depasturare nequeunt, qua de causa firmarius ibidem hujus staurum reliberavit': Cant. MS. M 13, xvii, mem. 7.

were actively pursued throughout the period. In 1411–12 no less than 1200 perches of marsh-land at Monkton were embanked at a cost of £25.[1] At the same time as these major embanking operations were in progress, large sums were spent on repairing the granaries, mills, dovecotes, and other appurtenances on the manors. Prior Chillenden was particularly active in causing new buildings to be erected and old ones to be repaired on most of the manors,[2] but nearly all his successors showed commendable diligence in this respect.[3] So, even if the monks suffered from a surfeit of good food and drink and greatly relaxed their standard of discipline, they never appear to have neglected their property or to have been careless in temporal administration. Indeed, the last century of their corporate existence saw two of their most ambitious achievements—the erection of the Angel steeple[4] at Canterbury and the reclamation of the Appledore marsh.

The last era of monastic life at Christ Church was fittingly symbolized by the visits of Erasmus, Colet, and Madame de Montreuil to the shrine of St Thomas. Erasmus in his *Peregrinatio religionis ergo*[5] showed a kindly yet critical spirit of scepticism which typified the new humanist approach to the miraculous, and Colet was frankly contemptuous of the exaggerated relic-worship which confronted him at Canterbury. Madame de Montreuil arrived at Canterbury on 31 August 1538 just before the shrine was demolished. 'I shoued her Saincte Thomas shryne', wrote Sir William Penison to Thomas Cromwell, 'and all such other thinges worthy of sight; at the which she was not little marveilled

---

[1] Accounts of *firmarius* and *bedellus*.

[2] *Lit. Cant.* III, pp. 116–20.

[3] Prior Molash spent £55. 9s. 4½d. on new buildings in 1436–37, including mills at Shamelsford and Borley, and £138. 2s. 7¾d. on repairing old buildings (Cant. MS. M 13, xvii, mem. 7). Prior Goldston I spent £85. 5s. on new buildings and £291. 16s. 5½d. on manorial repairs in 1453–54 (*ibid.* mem. 9) and £204. 8s. 3½d. on manorial repairs in 1455–56 (*ibid.* mem. 10). Prior Oxney and Prior Sellyng expended £293. 15s. 8d. and £387. 4s. 3½d. on the upkeep of the manors in 1467–68 and 1472–73 (*ibid.* mems. 11, 12).

[4] See Woodruff and Danks, *op. cit.* pp. 207–10, for an account of the building of Bell Harry, the crowning glory of Canterbury cathedral.

[5] This account of the visit of Erasmus and Colet to Canterbury c. 1513 is included in the *Colloquia*.

at the greate riches therof; saing to be innumerable, and that if
she had not seen it, all the men in the wourlde could never a
made her to belyve it. Thus overlooking and vewing more than
an owre as well the shryne as Saint Thomas hed, being at both
cousshins to knyle, and the Pryour openyng Sainct Thomas hed
saing to her 3 tymes "This is Saint Thomas hed" and offered
her to kysse it; but she nother knyled nor would kysse it, but
still vewing the riches thereof. So she departed and whent to
her lodging to dynner and after the same to interteyne her with
honest passetymes.'[1]

With this spirit abroad it is little to be wondered that the
dissolution of the cathedral priory early in 1540 caused little
disturbance and few tears. There were 53 monks at the time of
the suppression, 28 of whom joined the new collegiate establishment. The prior and the rest of the monks left the house with
handsome pensions.[2] An astonishing respect for legal forms
marked the whole Dissolution procedure.

[1] Quoted by D. Gardiner, *Canterbury* (1933 ed.), pp. 84–85.
[2] Woodruff and Danks, *op. cit.* pp. 218–20.

# Appendix I

## CHAPTER AND EXCHEQUER ORDINANCES,
### 1288–c. 1326

There have survived in five Canterbury MSS. a number of
chapter and exchequer ordinances covering the years 1288–c. 1326.
Four of these MSS. are bound registers partly or wholly compiled during the long rule of Henry of Eastry, 1285–1331. The
fifth is a single document now contained in the Rural Economy
section of the Dean and Chapter Library, Canterbury (R.E. II, 99),
consisting of one membrane and being an ordinance promulgated
at the exchequer in the year 1288. The relation of the four bound
registers to each other is a matter of some little complexity.
B.M. Cott. MS. Galba E iv (which contains the fullest set of
ordinances) has inscribed on its initial fly-leaf the title *Memoriale
Multorum Henrici Prioris*. It is, in other words, the private
memorandum-book of Prior Henry of Eastry. Canterbury
Register J is the *Registrum Johannis de Gore de redditibus et consuetudinibus Ecclesie Christi Cantuariensis tam infra curiam quam
in civitate ac eciam in Maneriis ejusdem cum quibusdam aliis
contentis*—a complete manual of estate management for a monk-
warden or any executive official of the priory. B.M. Add. MS.
6160 and Trin. Coll. Camb. MS. O. 9/26 are more selective in
their content. The former appears to have been a handbook for
a monk who filled successively the offices of an obedientiary and
a warden of the manors,[1] while the latter seems to have been
composed exclusively for the purposes of a monk-warden.

I have called these four registers A, B, C, and D in my text.
Clearly none of them is the original text and all are nearly contemporary in date, so I have had no alternative but to call the
ordinances enrolled in Galba E iv my Text A, giving reference
throughout to the foliation of the original. The last three
ordinances printed are peculiar to that MS. The rest (with the
exception, of course, of the first ordinance) are enrolled in
Canterbury Register J, fos. 306–8, which I have called Text B.

[1] 'It includes obedientiaries' accounts for the year 1299–1300, as
well as a mass of detail relating to estate management.'

In Add. MS. 6160, fos. 101 v.–102 v. (Text C) and Trin. Coll. Camb. MS. O. 9/26, fo. 107 (Text D) are enrolled the three ordinances printed on pages 214 and 215 of my text, without any additions in the case of Text C and supplemented only by the recital of carrying-services in that of Text D. Variant readings or substantial divergences in the four texts are indicated in the notes.

*Ordinacio facta ad scaccarium in die quatuor Coronatorum*
*de blado mittendo domi anno regni Edwardi xvi*

Cant. MS. R.E. ii, No. 99.

| | |
|---|---|
| De remanentia anni preteriti | ·xxix et dim. summe. |
| *De custodia de Eastekent* | |
| De Moneketon cum Broke, | cviii summe. |
| De Lyden cum molendino, | xx summe. |
| De Estria | cxviii summe. |
| De Ikham cum Bramblynge | cclviii summe. |
| De Adesham | lxxxvi summe. |
| De Chertham | iv summe. |
| De Godmersham | lxix summe. |
| De Broke | vi summe. |

Summa hujus = DCCXX summe, inde subtractantur lxiii summe, i bussellus missa ad granarium ad furniandum ante festum sancti Michaelis anno regni regis Edwardi xvi; remanent ad mittendum DCLVI summe, vii busselli.

| | |
|---|---|
| De Berthona | xc summe. |
| De Vestclyve | x summe. |
| De molendinis | xxiv summe. |
| De custodia de Waldia | cxx summe. |
| Item, de excremento, | xxv summe, vii busselli. |

Summa hujus = cclxviii summe, vii busselli.

Summa tocius frumenti missi et mittendi cum remanentia et excremento = DCCCCLVI summe, ii busselli.

### Ordeum

Ordeum mittendum ad Berthonam de custodia de Eastekent.

| | |
|---|---|
| De Moneketon cum Broke | cxiv summe, *defectus*, xii summe. |
| Item, de firmis | xx summe, vii busselli, *defectus*, v summe, |
| | i bussellus. |

| | nihil. |
| De Lyden, | *recipienda*, x summe. |
| De Eastria | xci summe. |
| | *item*, ix summe. |
| Item, de firmis | vii summe, iv busselli. |
| De Ikham cum Bramblynge | cclxx summe. |
| | *defectus*, vi summe, iii busselli. |
| Item, de firmis | viii summe, ii busselli. |
| | *defectus*, ii summe, vi busselli. |
| De Adesham, | cxliii summe. |
| Item, de Gavelkorn, | lxvi summe. |
| | *defectus*, i summa. |
| Item, de firmis, | iii summe, iv busselli. |
| De Chertham, | lxxvi summe, |
| | *defectus*, xxi summe, ii busselli. |
| Item, de firmis, | xii summe, i bussellus et dim. |
| | iii busselli (*defectus*). |
| De Godmersham | xxviii summe. |
| | *defectus* xiii summe. |
| Item, de firmis | xii summe dim. (*defectus*). |
| De Broke | nihil. |

Summa hujus = Dcccl et dim. summe, dim. busselli et *defectus*, lxxxi summe, ii busselli.

| De Berthona | nihil. |
| De custodia de Waldia, | cc summe, *item*, lx. (*defectus*). |
| De Vestclyve | xxx summe. |
| | nihil. |
| De empcione thesaurariorum | - cccxl summe. |

Summa hujus = DLXX summe.

Summa tocius ordei recepti et recipiendi cum excremento = MCCCCXX summe, iv busselli et dim.

Item, de excremento tocius ordei = xxvi summe.

Summa tocius ordei recepti et recipiendi cum excremento = MCCCCXLVI summe, iv busselli et dim.

### *Expensa*

| In metekorn quatuor servientium de braseria = xxxii summe. | |
| Item, pro aque ductu | iv summe. |

Summa hujus = xxxvi summe.

In lvi functuris, x summe, iv busselli et *dim.*, ultra de Mccccxxi summis, iv bussellis et dim. ultra ordei sicci. Inde faciendum est braseum, MDCCLXIII summe, ii busselli.

## Recepta avene

| | |
|---|---|
| De custodia de Eastekent | l summe. |
| De Berthona | x summe. |
| De custodia de Waldia, | c summe. |

Summa tocius avene recepte de utraque custodia cum Berthona = clx summe.

## Expensa

In x functuris, x summe ultra de clx summis avene. Inde faciendum est braseum, cxcii summe.

## Recepta de braseo

De remanentia anni preteriti = xli summe, i bussellus.

Item, de empcione thesaurariorum de veteri braseo  xx summe.

Summa veteris brasei = lxi summe, i bussellus.

## Recepta novi brasei, ordei et avene

De novo braseo ordei = MDCCLXIII summe, ii busselli.

Item, de novo braseo avene  cxcii summe.

Summa tocius novi brasei ordei et avene = MDCCCCLV summe, ii busselli.

Summa tocius brasei veteris et novi facti et faciendi = MMXVI summe, iii busselli.

Memorandum quod tenentes de Ycham debent facere cx averagia frumenti que continent lxxxi summas frumenti, scilicet, pro quolibet averagio vi busselli que amuntant in denariis ix sol. ii den., precium cujuslibet averagii i d. Inde allocantur xiii d. pro xii averagiis de uno wenland quod est in manu domini. Et debent facere cccvi averagia ordei que continent ccxxxvii summas, scilicet, pro quolibet averagio vi busselli, que amuntant in denariis xxvi sol. iv den., precium cujuslibet averagii i d. Et de avena dclvii averagia que continent ccxxviii summas, xii bussellos, videlicet, pro quolibet averagio viii busselli, et amuntant in denariis liv sol. ix den. ob., precium cujuslibet i den.

Item, x cotlandi de Eastri debent facere clx averagia que con-

[Text D.]
Trin. Coll.
Camb. MS.
O 9/26, fo.
107.

tinent lxxx summas frumenti, scilicet, pro quolibet averagio, dim. summe. Et amuntant in denariis xl sol., precium cujuslibet averagii iii den. Item, ibidem cotierés debent cariare ad curiam apud Cantuariam totum residuum frumenti cujuslibet nostris sumptibus, scilicet, recipiendo pro qualibet summa carianda, i denario, ob., et omnes tenentes debent averagia ad curiam apud Cantuariam de ordeo cccxvi averagia, que continent ccxxxvii summas, videlicet, pro quolibet averagio, vi busselli, et amuntant in denariis lxxix sol., precium cujuslibet averagii iii d. Et dclvii summas averagii de avena que continent cccxxviii summas, vii bussellos, scilicet, pro quolibet averagio viii busselli, et amuntant in denariis viii lib., iv sol., iv den. ob., precium cujuslibet averagii iii d. Summa averagii de Eastria, xiv libri, iv sol. iv d. ob.

Item, omnes tenentes de Adesham debent cvi averagia dim. frumenti que continent lxxx summas frumenti, scilicet, pro quolibet averagio vi busselli, et amuntant in denariis xiii sol. iv den., precium cujuslibet averagii i den. ob., et iidem tenentes debent cccxvi averagia ordei que continent ccxxxvii summas, videlicet, pro quolibet averagio vi busselli, et amuntant in denariis ad xxix sol. vi den., precium cujuslibet averagii i den. ob., et iidem debent dclvii averagia de avena que continent cccxxviii summas, xii bussellos, scilicet, pro quolibet averagio viii busselli, et amuntant in denariis iii lib. ii sol., ii den. quad. precium cujuslibet i den. ob. Summa averagii de Adesham in denariis, vi lib. xv sol. quad.

Memorandum quod xxiii juga et dim. de Godmersham debent claudere xlvii virgas dim. de bor heard circa curiam, et amuntant in denariis iii sol. xi den. ob., videlicet, de quolibet jugo, ii den.

[Text A]
B.M. Cott.
MS. Galba
E iv.

*Ordinaciones diverse facte per capitulum de custodia tem-*
*poralium et aliis.*[1] *Ordinacio facta per capitulum*[2]
*iv Idibus Aprilis anno Domini* MCCCIV

*De legalibus mensuris infra curiam et extra.*

Omnes mensure tam bladi quam brasei cujuslibet generis bladi et brasei sint unius assise et ejusdem quantitatis infra curiam et extra in maneriis[3] secundum standardum busselli et lagene[4]

[Text B]
Cant. Reg. J.

[1] *omit* Ordin.—aliis.
[2] per capitulum] in pleno capitulo.
[3] *omit* in maneriis.
[4] *omit* busselli et lagene.

Regis. Nec liceat alicui de cetero hujusmodi mensuras nec etiam justam ceruisie que continet unam lagenam et dimidiam secundum standardum Regis nec pondera aliqua augere vel minuere nec rectum modum mensurandi vel ponderandi mutare, capitulo inconsulto, sub pena inferius contenta.[1]

Item, quelibet functura bladi quamcito siccatur et bene mundatur statim quamcito fieri poterit separatim et per se moletur et ad curiam mittatur.

Item, totum bonum braseum et totum debile braseum tam vetus quam novum ordei et avene separatim et per se moletur et ad curiam separatim et per se mittatur. Et si misceri unum cum alio braseo debeat in braseria infra curiam per visum brasiatoris non alibi misceatur.

*De custodia brasei.*

Item, de eodem in folio leguntur.[2]

Item, in ostio[3] granarii braserie infra curiam sunt due serure et due claves diverse. Et subcelerarius[4] unam clavem inde habeat et berthonarius vel ejus lodarius, si voluerit, aliam clavem.[5]

Item, quandocumque braciator braciare debet, mensuretur braseum quantum braciare debet illa vice per visum subcelerarii[6] et per visum berthonarii vel lodarii sui, si voluerit, et aliud braseum braciatori liberetur braciandum per visum ipsorum. Et videant subcelerarius et braciator quod braseum sit bonum et non corruptum.[7]

Item,[8] subcelerarius[9] clavem suam de granario braserie infra curiam nulli tradat pro braseo mensurando braciatori liberando[10] nisi monacho professo.

---

[1] contenta] annotata.                                               [Text B]

[2] *omit* de—leguntur. The folio referred to in the text is probably Canterbury Register J.

[3] hostio.

[4] *add* vel granetarius interior (deleted in version A).

[5] *add* Item, quouscumque lodarius bertone aliquod braseum molaturus ad curiam cariaverit statim visu subcelerarii vel granetarii interioris mensuretur et fiat inde tallia contra berthonarium vel lodarium suum de tanto braseo ad curiam cariato.

[6] *add* vel granetarius interior (deleted in version A).

[7] *omit* Et videant—corruptum.                    [8] *add* nec.

[9] *add* nec granetarius interior.

[10] *omit* braciatori liberando.

Item, singulis annis in festo Sancti Michaelis vel ante vel statim post compotum berthonarius de braseria mensuret totum braseum quod remanebit post compotum in annum futurum per visum duorum fratrum[1] et, si aliquid inde deficiat, statim super compotum vendatur.

fo. 73 v.

*De juramento braciatoris et pistoris.*[2]

Item, juret magister braciator quod totam ceruisiam braciatam in bracino et similiter magister pistor quod totum panem furniatum in pistrino, videlicet, panem monachialem, smalpeys, fertiz,[3] pleinpain,[4] et panem coquine integre et sine diminucione de cetero mittant et portari faciant in celarium. Et de celario panem et ceruisiam recipiant qui recipere debent tam granetarius quam alii quicumque.

Item, cotidie liberet celerarius[5] refectorario panes sufficientes pro fratribus infra monasterium comedentibus et pro mixto servitorum ac eciam pro fratribus in refectorio certis temporibus cenaturis et ultra aliquos panes pro hospitibus casualiter venturis.

*De liberacione fratrum in maneriis vicinis morantium.*

Item, fratres qui[6] de licentia presidentis apud Icham vel Adesham, Chertham vel Godmersham vel Broke[7] per tres dies continuos vel ulterius moram fecerint[8] de celario panes et ceruisiam de coquina[9] recipiant sicut in refectorio reciperent si domi fuissent, et ultra prout celerario videbitur expedire. Pro fratribus vero in locis remocioribus quibuscumque degentibus sive pro capellano domini archiepiscopi panes ad refectorium non mittantur quousque redierint ipsi fratres.

*De boscis non vendendis.*

Item, nulli liceat sub quocumque colore aliquid de boscis conventus prosternare vel succindere absque consilio et assensu presidentis nisi tantummodo[10] pro domibus, molendinis et aliis eorum edificiis sustentandis, excepto subbosco pro fagottis faciendis et sepibus claudendis. Et si alique arbores prosternate

[Text B]

| | |
|---|---|
| [1] *omit* per—fratrum. | [2] *omit* De—pistoris. |
| [3] ffetys. | [4] pleynpayn. |
| [5] celerarius liberet cotidie. | [6] *omit.* |
| [7] *omit* vel Broke. | [8] facientes. |
| [9] *omit* et—coquina. | [10] tantum. |

fuerint de assensu presidentis et talwode vel fagotti, cortices
vel ramilla harum arborum seu aliqua silva cedua vel subboscus
per quemcumque seu ex quacumque causa vendantur, tunc prepositus manerii ad quod boscus ille pertinet respondet[1] conventui
fideliter et integre de precio hujus vendicionis in proximo compoto suo sequenti.

*De pena transgressorum predictorum.*

Premissa ordinata fuerunt die predicto et de communi assensu
capituli berthonario celerario et granetario interiori ac eciam
custodibus omnibus maneriorum et aliis quibuscumque in pleno
capitulo injuncta diligenter observanda in virtute sancte obediencie et canonica monicione premissa sub pena majoris excommunicationis quam incurrerent omnes contrarium facientes absque
consciencia presidentis.

.    .    .    .    .    .    .    .    .

*De novis operibus non faciendis intra vel extra ultra precium xl*
*solidorum sine consciencia presidentis.*

Memorandum quod vigilia Sancti Martini anno domini MCCCV,
presentibus priore et omnibus senioribus et obedienciariis ecclesie,
ordinatum fuit ad scaccarium et per priorem inhibitum quatuor
custodibus maneriorum et omnibus aliis obedienciariis intra et
extra sub pena in precedenti ordinacione contenta ne ipsi ex tunc
aliqua nova opera ultra custus xl solidorum in custodiis vel
officiis suis propria auctoritate incipiant vel fieri permittant, set
omnia molendina et alia quecumque in custodiis et officiis suis
prius facta custodiant et sustineant intra et extra in statu bono
et competenti et omnia alia necessaria ad eadem pertinentia.

*De blado non vendendo per granetarium et berthonarium.*

Item, eodem die, presentibus omnibus supradictis, ordinatum
fuit et inhibitum sub pena predicta incurrenda ipso facto granetario et berthonario ne ipsi vel eorum successores in officiis
eisdem aliquod genus bladi vel brasei quacumque causa vel
occasione alicui vendant seu sub colore mutui vel prestiti inde
aliquid alienent, nisi invitatis prius expresso consensu et consilio
presidentis.

[1] respondeat.                                              [Text B]

P

*De blado non vendendo in custodia de Eastkent sine consilio presidentis nec de waldis sine consilio custodis.*[1]

Memorandum quod IV Kalendis Junii anno domini MCCCIX ordinatum fuit ad scaccarium de communi consilio et consensu fratrum quod omnes prepositi de custodia de Eastkent, qui pro tempore fuerint in eadem custodia, jurent super sancta Dei evangelia coram custode et socio suo quod nullum genus bladi vendent, alienabunt, nec ammovebunt sub quocumque colore absque consilio et consensu presidentis qui pro tempore fuerit, nisi tantummodo pro terris seminandis, liberacionibus famulorum, prebenda hostilagii et custodis et ballivi et prebenda carucarum et potagio famulorum.

Item, consimiliter juramentum jurent omnes prepositi de custodia de Waldis et de marisco, qui pro tempore fuerint in eadem custodia, quod sine consilio et consensu custodis blada non vendant ut supra.

*De custodia animalium carucariorum et aliorum animalium.*[2]

Quamcito terre seminate fuerint post Pàscham statim examinentur stotti, boves, vacce et alia animalia per visum custodis et[3] clerici sui, et ea quae retinenda sunt in annum futurum ponantur in bona pastura ut labores estivales possint bene sustinere et ad labores autumpnales et yemales efficiantur insuper fortiores.

Item, omnia animalia quae non sunt retinenda in annum futurum ponantur in meliori pastura et impinguantur et nichil laborent in estate equi nec boves set cum pingues fuerint vendantur.[4]

[Text B]     [1] Memorandum quod IV Kalendis Junii anno domini MCCCIX, coram priore et suppriore et quatuor custodibus maneriorum et multis aliis fratribus, prepositi de Moneketon, Estria et Lyden, Adesham, Ikham, Chertham, Godmersham et Broke juraverunt super sancta evangelia quod ab illo die, quam diu fuerint in servicio conventus in maneriis predictis vel aliquo ipsorum, nullum frumentum, ordeum vel avenam vendent vel prestabunt sine consilio et consensu prioris vel supprioris, absente priore.

[Text C]<br>B.M. Add.<br>MS. 6160,<br>fos. 101 v—<br>102 v.     [2] A condensed version of this and the two following ordinances headed 'ordinaciones facte in scaccario ad Pascham anno Domini MCCC. Et debent custodes facere executionem primo torno post Pascham.'

[Text B]     [3] vel.

    [4] *add* vel ad terminum competentem prestentur.

Item,[1] provideant custodes quod numerus vaccarum et ovium in maneriis nullo modo minuatur per aliquam vendicionem qualitercumque factam vel faciendam set quamcito fieri poterit suppleatur numerus et augeatur. Et hoc idem injungatur omnibus prepositis inviolabiliter observandum in virtute prestiti juramenti.

Item, quandocumque vituli, agni et porcelli a matribus separantur ablactati, statim signentur communi signo conventus.

Item, animalia aliena non pascantur nec mittantur sub quocumque colore infra portas maneriorum conventus. Et si aliqua animalia inveniantur infra maneria signo communi conventus non signata, statim oneretur prepositus de his animalibus per indenturam, exceptis animalibus imparcatis.

### De terra marlanda.[2]

Item, in omnibus maneriis in quibus marla de facili haberi poterit provideantur marlatores in singulis maneriis et marletur tanta terra quanta poterit in estate.

Item, expensa pro terris marlandis, in stauro emendo ac minutis defectibus reparandis provideant custodes per totam custodiam suam secundum quod magis viderint expedire.[3]

### De defectibus reparandis.

Item, injungatur prepositis quod omnes minutos defectus tam in co-opertura domorum et murorum quam in clausura circa domos et curiam, nemora, campos et pasturas et alia reparari faciant sumptibus conventus infra terminum competentem eis assignandum. Alioquin custodes, hoc termino elapso, omnes tales defectus reparari faciant sumptibus prepositorum.

[1] et omnia animalia tam ad carucas quam ad staurum multiplicandum emantur tempestive. [Text B]

Item, emantur oves minores in singulis maneriis ad agistandas omnes pasturas ovium de ovibus propriis.

Item, vacce veteres vendantur cum pingues fuerint et juniores emantur quot maneria poterunt bene sustinere.

Item, sues et porcelli de exitu videantur et diligenter custodiantur et provideatur eis in estate de escaeta grangie aliter quam porcis masculis ut exitum habeant tempore competenti. Et quandocumque porcelli sanantur statim signentur signo communi conventus.

[2] *omit* De—marlanda.

[3] *add* salvo annuo redditu in thesaurum solvendo.

*De securitate prepositorum et bedellorum.*

Item provideant custodes maneriorum [1] quod habeant sufficientem securitatem de omnibus [2] prepositis et bedellis in custodia sua existentibus per quoscumque receptam et in futurum recipiendam [3] ad respondendum fideliter de omnibus exitibus maneriorum et ad solvenda arreragia compoti sui [4] termino assignato, et quod omnes servientes inutiles amoveantur annuatim post festum Nativitatis Sancte Johannis et ante autumpnum. [5]

*De blado misso ad berthonam ad braseum faciendum.*

Item, de avena recepta ad berthonam ad braseum faciendum nichil expendat nec allocet berthonarius in compoto suo de braseo nisi tantummodo ad braseum faciendum et in farina coquine et prebenda lodarii. Prebenda vero palefridi berthonarii provideatur de empcione vel de caruca berthonarii.

Item, de ordeo recepto ad berthonam nichil expendatur nisi in braseo faciendo et in metecorne duorum servientium facientium braseum et molendinarii et lodarii tempore tantummodo quo faciunt braseum et pro aque ductu. [6]

*De defectu panis cujuslibet furniati.*

Celerarius faciat memorandum quolibet quarterio quot panes deficiunt de qualibet furniatura cujuslibet generis bladi. Et in fine quarterii reddant molendinarii tantum de frumento quot panes deficiunt de summa bladi secundum estimacionem summe et non ipsos panes. Et de ipso frumento granetarius oneretur in compoto suo.

. . . . . . . .

*De equis [7] vendendis aliis obedienciariis et non extraneis personis.*

Memorandum quod die dominica in crastino Sancti Martini anno Domini MCCCXVIII ordinatum fuit in pleno capitulo et sub pena

[Text B]

[1] *omit.*                          [2] *omit.*
[3] *omit* exist.—recipiendam.        [4] compoti sui] sua.
[5] *omit* et quod—autumpnum.
[6] Prebenda palefridi et lodarii berthonarii ematur in principio anni et nichil expendatur de avenis receptis de maneriis nisi ad braseum faciendum et in farina.
Item, de ordeo recepto ad bertonam nihil expendatur nisi in braseo faciendo et in metecorne duorum servientium et molendinarii et lodarii tempore quo faciunt braseum et pro aque ductu.
[7] *add* obedienciariorum.

proprietatis et inobediencie firmiter inhibitum omnibus obedienciariis ecclesie interius et exterius, qui tunc equos tenuerunt et
in posterum pro suis officiis equos tenebunt, ne aliquis ipsorum
hos equos suos aliquo tempore vendat aliquibus extraneis personis, set cum hos equos suos vendere voluerit, illos alicui alteri
obedienciario ecclesie vendat qui his equis vel ipsorum aliquo pro
suo officio indigebit et qui pro eisdem equis vel equo justum
et racionabile precium solvere voluerit venditori.

Item, eodem die injunctum fuit eisdem obedienciariis sub
penis predictis incurrendis quod de omnibus infirmitatibus et
defectibus quos sciverint hos equos suos habere prominuant hos
obedienciarios emptores antequam precium horum equorum
recipiant ab eisdem.  Alioquin iidem venditores hos equos recipere
et rehabere et precium pro eisdem equis receptum restituere
emptoribus teneantur.

. . . . . . . . .

*De custodia prisonum in prioratu ecclesie Christi Cantuarie.*    fo. 74 v.

Juret portarius exterioris porte curie quod faciet indenturam inter
ipsum et gayolarium de die, anno, et nomine cujuslibet prisonis
qui portas curie intrabit.

Item, quod non permittet aliquem prisonem portas curie exire
sine speciali precepto capitalis senescalli libertatis prioris et conventus vel clerici libertatis locum senescalli tenentis, ipso absente.
Juret gayolarius quod faciet indenturam inter dictum portarium
et ipsum de die, anno, et nomine cujuslibet prisonis quum hos
prisones recipit in custodiam.

Item, juret quod omnes prisones custodiet in gayola et quod
non permittet aliquem prisonem portas curie exire sine speciali
precepto predicti senescalli vel clerici libertatis locum suum
tenentis, ipso absente.  Et si aliquis priso portas curie aliter
exierit, scire faciat senescallo in proximo adventu suo apud
Cantuariam nomen talis prisonis et per quem talis priso exivit.

Item, juret quod panem nec aliud quodcumque victuale petet
nec recipiet a celerario vel ab alio quocumque ad opus alicujus
prisonis, nisi ille priso sit de die et nocte commorans infra portas
curie.

Item, juret quod quolibet quarterio anni fideliter scire faciat
predicto senescallo in scriptura quid et quantum et cui quilibet

priso in custodia sua vel alius quicumque pro ipso prisone promittet vel dabit pro gratia habenda.

*De custodia brasei.*

Omnes servientes qui debent facere braseum conventus ad berthonam jurentur specialiter conventui quod bene et fideliter conventui servient in faciendo braseo suo quamdiu steterint in servicio suo.

Item, omnes servientes predicti vel adminus unus ipsorum in talibus magis expertus faciat berthonario pro seipso et sociis suis sufficientem securitatem per plegium quod facient ad berthonam bonum et competens braseum per visum et testimonium braciatoris conventus et aliorum qui braseum cognoscunt. Et si aliqua functura vel dimidia functura seu aliqua porcio brasei per defectum ipsorum predictorum servientium depereat, ita quod de eodem braseo competens ceruisia per testimonium predictum fieri non possit, tunc totum hujusmodi braseum sic consumptum predictis servientibus liberetur. Et iidem servientes infra mensem primum sequentem restituere teneantur berthonario tantam mensuram de bono braseo et competenti.

Item, jurent dicti servientes quod nullum braseum siccabunt antequam braciator conventus viderit si braseum bene gravimetur.

Item, jurent dicti servientes et molendinarius berthone quod nullum braseum facient molare antequam braciator conventus viderit si braseum bene ventetur et vannetur et competenter purgetur.

Item, braciator juretur specialiter conventui quod bene et fideliter braciabit et custodiet ceruisiam conventus, prout alias ordinatum fuit.

Item, semel in qualibet septimana examinetur panis conventus si fit de pondere legali.

Item, semel in qualibet quindena examinetur justa Lanfranci in celario ceruisie si liberaciones ceruisie fiant per rectam et legalem mensuram.

. . . . . . . .

fo. 177 v.    *Ordinacio facta pro numero animalium in maneriis restaurando.*

Omnia infrascripta assignentur pro maneriis instaurandis quousque melius instaurentur:—

Omnes denarios de coreis pellibus et pellectis boum et vaccarum et omnium aliorum animalium in morina.

Item, omnes denarios de lana agnina vendita.

Item, quartam partem de herbagio estivali venditam.

Item, de lana ovium singulis annis tres saccos lane pro stauro emendo.

Item, omnes obvenciones in pecunia numerata post mortem fratrum.

Item, omnia herietta in maneriis.

Item, omnes denarios receptos pro nutritura orphanorum.

Item, fines nativorum pro redempcione sanguinis et pro terris tenendis post mortem antecessorum suorum ad voluntatem conventus.

Item, de boscis vendendis in Waldia, xx libras.

Item, de boscis vendendis apud Halton, x libras.

Item, de boscis vendendis apud Ryselbergh, vi libras.

Item, de boscis vendendis apud Newenton, vi libras.

Item, omnia escaeta catallorum et terrarum dampnatorum parve mentis.

Item, de oblacionibus aliqua certa summa pecunie.

Annuatim quamdiu placuerit conventui.

Omnes denarii predicti annuatim colligantur et de illis denariis emantur animalia pro maneriis restaurandis per consilium et ordinacionem custodis et ballivorum maneriorum, et quod singuli custodes maneriorum respondeant conventui singulis annis in festo Sancti Michaelis qualiter denarios predictos expendiderunt.

# Appendix II

## A PLAN FOR REDUCING HOUSEHOLD
## EXPENDITURE, c. 1285[1]
### Canterbury MS. D.E. 87

Maneria nostra de Moneketone, Estrie, Yicham, et Edesham cum Knoldane et Terra de la Lee tradita sunt ad valorem quingentarum et quindecim librarum in blado et in denariis.

Item, maneria de Chertheham, Holingheburne, Berkesore, Leisdone, et Coptone tradita sunt ad valorem ccxviii lib. vi sol. viii den.

Item, Godmersham et Welles cum aliis maneriis de Waldis tradita sunt pro cccc lib. in blado et in denariis.

Item, Lose valet xv lib, Laningbledone et Moningeham xx sol, et Eylwortone v sol. . . . Orpintone lxxv lib., Surreya lxxx lib., Oxonia et Buckingeham lxxx lib., Waleworthe xxx lib., Londonium xxx lib., Depeham i marcam.

Ylle, Hallee, et Bockinge cum Merseye valent cv lib. sine operibus et consuetudinibus.

Lellinge et Mideltone lxxxx lib., Bercarie de Clive cxx. lib.; Feudofirme cum Doccumbe lxx lib., Cantuaria lxxx lib., Sandwiz lxxx lib.

De diversis locis et gabulis lxx lib., de Bertona et Coltona xl lib. De pensionibus cum Hybina ix lib.

De oblacionibus lxxx lib. De pistrino, bracino, et molendinis xx lib. De bosco vendito xxx lib.

Summa totius MMCCCxlix lib.

### Expensa

Ad hec expendendum providit dominus prior quod in stabulo suo sint tantum decem equi et x pueri, i nuncius et i messarius. Quilibet equus habeat per annum x summas de prebenda et pueri comedant in aula sicut prius.

[1] This undated document was composed shortly before 1290, when Sandwich, mentioned here as a possession of Christ Church, was ceded to the crown. It almost certainly represents a part of the reforming programme of Henry of Eastry, who acceded to the priorate in 1285.

Sacrista habeat per annum lx lib. de thesaurariis et redditus suos et provideat obediencie sue et equis et pueris preter liberacionem eorum qui habent turtas.

Camerarius habeat per annum cxx lib. et provideat obediencie sue et equis et pueris et cuilibet monacho in vestimentis et calciamentis ad valorem xviii sol., et turte liberentur sicut prius et pesepannes et suvelpanni.[1]

In stabulo celerarii sint i carectarius et ii equi carectarii, i palfridus, i summarius, et i runcinus, et ii pueri ad illos equos custodiendos, et tercius qui sit messarius pro tempore.

Ad panem conventus suficient qualibet ebdomada viii summe, et ad panem familie iiii summe, quod amuntat per annum dcxxiiii summas. Et pro festis, nebulis, et oblatis lxxvi summe, que valent in denariis clxxv lib., summa computata pro xl den.

Pro turtis, metecorn, pesepannes, et suvelpannis per totum annum lv lib.

Ad coquinam conventus suficient qualibet ebdomada c sol., quod amuntat per annum cclx lib.

Item, ad farinam potagii conventus, xxx summe de grossa avena que valet c sol., et de pisis lx summe que valent xv lib.

Pro Lamfrancis,[2] familia, et mandato lx lib. Ad vinum emendum l lib.

Pro festis et hospitibus lxxx lib. Ad prebendam emendam pro stabulo prioris c summe. Pro stabulo celerarii lx summe. Pro stabulo granetarii xv summe. Pro hospitibus et senescallo c summe. Pro palfrido et lodario de Bertona, xxv summe, que valent in den. xxxvii lib. x sol., summa computata pro xxx den.

Ad expensas celerarii sine esu et potu xlv lib. Ad expensas granetarii interioris in den. xx lib. Ad expensas bertonarii xvi lib.

Ad custodienda nemora, xi lib. viii sol. Capellano domini Prioris x sol. Carpentario x lib. Ad ligna trahenda lx lib.

Ad opera in villa xx lib. Ad pensiones et solidata cxx lib. Ad diversa negotia c lib. Ad dona fratrum x lib. Ad anniversaria xxx lib. Ad cereos domini Regis x lib.

Summa totius expensae in blado et in denariis, mdccxiii lib. iiii sol. viii den., sine allocamentis faciendis in maneriis que amuntabunt forte usque ad c lib. vel amplius. Et sic possunt remanere ad solutiones debitorum, dccc marce.

[1] Pittances of household servants.

[2] *Sic.* The reference is to the expenditure incurred on the obit-day of Lanfranc.

# Bibliography

## MANUSCRIPT SOURCES

### DEAN AND CHAPTER LIBRARY, CANTERBURY

(a) IN CUPBOARD F I.

Registers A, B, C, D, E, H, I, J, K, O, P, and Q. (See reports on their contents by Dr J. B. Sheppard in *H.M.C.* Appendices to VIIIth and IXth Reports.)

(b) IN CUPBOARD F II.

Treasurers' accounts, 1206–1384. (Called F ii and F iii in text.)
Treasurers' building accounts, 1436–43, 1471–c. 1520.

(c) IN CABINET AA.

(Drawer 32.) Accounts of 'progress' of warden of manors, 1463–99.

(d) IN ROOM XYZ.

*Account-Rolls.*

(In cupboard M 13.)

    i. Anniversarian, c. 1300–1533.
    ii. Shrine-Keepers, 1397 (and other miscellaneous accounts).
    iii. Garnerer, 1307–1505.
    iv. Serjeant of Barton, 1291–1471.
    v. Chaplain of prior, 1360–1424.
    vi. Bartoner, 1279–1428.
    viii. Almoner, 1284–1392.
    ix. Cellarer, 1392–1494.
    x. Bartoner as Keeper of Malthall, 1377–1460.
    xi. Court-rolls, plea-rolls, fine-rolls, and account-rolls of High Court of prior, and court-rolls of Sacrist's Court.
    xiii. Chamberlain, 1308–1468.
xiv, xv. Treasurers, 1282–1512.
    xvi. Sacrist, 1330–1475.
    xvii. Prior, 1396–1473.
    xix. Assisae Scaccarii, 1225–1336.

*Eastry Correspondence.*

Four Portfolios in cupboard M 13.

*Miscellaneous.*

MS. D. iv. Includes treasurers' accounts, 1198–1205. (Press-mark Y 7. 28.)

MS. E. vi. Day-book of Prior Goldston I. (Press-mark Y. 8. 16.)

(*e*)  IN ROOM ZA.

*Sede Vacante Scrap-Books.*

ii, 196, 199. Correspondence relating to *sede vacante* jurisdiction, 1240.

iii, 12, 13, 14. Statement of certain liberties of the priory, c. 1250.

*Miscellaneous.*

(In Box D.) Rental of the city of Canterbury, c. 1165. Account-rolls of the steward of the Liberty, fourteenth and fifteenth centuries.

(*f*)  IN BASEMENT.

Serjeants' and beadles' accounts, 1260–1432 (most of which are listed in *Bulletin of the Institute of Historical Research*, 1931, VIII, pp. 136–55):


DOMESTIC AND RURAL ECONOMY

(In various places; see catalogue in Dean and Chapter Library.)

D.E. 3.  Day-book of Priors Oxenden and Hathbrand, 1331–43.

D.E. 13, 14, 15. Fifteenth-century contracts for the purchase of cloth.

D.E. 25. Pittance-roll, 1464–65.

D.E. 29. Fifteenth-century list of household servants.

D.E. 58. Articles supplied to monks in infirmary, c. 1523.

D.E. 70. Accounts of 'progress' of warden of manors, 1518.

D.E. 74. List of monks, c. 1480.

D.E. 87. Plan for reducing household expenditure, c. 1285 (printed in Appendix II).

R.E. 6.  Accounts of 'progress' of warden of manors, 1493.

R.E. 40. Accounts of 'progress' of warden of manors, 1447.

R.E. 99. Exchequer ordinance on delivery of food-farm, 1288 (printed in Appendix I).

R.E. 100. Court-rolls of bartoner's court, 1434–1522.

R.E. 131. Accounts of 'progress' of warden of manors, c. 1490.

## LAMBETH PALACE LIBRARY

Register of Walter Reynolds, 1313–26.
MS. 1212. Cartulary of Christ Church.
MSS. 242, 243. Treasurers' accounts, 1257–1391.

## BRITISH MUSEUM

COTTONIAN MSS.
Galba E iv. Memorandum-book of Prior Henry of Eastry, 1285–1331.
Cleopatra c. vii. Contains part of a Christ Church register.

ADDITIONAL MSS.
6159, 6160. Early fourteenth-century Christ Church registers.

## CAMBRIDGE UNIVERSITY LIBRARY

Ee. v, 31. Register of letters close and patent of Christ Church, 1285–1331.

## TRINITY COLLEGE, CAMBRIDGE, LIBRARY

O. 9/26. Early fourteenth-century Christ Church register.

## PRINTED ORIGINAL SOURCES

### (a) RELATING TO THE HISTORY OF CHRIST CHURCH

*Christ Church Letters*, 1334–c. 1539, ed. J. B. Sheppard (Camden Soc. 1877).
'Chronicle of John Stone, 1415–71', ed. W. G. Searle in *Camb. Antiq. Soc. Publ.* XXXIV (1902).
'Chronicle of William Glastynbury, monk of Christ Church Priory, 1418–48', ed. C. E. Woodruff in *Arch. Cant.* XXXVII (1925).
*Epistolae Cantuarienses*, ed. W. Stubbs (Rolls Series, 1865).
Gervase of Canterbury, *Opera*, ed. W. Stubbs, 2 vols. (Rolls Series, 1879–80).
*Historical Manuscripts Commission*. Reports by J. B. Sheppard in Appendices to Vth Report (1876), to VIIIth Report (1881), and to IXth Report (1883).
Report by H. T. Riley in Appendix to VIth Report (1877).

*Literae Cantuarienses*, ed. J. B. Sheppard, 3 vols. (Rolls Series, 1887–89).
'Monastic Chronicle of Christ Church, 1331–1415', by an anonymous chronicler, ed. C. E. Woodruff in *Arch. Cant.* XXIX (1911).


## (b) GENERAL

*Accounts of the Obedientiars of Abingdon Abbey*, ed. R. E. G. Kirk (Camden Soc. 1892).
*Annales Monastici*, ed. H. R. Luard (Rolls Series, 1869), IV.
*Calendar of Charter Rolls.*
*Calendar of Letters Close.*
*Calendar of Letters Patent.*
*Cartularium Monasterii de Rameseia*, ed. W. de G. Birch, 3 vols. (Rolls Series, 1884–93).
*Cartulary and Terrier of Bilsington Priory, Kent*, ed. N. Neilson (British Academy Records, VII, 1928).
*Chapters of the English Black Monks*, 1215–1540, ed. W. A. Pantin (Camden Third Series, XLV, XLVII, LIV, 1931–37).
*Charters of Romney Marsh* (1846 ed.).
*Chronicon Abbatiae de Evesham*, ed. W. D. Macray (Rolls Series, 1863).
*Chronicon Petroburgense*, ed. T. Stapleton (Camden Soc. 1849).
*Coenobii Burgensis Historia*, ed. J. Sparke (1727).
*Compotus Rolls of the Obedientiaries of St Swithun's Priory, Winchester*, ed. G. W. Kitchin (Hants Record Soc. 1892).
*Compotus Rolls of the Priory of Worcester in the xivth and xvth Centuries*, ed. S. G. Hamilton (Worc. Hist. Soc. 1910).
*Concilia Magnae Brittaniae*, ed. D. Wilkins, 3 vols. (1737).
*Custumale Roffense*, ed. J. Thorpe (1788).
*Gesta Abbatum Sancti Albani*, ed. H. T. Riley, II (1867).
'Lanfranci Opera' in Migne's *P.L.* CL (1854).
*Monasticon Anglicanum*, ed. W. Dugdale, I (1846 ed.).
*Novum Repertorium Ecclesiasticum Parochiale Londinense*, ed. G. Hennessy (1898).
*Papsturkunden in England*, ed. W. Holtzmann, II (Berlin, 1935).
*Placita de Quo Warranto* (Record Commission, 1818).
*Registrum Epistolarum Johannis Peckham*, ed. C. T. Martin, 3 vols. (Rolls Series, 1882–85).
*Registrum Roberti Winchelsey*, ed. R. Graham (Canterbury and York Soc. 1917–      ).

*Repertorium Ecclesiasticum Parochiale Londinense*, ed. R. Newcourt (1708–10).

*Rotuli Hundredorum*, I (Record Commission, 1812).

*Rotuli Litterarum Clausarum* (Record Commission, 1844).

*Sancti Benedicti Regula Monachorum*, ed. Dom C. Butler (Fribourg, 1912).

*Valor Ecclesiasticus*, I (Record Commission, 1810).

*Walter of Henley's Husbandry*, ed. E. Lamond (1890).


## SECONDARY SOURCES

### (a) RELATING TO THE HISTORY OF CHRIST CHURCH

BOX, E. G. 'Donations of Manors to Christ Church, Canterbury, and Appropriations of Churches' in *Arch. Cant.* XLIV (1932).

BRITTON, J. *History and Antiquities of the Church of Canterbury* (1821).

DART, J. *History and Antiquities of Canterbury Cathedral* (1726).

HASTED, E. *History of Canterbury*. 3 vols. in 1. (Part of his *History of Kent*, 1799.)

HOPE, W. H. St JOHN. See Legg, J. Wickham.

KISSAN, B. W. 'Lanfranc's Alleged Division of Lands between Archbishop and Community' in *Eng. Hist. Rev.* LIV (1939).

KNOWLES, Dom DAVID. 'The Early Community at Christ Church, Canterbury' in *Journal of Theological Studies*, XXXIX (1938).

—— 'The Canterbury Election of 1205–6' in *Eng. Hist. Rev.* LIII (1938).

LEGG, J. WICKHAM and HOPE, W. H. St JOHN. *Inventories of Christ Church, Canterbury* (1902).

NICHOLS, J. F. *Custodia Essexae*. (An unpublished London Ph.D. thesis, 1930.)

—— 'An Early Fourteenth Century Petition from the Tenants of Bocking to their Manorial Lord' in *Econ. Hist. Rev.* II (1930).

ROBINSON, J. ARMITAGE. 'The Early Community at Christ Church, Canterbury' in *Journal of Theological Studies*, XXVII (1926).

—— 'Lanfranc's Monastic Constitutions' in *Journal of Theological Studies*, X (1909).

SMITH, R. A. L. 'The Central Financial System of Christ Church, Canterbury, 1186–1512' in *Eng. Hist. Rev.* LV (1940).

SOMNER, W. *Antiquities of Canterbury* (ed. N. Battely, 1703).

SYMONS, Dom T. 'The Introduction of Monks at Christ Church, Canterbury' in *Journal of Theological Studies*, XXVII (1926).

WILLIS, R. *History of the Conventual Buildings of Christ Church, Canterbury* (1869).

WOODRUFF, C. E. 'The Financial Aspect of the Cult of St Thomas of Canterbury' in *Arch. Cant.* XLIV (1932).

—— 'The Sacrist's Rolls of Christ Church, Canterbury' in *Arch. Cant.* XLVIII (1936).

WOODRUFF, C. E. and DANKS, W. *Memorials of Canterbury Cathedral* (1912).

WOOLNOTH, W. *History and Description of Canterbury Cathedral* (1816).

## (b) RELATING TO THE HISTORY AND TOPOGRAPHY OF KENT

ADLER, M. 'The Jews of Canterbury' in *Jewish Hist. Soc. Trans.* VII (1915).

BOYS, J. *A General View of the Agriculture of the County of Kent* (1796).

BOYS, W. *Collections for an History of Sandwich* (Canterbury, 1792).

BURROWS, A. J. 'Romney Marsh, Past and Present' in *Trans. of Surveyors' Institution*, XVII (1885).

COTTON, C. *The Greyfriars of Canterbury* (1926).

DERVILLE, M. TEICHMAN. *The Level and the Liberty of Romney Marsh* (1936).

FURLEY, R. *History of the Weald of Kent.* 3 vols. (1871–74).

GARDINER, D. *Canterbury* (1933 ed.).

—— 'Merchants of Canterbury in the Middle Ages' in *The Parents' Review*, XXXVI (1925).

HAINES, C. R. *Dover Priory* (Cambridge, 1930).

HASTED, E. *History of Kent.* 12 vols. (Canterbury, 1797–1801).

JOLLIFFE, J. E. A. *Pre-Feudal England. The Jutes* (Oxford, 1933).

LAMBARD, WILLIAM. *The Perambulation of Kent* (1656 ed.).

PELHAM, R. A. 'Some Aspects of the East Kent Wool Trade in the Thirteenth Century' in *Arch. Cant.* XLIV (1932).

SMITH, R. A. L. 'Marsh Embankment and Sea Defence in Medieval Kent' in *Econ. Hist. Rev.* XII (1940).

*Victoria County History. Kent*, ed. W. Page, II and III (1926–32).

WOODRUFF, C. E. and CAPE, H. J. *History of the King's School, Canterbury* (1908).

## (c) GENERAL

ABBOTT, E. A. *St Thomas of Canterbury. His Death and Miracles.* 2 vols. (1898).

ADAMS, G. B. 'Private Jurisdiction in England' in *American Hist. Rev.* XXIII (1918).

ASHLEY, Sir WILLIAM. *Bread of Our Forefathers* (Oxford, 1928).

AULT, W. O. *Private Jurisdiction in England* (Yale Hist. Publ. X, 1923).

BENNETT, H. S. 'The Reeve and the Manor in the Fourteenth Century' in *Eng. Hist. Rev.* XLI (1926).

BENNETT, M. K. 'British Wheat Yield Per Acre for Seven Centuries' in *Economic History* (a Supplement to the *Economic Journal*, 1937).

BERLIÈRE, Dom URSMER. 'La Familia dans les Monastères Bénédictins du Moyen Age' in *Mémoires de l'Académie Royale de Belgique*, XXIX (Brussels, 1931).

—— 'Le Sceau Conventuel' in *Revue Bénédictine*, XXXVIII (1926).

BEVERIDGE, Sir WILLIAM. 'The Yield and Price of Corn in the Middle Ages' in *Economic History* (1929).

BEVERIDGE, Sir WILLIAM, and others. *Prices and Wages in England* (1939–    ).

BISHOP, T. A. M. 'The Rotation of Crops on the Manor of Westerham' in *Econ. Hist. Rev.* X (1938).

BRITTON, C. E. *A Meteorological Chronology to* A.D. 1485 (H.M. Stationery Office, 1937).

CAM, H. M. *The Hundred and the Hundred Rolls* (1930).

—— 'The King's Government, as administered by the Greater Abbots of East Anglia' in *Camb. Antiq. Soc. Proc.* XXIX (1928).

CARRIER, E. H. *The Pastoral Heritage of Britain* (1936).

CHENEY, C. R. *Episcopal Visitation of Monasteries in the Thirteenth Century* (Manchester, 1931).

—— 'Norwich Cathedral Priory in the Fourteenth Century' in *Bulletin of John Rylands Library*, XX (1936).

—— 'The Papal Legate and English Monasteries in 1206' in *Eng. Hist. Rev.* XLVI (1931).

CHEW, H. M. *Ecclesiastical Tenants-in-Chief* (Oxford, 1932).

CHURCHILL, I. J. *Canterbury Administration.* 2 vols. (1933).

COULTON, G. G. *Five Centuries of Religion*, II and III (Cambridge, 1927–36).

DENHOLM-YOUNG, N. *Seignorial Administration in England* (Oxford, 1937).

*Dictionary of National Biography*, ed. L. Stephen and S. Lee (1885–  ).

DUGDALE, WILLIAM. *History of Imbanking and Draining* (1772 ed.).

GRAS, N. S. B. *The Evolution of the English Corn Market* (Cambridge, Mass. 1915).

GRAY, H. L. *English Field Systems* (Harvard, 1915).

HARROD, H. 'Some Details of a Murrain of the Fourteenth Century' in *Archaeologia*, XLI (1867).

HEARNSHAW, F. J. C. *Leet Jurisdiction in England* (Southampton, 1908).

HUTTON, W. H. *Thomas Becket* (1926 ed.).

JOHNSTONE, H. 'Poor Relief in the Royal Households of Thirteenth-Century England' in *Speculum*, IV (1929).

KNOWLES, Dom DAVID. *The Monastic Order in England, 943–1216* (Cambridge, 1940).

KOSMINSKY, E. A. 'Services and Money Rents in the Thirteenth Century' in *Econ. Hist. Rev.* VII (1935).

LEVETT, E. *Studies in Manorial History* (Oxford, 1938).

LEVILLAIN, L. 'Les Statuts d'Adalhard' in *Le Moyen Age* (1900).

LOBEL, M. D. 'The Ecclesiastical Banleuca in England' in *Oxford Essays in Medieval History presented to H. E. Salter* (Oxford, 1934).

LUCAS, H. S. 'The Great European Famine of 1315–16 and 1317' in *Speculum*, V (1930).

LUNT, W. E. *Financial Relations of the Papacy with England to 1327* (Cambridge, Mass. 1939).

MACDONALD, A. J. *Lanfranc* (1926).

MAITLAND, F. W. *Domesday Book and Beyond* (Cambridge, 1907 ed.).

MELVILLE, A. M. M. The Pastoral Custom and Local Wool Trade of Medieval Sussex, 1085–1485. (An unpublished London M.A. thesis, 1930.)

MILLER, E. 'The Estates of the Abbey of St Alban' in *St Albans and Herts. Architectural and Archaeological Soc. Trans.* (1938).

MURRAY, K. M. E. *The Constitutional History of the Cinque Ports* (Manchester, 1935).

NEILSON, N. *Customary Rents* (Oxford Studies in Social and Legal History, ed. P. Vinogradoff, 1910).

ORWIN, C. S. and C. S. *The Open Fields* (Oxford, 1938).

PAGE, F. M. *The Estates of Crowland Abbey* (Cambridge, 1934).

—— 'Bidentes Hoylandie' in *Economic History*, I (1927).

PANTIN, W. A. 'The General and Provincial Chapters of the English Black Monks, 1215–1540' in *Trans. Royal Hist. Soc.* Fourth Series, x (1927).

PEARCE, E. H. *Thomas de Cobham* (1923).

PETIT-DUTAILLIS, C. and LEFEBVRE, G. *Studies Supplementary to Stubbs' Constitutional History*, III (Manchester, 1929).

POLLOCK, F. and MAITLAND, F. W. *History of English Law.* 2 vols. (1923).

POOLE, R. L. *The Exchequer in the Twelfth Century* (Oxford, 1912).

POSTAN, M. M. 'The Chronology of Labour Services' in *Trans. Royal Hist. Soc.* Fourth Series, xx (1937).

—— 'Credit in Medieval Trade' in *Econ. Hist. Rev.* I (1929).

—— 'Medieval Capitalism' in *Econ. Hist. Rev.* IV (1933).

—— 'The Fifteenth Century' in *Econ. Hist. Rev.* IX (1939).

POWER, E. E. *The Wool Trade in English Mediaeval History* (Oxford, 1941).

RICHARDSON, H. G. 'The Early History of Commissions of Sewers' in *Eng. Hist. Rev.* XXXIV (1919).

ROGERS, J. E. THOROLD. *The History of Agriculture and Prices*, I and II (1866).

SAUNDERS, H. W. *An Introduction to the Rolls of Norwich Cathedral Priory* (1930).

SIMON, A. L. *History of the Wine Trade.* 2 vols. (1906).

SNAPE, R. H. *English Monastic Finances in the Later Middle Ages* (Cambridge, 1926).

STEPHENS, W. R. W. *Memorials of the See of Chichester* (1876).

SUTCLIFFE, DOROTHY. 'The Financial Condition of the See of Canterbury, 1279–1292' in *Speculum*, x (1935).

THOMPSON, A. HAMILTON. *Cathedral Churches of England* (1925).

—— *English Monasteries* (Cambridge, 1923 ed.).

—— *The Premonstratensian Abbey of Welbeck* (1938).

—— 'A Corrody from Leicester Abbey, A.D. 1393–4, with some Notes on Corrodies' in *Trans. Leicestershire Arch. Soc.* (1925).

TOUT, T. F. *Chapters in Medieval Administrative History.* 6 vols. (Manchester, 1920–33).

—— *History of England*, 1216–1377 (1905).

WHITWELL, R. J. 'English Monasteries and the Wool Trade in the Thirteenth Century' in *Vierteljahrschrift für Social- und Wirtschaftesgeschichte*, II (1904).

WRETTS-SMITH, M. 'Organization of Farming at Crowland Abbey' in *Journal of Economic and Business History*, IV (1932).

# Index